The Spirituality Gap

The Spirituality Gap

Searching for Meaning in a Secular Age

ABI MILLAR

First published in the United Kingdom by September Publishing in 2025

September Publishing, an imprint of Duckworth Books Ltd
1 Golden Court, Richmond, TW9 1EU, United Kingdom
www.duckworthbooks.co.uk

For bulk and special sales please contact info@duckworthbooks.com

© Abi Millar, 2025

All rights reserved. No part of this publication may be reproduced,
stored in a retrieval system, or transmitted, in any form or by
any means electronic, mechanical, photocopying, recording or
otherwise, without the prior permission of the publisher.

The right of Abi Millar to be identified as the Author of this Work has been
asserted by her in accordance with the Copyright, Designs and Patents Act 1988.

A catalogue record for this book is available from the British Library

Book design by Danny Lyle

Printed and bound in Great Britain by Clays Ltd, Elcograf S.p.A.

1 3 5 7 9 10 8 6 4 2

Trade paperback ISBN: 9780715655153
eISBN: 9780715655160

To all the sceptics and seekers

Contents

Introduction	1
1. Ayahuasca: To Narnia and Back	15
2. Yoga: Practice, Practice and All Is Coming	37
3. Tarot: The Fool's Journey	57
4. Astrology: Star Stuff	75
5. Manifestation: Magnetic Thoughts and Vision Boards	91
6. Reiki: A Spoonful of Wellness	107
7. Atheist Churches: Pentecostalism for the Godless	127
8. Exercise: A Pilgrim's Progress	147
9. Meditation: The Hurricane in Your Head	167
10. Nature Spirituality: The Door to the Temple	185
11. Shamanism: Beyond the Veil	203
12. Raves: God Is a DJ	221
Epilogue	237
Notes	243
Bibliography	261
Acknowledgements	265
Index	269

Introduction

When I tell people I'm writing a book about spirituality, it's often with a note of apprehension. Of course, it should be obvious that I'm not a guru. I'm a harried-looking woman who swears like a sailor and who probably, by this point in the conversation, has a glass of red wine in her hand. I have never attained *samadhi*, had a 'Road to Damascus conversion', or communed with my spirit guides.

But just in case you think I do have pretensions towards enlightenment, I've fallen into the habit of describing this as 'a book about spirituality for sceptics', or even 'a book about spirituality for people who wouldn't be caught dead in the spirituality section of the bookshop'. That puts paid to any miscommunication, even if it might lead you to question the point of writing such a book at all.

In truth, I'm not interested in convincing anyone that there is such a thing as an immaterial realm. I have spent much of my career as a science journalist, which means I have never grown out of the small child's obsession with asking 'why'. I always get frustrated by New Age books that don't back up their claims.

Equally, though, I'm not interested in rubbishing the whole enterprise. So often in irreligious circles, spiritual beliefs are treated as akin to superstition, a throwback to more intellectually primitive times. The idea seems to be that our emerging knowledge of how the brain works, or of the physical laws governing the universe, negates this entire area of human experience. Beliefs about the soul, or gods, or spirits, or an afterlife, or some overarching cosmic meaning, are taken as nothing more than self-deception – an evolutionary adaptation with little relevance to the nature of reality.

The battle lines are drawn: in one corner you have the rationalists, spearheaded by 'New Atheist' thinkers like Richard Dawkins; while in the other you have the gullible masses, sucked in by every wild theory they find on YouTube. I think in this rather misanthropic rendering something important gets lost.

Spirituality has always struck me as a fascinating subject precisely because it's so tricky to pin down. Attempts at definition often slip into tautology – the *Oxford English Dictionary* claims that spirituality is 'the quality of being concerned with the human spirit or soul, as opposed to material physical things', which of course raises the question of what 'spirit' means in the first place. Is it supposed to be the part of you that survives death, the part summoned by creepy TV mediums or that haunts some decrepit B&B? I like a good ghost story as much as anyone, but it's hard to work out what might be left of you upon the extinguishing of body and brain.

Is it just another way of describing someone's 'vibe', their presence, the sum of their attributes? Well, that's nice, but hardly informative. You aren't invoking anything that can't be explained through other means.

In my younger years, inspired by the New Atheists, I saw anything earmarked spiritual as New Age woo. Sure, you could talk about spirit in a metaphorical way – a 'spirited' person, a 'spirit' of resistance, the 'spirit' of the times – but otherwise you needed to back up and define your terms.

Today, I've become more comfortable with a certain level of imprecision, which reflects how the word 'spirit' is routinely used. There's a school of thought that suggests many of our philosophical problems are, in essence, language problems. We tie ourselves in knots because our language is dualistic: it conditions us to think of mind as being separate from body, subject as distinct from object, and the human spirit as being a kind of 'ghost in the machine'.

Introduction

One way of clearing the confusion is to argue that our metaphysics has got things twisted. A contemporary proponent of this view is the idealist philosopher Bernardo Kastrup, who thinks that matter emerges from consciousness, rather than the other way round. This may seem like an inconsequential distinction but it's actually quite a radical one. And if you follow this logic, many spiritual concepts start to make a bit more sense.

To break it down a little: in our culture, we tend to think that minds emerge from brains made from physical building blocks. (Science still can't really explain how – this is the so-called 'hard problem of consciousness', first described by David Chalmers, which keeps many a philosophy student up at night.) These minds have access to a shared physical reality, the domain of the empirical sciences. Anything outside of that reality – things like reiki energy, synchronicities, shamanic trances, near-death experiences and psychedelic visions, not to mention religious concepts like hearing the word of God – are open to question through dint of being purely subjective. It conditions people to ask: was that experience real, or was it all in my head?

In an idealist framework, 'real' versus 'in my head' are no longer opposed. Consciousness is the very foundation of reality, rather than a by-product of something physical, which means you can explain unusual mental phenomena without needing to use loaded terms like 'hallucination'. 'It is mind that is the broader framework, encompassing the brain but also the rest of existence. Our heads are in mind, not mind in our heads. The brain is merely an image in mind of a process of mind,' writes Kastrup, rather mind-bendingly, in his book *Why Materialism Is Baloney: How True Skeptics Know There Is No Death and Fathom Answers to Life, the Universe, and Everything*.[1] (Personally, I'm suspending judgement on whether he's right.)

Some Eastern philosophies, meanwhile, try to sidestep the problem by training our attention on the limits of language. There's a well-known Buddhist proverb about a 'finger pointing to the moon'. The idea is that truth can only be known experientially rather than conceptually, and that obsessing too much about the 'finger' – linguistic constructs – can blind you to the 'moon' – reality. Zen Buddhism uses a device called the koan to hammer this point home; these are nonsensical-seeming riddles that leave the student intellectually frustrated and, in doing so, open the mind to deeper truths.

I must admit that koans leave me cold – I can't get past the intellectual frustration part – but I don't doubt that language and spirituality are an awkward fit. Even as I try to find a working definition of spirituality, I'm aware that anything I devise will be so vague as to mean almost nothing at all. What I will say is that, when people use the word, they're generally talking about something significant and even sacred. Try to dissect it further than that, and the matter in question has a frustrating habit of wriggling out of your grasp.

If all this sounds a little dry or academic so far, I hope to make the case that bridging the spirituality gap holds some urgency. In fact, the solutions to our problems, both personal and planetary, are often taken to be spiritual in nature. As the late David Foster Wallace put it in his famous commencement speech, *'This Is Water'*, 'Everybody worships. The only choice we get is what to worship. And the compelling reason for maybe choosing some sort of god or spiritual-type thing to worship … is that pretty much anything else you worship will eat you alive.'[2]

He goes on to mention money, power, the intellect, physical beauty; if any of those are front and centre in your life, they'll be corrosive. What you have will never be enough, and you'll feel needy, weak, stupid and ugly, respectively. Extrapolate that out to an entire planet, and you have a world of unchecked consumption, driven by insecurity, that looks worryingly like the one we inhabit right now. For Foster Wallace, orienting yourself towards some 'spiritual-type thing' is the only way to avoid the shadow side of your fixations.

It's an idea that looms large in folk wisdom, as well as in myths, legends and religions. As the Buddhists would point out, everything we prize is subject to change and is inherently unstable. However hard you cling on to things – possessions, prestige, even relationships – all you can really achieve in doing so is a heightened state of anxiety. You can't fight the fact that, a few decades from now, you, your partner, your home security system and your professional accolades will have vanished into the ether. Far better to pay attention to what lies beneath all this noise.

This idea is prevalent in the Abrahamic religions too (although it doesn't seem to have filtered down to the kinds of megachurches that preach a 'prosperity gospel'). Take Matthew 6:20: 'Lay up for yourselves treasures in heaven, where neither moth nor rust doth corrupt.'

Even within the notionally secular sphere of therapy and self-help, plenty of concepts seem all but meaningless without a spiritual grounding. For instance, if we are just chance collections of atoms in a blind universe, it's hard to see *why* we should hold ourselves in 'unconditional positive regard'. Nor is it clear what 'personal growth' means – which part of you is 'growing' and what is its organising principle or destination? And while many an inspirational Instagram account will inform you that 'fear' stands for 'False Evidence Appearing Real', that isn't much consolation to those who see death as genuine oblivion.* There is a thin line between depression and philosophical nihilism, and the latter seems hard to counteract without using explicitly spiritual concepts. The overlap between spirituality and mental health is one that will recur in various guises throughout this book.

Our species has probably had spiritual teachings for as long as we've had language. These have offered ways to make sense of life, to live as well and as meaningfully as possible, and to tell stories about the numinous. Even today, those who follow some kind of spiritual teaching usually profess to be happier than those who don't. And while this isn't an argument for the veracity of those teachings, it is an argument for looking carefully at the needs that are being addressed.

I'd go further and say, with our planet in crisis, we are bumping up against the limits of our dominant secular narratives – especially those around progress, dominion over nature, and the belief that we should be growing GDP at all costs. We're in a polycrisis – defined by the World Economic Forum as a state 'where disparate crises interact such that the overall impact far exceeds the sum of each part'.[3] Many of us are desperately worried about the condition of the world, to the point that a high proportion of millennials and

---

* I'm not sure these accounts are fact-checked, to be honest.

Gen Z are foregoing having children. It's as though 'life's longing for itself'[4] – a beautiful phrase by the poet Kahlil Gibran – is being overshadowed by our fears about what's to come.

If we are to find hope amid the polycrisis, we sorely need new ways of understanding the world and our place in it. These kinds of narratives could play a key role in systems change, giving us a conceptual footing for building a better world and a rope to pull ourselves back from the brink. At the very least, the stories we tell can help us on an individual level, imbuing our lives with meaning as so much of what we hold dear sputters out.

All this said, the question of *which* stories to buy into is far from simple. Presumably it was easier many centuries ago – you'd opt for whichever rain god or hunting goddess belonged to your immediate tribe. Even fifty years ago, it was the done thing for the average British person to spend their Sunday mornings in church. It's a different matter if you grow up in a multicultural society with the mores of an entire planet just a few clicks away. How on earth are you supposed to select your 'god or spiritual-type thing' in the information age?

I write this with the obvious caveat that, in many parts of the world, traditional religion hasn't gone anywhere. In places like Iran or northern Nigeria, apostasy is serious stuff, and the vast majority of people would call themselves believers.[5] Right-wing Hindu nationalism is rife in India, while Islamic revivalism is a global phenomenon. In the US, the Christian Right is as vocal as ever, with many political rallies now serving up their 'America First' sloganeering with a side of evangelical praise music.[6]

However, the general shift away from organised religion has been confirmed by studies from Chile to South Korea. According to a World Values Survey, the importance of God dwindled in 39 out of 44 countries between 2007 and 2019.[7] In the UK's 2021 census, less than half of British adults described themselves as Christian – making Christians a minority for the first time.[8] More than a third of respondents said they had no religion, including more than half the nation's twenty-somethings. Even in the comparatively God-fearing US, the trend is all one way. As of 2024, 28 per cent of American adults say they do not have a religious affiliation, up from 16 per cent in 2007.[9] Colloquially, the unaffiliated are known as 'nones'.

Of course, a shift away from religion doesn't necessarily mean a shift towards non-belief. In fact, many new 'gods or spiritual-type things' are being forged in the crucible of online spaces. Alongside the more nefarious examples, which often include an element of conspiracy theory,[10] are those that just sound a bit nutty. I recently learned about Bashar, a multidimensional, extraterrestrial 'friend from the future' who speaks through a man called Darryl Anka. He provides 'cutting-edge information' on everything from parallel realities to the history of the universe, and currently has 143,000 followers on Instagram.

At the same time, digital culture is driving scepticism, with the information at our disposal making it easier for individuals to pick holes in the stories we've inherited. I think I speak for a lot of people today when I say I'm suspicious of pre-packaged belief systems. It doesn't matter whether those systems come from the Church or have been unspooled from some online rabbit hole at 4am – I'm not going to take their claims at face value.

People like me haven't signed up to living a life devoid of meaning and purpose. What we want is to define that purpose in our own terms. And for many of us 'nones' – those who reject both organised religion and the unsavoury melting pot of conspirituality – that does include an element of the spiritual. My aim throughout this book is to explore what this might look like. What are my fellow 'nones' doing to fill the spirituality gap?

Now, you may wonder what qualifies me to write such a book at all, given my lack of guru status. It's precisely because I haven't found any definitive answers, precisely because I'm an avowed agnostic who baulks at religion and feels out of place in New Age spaces, that I'm so aware of the spirituality gap. I am someone who feels a spiritual hunger very acutely, yet I struggle to define what that hunger represents, and I haven't found a reliable formula for sating it. Like the physicist Richard Feynman, I believe: 'It's much more interesting to live not knowing than to have answers which might be wrong.'[11] I'm also fascinated by those who say they *do* have answers – how did they acquire them and what effect, in the end, does that have on their life?

My route towards this point was a little unusual. I was brought up a Christian, and not the kind of Christian who only goes to church at Christmas and prays to an old man in the clouds. My church was part of Newfrontiers (then New Frontiers International or NFI), a socially conservative band of churches that insisted on biblical literalism. If you believed in Jesus, you went to heaven, and if you didn't, you went to hell. It was that stark. There was also the small matter of the Holy Spirit, who was supposedly sweeping the nation's churches in a wave of religious revival. During an average Sunday service, it was common to come across someone speaking in tongues, someone bringing a prophesy, and someone falling to the floor and writhing around uncontrollably (we called this being 'zapped').

Regarding the heaven vs hell thing, your eternal destiny was supposedly unrelated to your moral mettle. In theory, you could devote all your time to opening soup kitchens and rescuing drowning puppies from whitewater rapids but still go to hell. Or you could live your life as a murderous maniac, convert on your deathbed, and go to heaven. It all came down to belief. While there might be special dispensation for babies, or those who'd been born in a different historical era, the typical non-believer had no excuse. Those who had failed to accept the 'Good News of Jesus Christ' would be tormented for their thought crimes for all eternity.

Naturally, this was a recipe for neurosis, and I started to have my doubts very young. It began with 'What about the dinosaurs?' – if the Genesis creation story was true, where did my beloved diplodocus toy fit in? A woman at church thought she'd cracked it: dinosaurs had never existed, and the devil had planted their bones to hoodwink scientists. A little later, I was assured that the theory of evolution is only that, a theory, and therefore doesn't count for much against the infallible word of Genesis 1.

Not everyone at church was so face-smackingly literal. Lots of people (my parents included) maintained that the biblical creation story was metaphorical, and that the religion was compatible with mainstream science. However, my appetite for answers wasn't so easily satisfied. By my early teens, I was hoovering up books that purported to explain exactly why this mystifying worldview made sense. It was as if, by finding the answers, I could cast out my badness. I would finally be a true believer, St Peter stamping my hand in approval as he nodded me through the pearly gates.

Each time I found an answer, I'd be temporarily appeased, assured of my own heavenly destiny for a day or two. Still, there was one thing I couldn't get my head around, and it related to that whole hell business. I got it, you went there unless you were a Christian. But...what actually constituted a Christian? George W. Bush was supposed to be a Christian – never mind that thousands of innocent civilians had perished in his invasions of Iraq and Afghanistan – and likewise his good friend Tony Blair. The American Bible Belt was full of Christians, often quite racist ones, along with sects like the Mormons and Jehovah's Witnesses that you could maybe class as Christian and maybe not. You had the Quakers – peaceful, thoughtful people by all accounts, and ostensibly Christian, but with some members who didn't believe in God. You had people who called themselves Christian, but only believed certain bits of the Bible, schizophrenics who thought they were channelling Jesus, and billions who rejected the 'Good News' because they'd been brought up a Hindu, Buddhist, Muslim or Jew. The more I looked, the more gradations I saw: a rich spectrum of spiritual practices, shaped more by background and disposition than anything resembling 'free will'. Wherever you put the dividing line for salvation, it didn't make much sense.

I knew, of course, that 'God moves in mysterious ways'. But was it really mysterious or was it just petty-minded? This was a God who rewarded blind faith while penalising intellectual inquiry, a patriarchal God who wanted to pen you into a fear-based set of doctrines that collapsed under the slightest bit of analysis. I was a teenage girl, for goodness' sake, and I knew better than that. Around the age of seventeen, I made my choice: I refused to believe in a deity who was less intelligent and less humane than I was.

By the time I came of age, right in the middle of the New Atheists' heyday, the non-existence of God (or this God anyway) was so obvious to me as to be barely worth my attention. I had already gone through the arguments for and against, weighing up Pascal's wager against Occam's razor against Russell's teapot. I'd become convinced that the atheist arguments had the upper hand, and that the only way anyone believed in God was through a combination of logical fallacies and wishful thinking.

I wouldn't have called myself spiritual either. There was a shop named Guru Boutique in my hometown, which sold incense, crystals and henna tattooing cones. I liked the smells in there, and enjoyed the faintly transgressive feeling of being in there, as though I'd stumbled across a New Age Aladdin's cave. But I was a tourist in spaces like these, and a snarky one at that. Just as I didn't waste my time arguing against an imaginary God, I didn't lie awake at night pondering the colour of my aura or the workings of homeopathic water memory.

For me, atheism was simply part of a broader worldview that trusted facts over hunches, evidence over ideology, and the replicable and experimentally validated over subjective experiences. Religion was an unfortunate relic, and so was its wishy-washy, wind chime-wielding cousin 'spirituality'. Both spoke to the human tendency for self-deception, and our unwillingness to confront life's harsher truths. I became a science journalist and committed myself to rooting out sloppy thinking.

If things had ended there, this would have been a very different kind of book. But over time, something in me shifted. Intellectually, I still bought into all the arguments that had made me an atheist in the first place. It was just that something kept tugging at the edges of my consciousness, something that vanished as soon as I turned to look at it. I started calling myself an agnostic. Then I lost my father very suddenly, two months after his sixtieth birthday, and the big existential questions became all I could think about.

This book was dreamed up in the aftermath of my dad's death, in November 2018. Grief-stricken, I took part in an ayahuasca ceremony, which gave me an entirely new perspective on what spirituality might mean. Then came a move across an ocean, a pandemic, a marriage, a baby. My daughter was born in November 2022, and I wrote the first draft of this book while on maternity leave.

As psychedelic researchers David Yaden and the late Roland Griffiths have written, people 'frequently rate their psychedelic experiences as among the most meaningful of their entire lives and they are sometimes compared to the birth of a first-born child or death of a parent'.[12] You'll note that I experienced all three of these 'narrative inflection points', as Yaden and Griffiths describe them, during the time when this book was in gestation. They heightened my sense that spirituality is not about beliefs at all (although beliefs may be useful in its pursuit), but about something more integral to our humanness. Spirituality is the part of us that comes to the fore when something big happens, our basic programming, the very deepest stratum of our lives. It also intersects with the question of hope in rocky times, and why 'life's longing for itself' persists even when it's hard to rationalise.

If you're a person of strong religious faith or spiritual conviction, you might feel I'm missing something. I'm aware that 'the spirituality gap' has echoes of what some Christians call 'the God-shaped hole', a void that can only be filled with God. From that perspective, practices like 'getting a birth chart reading' and 'going to a rave' will probably seem flimsy substitutes. The same applies if your gut reaction, on encountering any form of spiritual talk whatsoever, is to feel that something is being intellectually bypassed. As I look into topics like tarot and reiki, you may be of the view that I don't treat my subject matter critically enough.

But I'd wager that many of us are caught somewhere in the middle – 'nones' who are struggling to find a framework for what feels like an authentic spiritual impulse. Maybe, like me, you've had mystical or transcendental experiences, or been blindsided by an inexplicable comfort during a dark time in your life. Maybe you have met God on LSD or have experienced synchronicities that you don't want to call coincidences. Or maybe you haven't had these experiences but are intrigued by the accounts of those who have. Perhaps you *do* think that personal experience has something to tell us, and that the scientific method, however important, is not our only means of gleaning truthful information about the world.

My question, then, is this: do we have to pick a side? Or can I embrace something vital at the heart of spirituality while rejecting dogma, wishful thinking and pseudoscience?

It would be ridiculous for me to attempt a comprehensive overview of contemporary 'secular spirituality'. There are probably as many variants as there are people. Instead, I've selected a few practices that seem to be growing in prevalence among the 'nones' – or at least those in my own limited frame of reference.

Over the next twelve chapters, I will meet people who swear by the Law of Attraction or ultrarunning or Gaia theory as a means of channelling their spiritual impulses. I will receive a shamanic healing, have a birth chart reading, train as a reiki practitioner, try ecstatic dancing, have a spiritual experience in a swimming lake and attend an atheist church. Some of the practices I cover – tarot, astrology, energy medicine – fall neatly into the New Age bracket, while others – exercise, raves, mindful meditation – would generally be considered secular. Some of them mesh easily with my own sensibilities, while others don't. All of them, though, seem to be gathering steam among my own cohort of godless metropolitan millennials.

To make my own position explicit: I'm a white, university-educated woman in my thirties, living in London. I'm part of a demographic that's immensely privileged in most ways, but maybe not so much when it comes to spirituality. As I will explore further throughout this book, many people like me lack any strong ancestral tradition to call on. Our attempts to locate spiritual practices can often feel forced or phoney. Many of the 'gods or spiritual-type things' that are packaged for us are tarnished by consumerism. At worst, this commodification can lead us to treat the rest of the world as our grab bag, snatching a little from this culture and a little from that, because our own doesn't appear to have the goods. Or we fall back on secular traditions for spiritual sustenance, often mediated by the language of mental health.

If there's a bright spot here, you could say the spiritual path is often framed in terms of 'seeking'. What better opportunity for seekers than to live in a society with multiple entry points to the maze?

As I wade into these types of practices, it's inevitable that some thorny questions will arise, which I'll attempt to answer with the help of experts. Throughout, I aim to take my subject matter seriously, while doing my best not to descend into sloppy thinking. Depending on your proclivities (or my own unchecked biases) you might think I go too far in one direction or the other. Nonetheless, I will do all I can to strike a balance, and, per that Buddhist proverb, see what all these pointing fingers have to tell me about the directional coordinates of the moon.

Chapter 1

Ayahuasca: To Narnia and Back

In January 2019, during what was probably the worst time in my life, I caught a train to an industrial estate just outside of Amsterdam and made my way to an unmarked door. Despite Google Maps' assurances, I appeared to be standing outside a lorry depot. It was a dreary day, with slab-grey buildings set against a similarly grey sky. There was nothing here suggestive of spiritual healing.

I waited there without knocking, frozen with anxiety. A few minutes later, another woman joined me, looking as incongruous as I was.

'Are you here for the...uh, ceremony?' I asked her, clocking the white pyjamas under her coat.

'The ayahuasca ceremony, yes,' she said, as though this were a perfectly normal way to spend a Tuesday lunchtime. 'Shall we go in?'

She pushed open the door, and I followed her upstairs. It wasn't a lorry depot, but nor was it the magical jungle enclave you might expect if you've read any other ayahuasca trip reports. In one room, six mattresses were laid out as for a teenage sleepover, albeit with a bucket and a roll of toilet paper beside each one. In another room, our facilitators (it didn't feel right to call them shamans) were meeting and greeting participants. As per the instructions received, we were all wearing white from head to toe, which set my cult radar into overdrive.

Toilet paper and sick buckets aside, this was the most unabashedly New-Agey room I'd ever visited. It featured a dreamcatcher, tarot cards, incense, a sculpture of the elephant-headed Hindu god Ganesh, a circle of candles in the central ring of a spiralling Afghan rug. This was where I'd spend the next two days, using my mattress both for sleeping and… well, it remained to be seen. Confronting my demons? Undergoing psychic surgery? Unravelling the fabric of spacetime? Puking my guts out? That mattress had seen some shit – possibly literally.

I was here to sample one of the most powerful psychedelics known to humanity. A psychoactive brew concocted from two plants, ayahuasca comes from the Amazon basin, where tribal societies have been using it medicinally for hundreds of years. In many traditions, the idea of drinking it for personal healing would have sounded as odd as a patient wielding a scalpel – it was down to the *curanderos*, or healers, to drink the brew. They'd embark on journeys through unseen realms, trying to uncover the source of their patient's malady or even to rescue their soul. In other traditions, ordinary people drank it recreationally, or used it to visit their family members from afar.[1]

Very few Westerners caught wind of these practices – and the ones who did responded in predictable ways. Take the seventeenth-century Jesuit missionaries who described the brew as the work of the devil. 'When the sorcerer sees the assembled people possessed and fixed in fear, he screams and says…"You will hear, you will hear",' reads the first written report of an ayahuasca ceremony, dating to 1675.[2] A century later, ayahuasca caught the attention of the Victorian explorer and botanist Richard Spruce, although it remained little known outside of anthropology departments for quite some time.[3] Then, in the 1950s, Beat author William S. Burroughs embarked on a Holy Grail-like quest for *yagé*, another name for ayahuasca, trekking through Colombia, Panama and Peru in search of the 'elixir'. 'Yagé may be the final fix,' he wrote in his novel *Junky*, laying the groundwork for the ayahuasca boom to come.[4]

Over the subsequent decades, the medicine has been popularised among Westerners. South America has seen an upsurge in ayahuasca tourism, while ceremonies of varying degrees of legality have been cropping up across Europe and North America.

From what I'd heard, the stuff was downright terrifying. People had reported visiting their personal hell and doing battle with their deepest fears, often while undergoing dramatic hallucinations involving demons and alien surgeries. Oh, and then there was the puking. Lots and lots of puking. You supposedly hurled your guts up in a bucket and you were lucky if it just came out the top end. Ayahuasca, a Quechuan word meaning 'the vine of the dead', made magic mushrooms sound like a teddy bears' picnic.

On the other hand, it was meant to be the real deal, the most powerfully therapeutic of all the psychedelics. One ceremony was supposedly equivalent to ten years on the therapist's couch, ideal for somebody as impatient as I was.

Our facilitators, whom I'll call Abdul and Joost, were two old friends with dramatic transformation stories. A little dubiously, they claimed that ayahuasca had cured them of years of criminality and addiction. After dozens of ceremonies, they were family men: clean-living, life-loving and spiritual.

Abdul 'smudged' the room with white sage, a ritualistic manoeuvre designed to 'cleanse its energies'; he then made us inhale a kind of tobacco called rapé, which might as well have been a blowtorch up the nose. We were instructed to light a candle and each set our intention. 'Teach me in the way I need to be taught, and heal me in the way I need to be healed,' I mumbled, sticking with something generic and open-ended that I'd sourced from an internet forum the night before. I felt sure that doing this ceremony would open a can of worms, but which kind of worms, specifically, remained to be seen.

The idea that psychedelic drugs can function as a tool for self-enquiry, or even as a conduit to mystical experiences, is hardly a radical one. Think of the Bill Hicks quote: 'Today a young man on acid realised that all matter is merely energy condensed to a slow vibration, that we are all one consciousness experiencing itself subjectively, there is no such thing as death, life is only a dream, and we are the imagination of ourselves. Here's Tom with the weather.'[5]

It's funny because it's accurate. Of course the young man on acid would have a grandiose revelation about the nature of reality, one that to him seems ground-breaking and newsworthy, but comes off as faintly absurd to anyone else. This trope was spoofed more recently in the existential comedy *The Good Place*, in which photos of a 'stoner kid' named Doug Fawcett adorn the walls of the afterlife. Apparently Doug had got high on mushrooms, and correctly described 92 per cent of what happens after we die.

Psychedelic substances have been a source of profundity, or pseudo-profundity, for as long as there have been people willing to consume them. They have been used for thousands of years in shamanic cultures, shaped many religions, and are still in use in rituals today. When used for spiritual purposes they are called 'entheogens', a term coined in 1979 from the Ancient Greek word *éntheos*.*

Modern Westernised culture, in fact, is very much an anomaly in its attitude to psychedelics. Since 1970, when the US Controlled Substances Act and its international counterparts were signed into law, the likes of LSD, psilocybin, DMT, mescaline and ayahuasca have been prohibited in most countries. For several decades, research in the field almost ground to a halt, and public information campaigns further entrenched the stigma. Just think of the 'This Is Your Brain on Drugs' adverts from the 1980s, which depicted said brain on drugs as a sizzling egg, or the 'Just Say No' campaign that followed it. I grew up thinking that all drugs were bad and that psychedelics were the worst of the worst – my brain would be staying unsizzled, thank you.

Before that, though, psychedelics enjoyed a brief grace period, during which thousands of scientific experiments were conducted into psilocybin and LSD. If you tried to tell the story of the hippie movement without mentioning psychedelics, you wouldn't have much to talk about – no Woodstock, no Timothy Leary, no 'Lucy in the Sky with Diamonds', and certainly no tie-dye.

At the time, these substances were considered a great hope for psychiatry – and for many contemporary thinkers, their

---

* Usually translated as 'possessed by a god', or 'inspired'.

spiritual potential was obvious. As Alan Watts wrote in his 1968 essay 'Psychedelics and Religious Experience': '[Mystical] states of consciousness induced by psychedelic drugs ... are virtually indistinguishable from genuine mystical experience ... The quality of these experiences depends considerably on one's prior orientation and attitude to life, although the now voluminous descriptive literature of these experiences accords quite remarkably with my own.'[6]

While psychedelic research languished in the wilderness for several decades, a casualty of anti-hippie sentiment and the War on Drugs, the last twenty years have seen the makings of what is being called a 'psychedelic renaissance'. In 2005, the British medical press published its first editorial on psychedelic therapy in decades. This was followed by a symposium at the Royal College of Psychiatrists and a major international conference. Since then, dozens of studies have got underway, attempting to determine whether the likes of LSD, psilocybin, MDMA and ketamine might be used to treat mental health conditions.

'We have a drug classification scheme that is not fit for purpose,' said the writer and psychiatrist Dr Ben Sessa, when I spoke to him for an article in 2016. 'It's not based on any science whatsoever. Drugs like psilocybin and LSD are incredibly useful in psychiatry, and they're virtually inert physiologically – there have been no recorded deaths from toxicity. As a pharmacologist I look beyond what the government arbitrarily calls legal or illegal, and I look at the relative benefits of the compound. When you do that, it's a very frustrating arena in which to work.'[7]

Sessa was an interesting person to interview. He had been involved with the research revival from the outset, both as a doctor and as a research subject – in 2009 he became the first person in thirty-three years to be legally administered a psychedelic drug in the UK. He also had strong views on why these studies were so hard to conduct, and why the pharma industry had so little interest in funding them.

'Most psychiatric drugs, like SSRIs, are maintenance therapies – you take them day in, day out, sometimes for years, and they mask the symptoms,' he told me. 'But MDMA or psilocybin therapy is, if I dare use the word, somewhat curative, so there's no product there for the pharma industry. Why would they throw tens of millions of dollars at this product when there's very little profit to be made from its use?'

This might sound like your classic conspiracy theorist, anti-Big Pharma tirade, if it weren't for Sessa's legitimacy in the field and the many others corroborating his viewpoint. I became fascinated by this area of research. And not, I must admit, for purely disinterested journalistic reasons. I wanted to know whether psychedelics might help me.

Here on this grimy mattress, I was about to find out. By this point, I wasn't a stranger to psychedelic experiences; I lived in Amsterdam, where magic truffles are legal. But, right now, I needed more. I'd had a relentless year, spanning a bad breakup, six weeks sleeping on a friend-of-a-friend's couch, an intense fling followed by another breakup, a tax bill I couldn't pay, a cat no longer in my custody, and an ongoing stretch of career stagnation. And just seven weeks previously, my apparently healthy father had died of a cardiac arrest while on a bike ride. My grief was blinding. Coming here would have seemed foolhardy if I'd had anything to lose.

We drank the brew in two parts: ayahuasca vine first (*banisteriopsis caapi*), followed by chacruna leaves (*psychotria viridis*). The first cup worked as a monoamine oxidase inhibitor, meaning it blocks the activity of a particular enzyme and allows your body to process the second cup. Cup number two contained DMT (N, N-Dimethyltryptamine), a potent hallucinogen that, following research by the psychiatrist Rick Strassman, has become widely known as 'the spirit molecule'.[8] Both came in a shot glass and, like most things that come in shot glasses, were variations on a theme of repulsiveness.

Medicine administered, I lay back on the mattress and tried to focus on my breathing. In – and out – and in – and out. The hardest part was keeping the nausea down. The girl beside me threw up, loudly, five minutes in, followed by another participant two minutes later. Since the medicine hadn't kicked in yet, both were required to drink again.

Aside from trying not to puke, not much else seemed to be happening. I wondered if I was going to be one of those rare participants who doesn't get anything from ayahuasca; someone whose physiological makeup, or maybe psychological blockages, debars them from the psychedelic realm. I hoped that wasn't the case. Demons I could deal with, I prided myself. But I wasn't sure I could handle a total anticlimax.

'Come on,' I thought, addressing the plant a little indignantly, 'don't you know what things have been like for me? Aren't you going to show me the way through, let me purge it?'

Suddenly, I became aware of a warm, protective presence, 'Mother Ayahuasca' herself. Right on cue came some visuals: a vision of myself as a baby, being cradled by a maternal figure all in blue. She was rocking me back and forward as I cried, making conciliatory noises.

'Don't worry,' she seemed to say. 'You've been through the worst of it already. You don't need a dark, difficult ceremony to strip down your ego, because you've already been stripped down. You've reached a new point in the life cycle, the rebirth.'

Now, I know that when I speak of ayahuasca 'saying' something, or position it as a character in my psychodrama, I sound more than a little unhinged. There are lots of theories on what happens during a ceremony, some of which accord more easily than others with a typical Western mindset. There are those who believe the plants themselves are communicating with the journeyer, and others who believe the medicine forges a direct connection with the spirit realm. You can take a Jungian perspective and posit that it puts you in touch with your higher self or the collective consciousness, or that it allows you to integrate the unconscious material lurking within your shadow. There are also ways of viewing the experience that are compatible with no-frills scientific materialism. I'll come to these later on.

But for now, I'll just say that the hallmark of the ayahuasca experience was the sense that something else had taken the reins, an unfamiliar intelligence that wasn't 'me' as I normally understood myself. I was variously punished, rewarded, toyed with, given tough love, given gentle love, shown things about myself I hadn't realised, and even subjected to some high-concept hijinks as Mother Ayahuasca played tricks on me. I was grappling with a powerful unknown here, and all I could do was hang on for the ride.

'I don't think there's any doubt that tripping is all in the mind,' I wrote in my notes after the ceremony, 'although what the mind actually *is* is open to question.'

While this wasn't the trip to hell I'd envisaged, you could call it a kind of sensory purgatory. Much like the 'baby' I had become, I wanted to cry one minute and laugh the next and was constantly on the cusp of overwhelm. According to one theory, pioneered by Dr Alison Gopnik at UC Berkeley, there are remarkable similarities between young children's brains and those of adults using psychedelics. 'The short summary is, babies and children are basically tripping all the time,' she says in Michael Pollan's seminal book on the subject, *How to Change Your Mind: The New Science of Psychedelics* (2018).[9] The default mode network, a cluster of brain regions heavily influenced by psychedelics, serves to filter out 'unnecessary' information (i.e., whichever information is less relevant to survival). It isn't yet operational in young children, giving them access to a rich, untempered and thoroughly exhausting world of magic. The same applies to adults tripping balls.

Seven hours after I drank the first cup – although it could just as easily have been seven minutes or seven days – Abdul handed me a bowl of fruit, and I began to edge back towards grown-up consciousness. 'I don't think I'm going to stay for the second day,' I told him, convinced I'd wrung just about everything I could from the experience.

'Sleep on it,' he said knowingly. 'The medicine is only just getting started.'

How psychedelics work is a puzzle we are only now beginning to unravel, thanks to a trickle of research studies in the field that is starting to become a flood. I called up Dr James Cooke, a neuroscientist and psychedelics researcher at University College London and Trinity College Dublin, to ask him what's going on neurologically when we trip.[10] He gave me a quick primer on the role of the cortex, the part of the brain that builds up models of the world. During normal perception, the brain receives all kinds of inputs that it transforms into a working map of reality. The mapping process isn't perfect – that's why we have optical illusions – but it's robust enough for our day-to-day purposes. It's a kind of perceptual shortcut, saving time as you move though the world.

When you take a classic psychedelic like LSD or psilocybin, the compound binds to receptors in the cortex called 5-HT2A. This seems to mess with the mapping process, meaning the brain has a harder time matching sensory input to its models.

'As I'm looking at a tree, there are circuits in my visual cortex that, based on learning, have encoded a template of what a tree looks like, which gets matched to the visual input,' says Cooke. 'There's an implicit assumption that the tree trunk is not going to suddenly turn into a cow – that's not in my model. But psychedelics take away how tightly you hold on to those expectations. Suddenly, you're looking at a tree trunk and might start to see faces in the bark.'

There are lots of 5-HT2A receptors in the visual cortex specifically, which is why psychedelics typically have strong visual effects, and fewer auditory ones, for instance. Where things get really interesting, however, is in the default mode network (DMN) which, in addition to filtering information, also seems to play a role in generating our sense of self.

'Robin Carhart-Harris at Imperial has argued that this effect of dissolving your models also happens at the top of hierarchy, where you have these very sophisticated models of the self,' says Cooke. 'It's like knocking out a dictator. The brain is pushed into a more anarchic situation where memories can be associated with new things, and everything starts bubbling up.'

To use a different analogy, coined by Carhart-Harris himself, we might think of the mind as a ski slope. As we ski down the slope, we create deep grooves in the snow, habitual patterns of mind that become further entrenched each time we ski. It becomes harder and harder to avoid them. A psychedelic works like a snowstorm – a state of entropy that covers up those tracks and gives us the chance to forge new pathways.[11]

That seems to be part of why psychedelics can have therapeutic effects: for the duration of the trip, you have the cognitive flexibility to dislodge old patterns of thinking and let new ones take root. But it's also why the psychedelic watchwords 'set and setting', mindset and environment, are so important. If these substances cause you, in effect, to revert to a childlike neurology, then with that comes a childlike vulnerability. You're more suggestible to outside influences, for better or worse, and tripping with the wrong people or in the wrong environment can do real harm. There is a case to be made for taking these substances in controlled therapeutic settings, with experienced guides on hand to help.

Most relevant for our purposes: the DMN may also hold the key to mystical states. This is a subject close to Cooke's heart, following an ego death experience he had as a teenager.

'I was a very scientifically oriented kid who happened to have a stress-induced spiritual experience,' he tells me. 'The nature of the experience was non-conceptual. It was like the thinking mind, the mind that labels things, stopped as a result of stress. And what was left was the perception of reality as a whole. I was part of it in a way that felt incredibly positive, and more real than the way I usually think.'

During his PhD research, Cooke became interested in how the brain pulls off this ruse. How does it take a unified reality, and fool us into thinking it's made up of discrete objects, not least a so-called 'self' that's separate from the rest of the world?

'There's an interesting thing that happens with [an individual human] life, which is that it attempts to pull away from the rest of the world for a time,' remarks Cooke. 'And then eventually, with death, we dissolve back into it. But all of our evolved instincts work to keep this process of separation going, and because it's based on survival there's a lot of suffering that goes along with it.'

Reduced activity in the DMN can be occasioned by extreme stress, meditation and even starvation as well as psychedelics; in this state, the illusion of a separate identity briefly falls away, giving rise to a sense of merging with all that is. As powerful experiences go, this one's up there. According to a 2018 research paper, between 66 per cent and 86 per cent of participants in psychedelic trials rated their experiences as one of the top five most meaningful and spiritually significant events of their lives.[12]

'Psychedelics can act on the circuits in the brain that mediate the sense of self, and artificially, for a time, bring down activity there,' says Cooke. 'Physiologically what's happening is that the circuits that produce this struggle and negativity and separation are being relaxed for a while. And what that feels like is coming closer to a feeling of being connected to the rest of the world, coming to this perspective of the universe in which it's actually fine that I'm going to die one day. One of the first studies that sparked the psychedelic renaissance showed that psilocybin in high doses can alleviate fear of death.'[13]

My second ayahuasca ceremony, which took place the next day, did not alleviate my fear of death. But it did plunge me right into the midst of it. Appositely enough for something called 'the vine of the dead', this ceremony was one long *memento mori*. It almost seemed academic that my dad was dead already, while the rest of us would be dead in the future. If you take the view that time is an illusion, which somehow seemed to go without saying here, everything and everyone is marked by certain loss.

I thought about how, most of the time, we distract ourselves from this knowledge. It's like looking at the sun; we can't glimpse it for more than a second without averting our eyes. But every single one of us is just a dying animal without a clue how we came to be here.

This macabre train of thought led me on to something so bizarre I feel quite embarrassed to recount it. I was mulling over the fear of death, and how it can lead to stupidity and brutality. If I can make *you* a victim, I can make *myself* a victor, and kid myself I've outsmarted the Grim Reaper. It struck me that this might apply to the way we treat farm animals. We exploit and abuse them because they remind us of our own weakness; we 'other' them because we want to believe we can transcend our vulnerable animal selves.

Suddenly, I found myself in the body of a chicken, or in a state of bizarre hyper-empathy with a chicken, looking out on a factory farm through chicken eyes. The sensation was one of uncomprehending terror. I seemed to become other chickens after that, and maybe a pig or cow, my normal human cognition gone but my sense of subjectivity frighteningly intact. The point seemed to be that each animal is its own locus of consciousness, that as per Thomas Nagel's famous essay, 'there is something that it is like to be a bat'.[14]

The Spirituality Gap

For sure, this was just a drug-induced vision, as opposed to a philosophical treatise on animal consciousness. But it permeated deeply, and I realised my own lacklustre embrace of Meatless Mondays was no longer going to be enough.

'Oh shit, I have to stop ignoring animal exploitation, don't I?' I thought, miserably. 'But ugh, vegans are such sanctimonious bores. And are you really telling me that I can *never eat cheese again*?'

I saw a piece of cheese in the middle distance, vanishing like a mirage as I approached it.

'If you can handle losing your dad, you can handle losing cheese,' said Mother Ayahuasca, not sternly or reproachfully so much as factually. I understood that I was to mourn mozzarella, grieve gruyère, but that I was to let it go anyway – along with scrambled eggs and salmon and my own swaggering identity as someone who'd eat whatever you put in front of me. This wasn't just a fever dream: I've been a vegan ever since.

The call came round for the second dose, but I decided against it. While I was clearly high as a kite (I mean, I had just turned into a chicken and renounced whole food groups), I was also quite lucid and wanted to retain that. There was less random mental static than previously, as though my brain were a radio receiving a better signal.

I opened my eyes onto a faraway land, with a man I didn't recognise looming above me. Somehow, I knew that in this reality, I was an extremely beautiful woman, the type of woman who inspires fairytales. The type of woman men yearn for, whose face launches a thousand ships, who exists as the sort of Platonic ideal of a woman against whom all others are found wanting.

In my own life as a regular woman, I suppose this kind of goddess would stir up complicated feelings at best. And yet here inside her body, looking out through her eyes, it struck me that it had just been 'me' all along – that familiar sense of being 'I', carried through to a different body and identity. What's more, if people persisted in projecting their shit onto me, my life as the Platonic Ideal of All Women might not be all that rosy.

'Why would anyone envy me, when it's just *me* in here?' I wondered, cutting through thirty-two years of beauty-related insecurities.

I became other people, living other lives. A normal man, working a normal 9–5 before going home to watch *Gogglebox*. A person with facial deformities. A single mother on the breadline working multiple jobs to get by. All of them struggling, some more than others, with their individual flavour of struggle being shaped by the bodies they were born into. I was slapped in the face by the fact of my own white, middle-class privilege. But it also seemed clear that privilege was no bulwark against existential terror, and that the only logical attitude to *any* human was compassion. It seemed risible that we took our differences seriously, when it was just the same 'I' every time, working its way through another set of life experiences.

Of course, that isn't exactly an earth-shattering concept, the idea that my 'I' is identical to your 'I' and that in the sense of being subjective entities we're all the same. If anything, it's an embarrassingly obvious idea: the sort of stoner philosophy you might hear espoused during the dregs of a house party.

Some people come out of their ceremonies aglow with the sense that 'love is all you need' or 'we're all connected' or 'you should appreciate what you have'. These are the kinds of ideas you might find superimposed onto a sunset, in a curly font, on some cringey inspirational Instagram account. And yet ayahuasca has a habit of taking these intellectually unexciting points and making you *feel* them. Under its spell, faded truisms become technicolour realities.

In my case, I was chilling on my mattress, flipping between identities, experimenting with becoming a Brexit supporter or a woman hater, when the true purpose of this psychological costume changing became apparent. Uh-oh. The ayahuasca was going to show me what it was like to be *myself*.

Now, I had been able to muster compassion for just about every character in whom I had taken tenancy. Even the woman hater: when I took my personal emotions out of the equation, I was able to see how the most reprehensible behaviour came from a wounded place. This being so, it seemed jarring that self-compassion had always been such a struggle for me. I prodded round inside and observed what it was like to be this person. She had been through a lot. She had always tried her best. She had made her fair share of mistakes, some of which were shameful to recount, but had always attempted to learn from them. The other characters in my roll call deserved some empathy – could she really be the exception to the rule?

'You haven't been nice to yourself,' said Mother Ayahuasca. 'Well, it's time to be.'

I had never really understood what self-compassion meant before. The idea had always struck me as icky, a cloying piece of therapy-speak on a par with 're-parenting your inner child'. Now, though, something clicked, and I saw how much easier life would be if I harnessed it.

At that moment, I was overcome with a rush of euphoria, far calmer and more expansive than anything I'd thought possible. I seemed to intuit, while in this blissed-out state, that all our struggle was *for* something: that there was a purpose to life and its cycles and something good underlying it all. What form this good took I hadn't a clue – perhaps the next level of the Matrix, perhaps an evolving strain of divinity within humanity – but here it manifested as something warm and even paternal. I saw my dad now, as though he'd never left. He was smiling as though he knew something.

I wasn't quite able to hold on to these beliefs outside the ceremony, although they felt real at the time. I have subsequently gone back and forth on whether, and to what extent, I can trust them. But as I left the centre the next morning, stepping out into a world washed clean, I felt as though I'd been through a conversion.

'It's such a profound and powerful medicine,' says Kerry Moran, an ayahuasca integration therapist, when we speak via Zoom.[15] 'I'm in awe of the intelligence at work here. And I always point out to people, it's not just the intelligence of the medicine, although it clearly is an intelligent spirit. It's also working with your own inner healing intelligence. It's an experience of your deepest self mediated by this amazing plant.'

Splitting her time between Portland, Oregon and Peru, Moran is one of only a handful of therapists worldwide who specialises in helping people make sense of their ceremonies. I'd found her website after my own ayahuasca journeys, when I googled 'ayahuasca integration tips'; how exactly was I supposed to go back to my normal life when I'd just met God and turned into a chicken?

Feeling that my work wasn't done yet, I'd returned to the centre a couple of months after my first visit, and if anything, that experience was even more powerful. That time, the take-home message seemed to be: spirituality is real and important, but it can't be neatly encapsulated in words and concepts. As soon as I think I've found a formulation, I'll find flaws in it, and as soon as I find the flaws in it, I'll end up trashing spirituality.

'Over-intellectualising everything will take you away from the truth about things, rather than towards it,' and 'Learn to have faith without belief,' I wrote, somewhat mysteriously, in my notes.

I had grappled with what it might mean to trust and let go, even when I didn't know what I was surrendering to. I had uncovered some of the mechanisms behind my chronic anxiety. I had come to believe, at least for the duration of my journeys, that there was an unseen pattern behind life's processes, and that death was simply part of this bigger picture.

Life-changing stuff, but in the cold light of day I wasn't sure what to think. I felt like I'd been to Narnia and back – I'd had all these mad adventures, of questionable ontological value, and had emerged from the wardrobe to find that nobody else had left the building. What on earth was I supposed to make of it?

I wanted to talk to Moran because her work bridges so many different approaches: traditional plant medicine, Tibetan Buddhism, somatic therapy and Jungian depth psychology among them. If anyone could explain to me what actually happens during an ayahuasca journey, surely she could.

'It's like we enter a different dimension, or set of dimensions, that we don't normally have access to with our conscious mind,' she tells me. 'It breaks down the barriers and opens things up, so we start to sense things that are not normally available to us. And one facet of that dimensionality is certainly the personal unconscious. I always say it goes down to the root chakra and just starts cleaning out whatever we've repressed or forgotten or avoided. But there are also things that are beyond your personal unconscious that come up – the collective psyche, certainly. And also the world of spirits: plant spirits, invisible healers, the spirit of ayahuasca.'

At first, I suppose I was a bit disappointed with this answer. I wasn't sure I was enough of a hippie to get on board with chakras and spirits. And yet purely scientific explanations seemed unsatisfactory in their own way, like interpreting love as a by-product of hormones or trying to understand humour through reference to linguistic structures. Sure, you could use this paradigm, but some might say you weren't very romantic or didn't get the joke.

In any case, the healing powers of ayahuasca don't seem to be limited by what you believe about them. Moran's view is that the medicine works more by mitigating our sense of separation.

'Traditional healers see everything as this web of connection,' she says. 'We Westerners show up, and we're so broken and so disconnected that healing becomes a process of reconnection. Psychedelics connect us back to nature, they connect us to our broken lineages, to our ancestors, to our souls, to what's bigger than us and what holds us.'

Her mention of nature struck a chord with me. Aside from turning vegan, I seemed to have gone full Earth Mother since my ceremonies: mainlining David Attenborough documentaries and even engaging in the occasional bout of tree-hugging. The comedian Simon Amstell has talked openly about both veganism and ayahuasca (although I'm not sure which of the two came first in his case),[16] while Gail Bradbrook, co-founder of Extinction Rebellion, has said she received the 'codes for social change' during an ayahuasca ceremony.[17]

As the writer Alexander Beiner has pointed out: 'We can't (and definitely shouldn't) put LSD in the water and hope that everyone will turn into a super-conscious environmentalist'.[18] But it seems reasonable to hope that psychedelics could play a role in sparking climate action. A recent paper from researchers at the University of Greenwich concluded that 'psychedelics have the capacity to elicit a connection with nature that is passionate and protective, even among those who were not previously nature oriented.'[19] Unsurprisingly, there are many psychedelic evangelists out there who believe these 'medicines' could be key to sorting out our messes.

Although my integration process had been complicated, I *had* felt more a part of things since my ceremonies. I no longer felt like I carried something repellent inside me, something that served as a barrier to connection. I was sold on ayahuasca's potential to help people – and I wanted to know how Moran thought plant medicines should be integrated into Western cultures. We hear a lot about cultural plundering in this context, and there's something uneasy about rich Westerners trekking into the jungle and misappropriating an Indigenous tradition. On top of that, the underground nature of the scene makes it sketchier than it needs to be. What might ayahuasca retreats look like in Europe and North America once the legal obstacles are overcome? How might they serve people who don't necessarily have a shamanic understanding of spirituality?

'Certainly, it's not the medical model – you don't put ayahuasca in a pill, and calibrate the dosage,' suggests Moran. 'Every brew is different, the whole delivery system in a ceremony is not conducive to laboratories. And I don't believe it should be like the legalised cannabis market, where you just go buy some and take it home. What I'd love is to see it embedded into spiritual community. There's an excitement in creating it as we go along, and finding out what works for the Western mind – meeting ourselves as we are.'

She is adamant that, when done correctly, ayahuasca tourism doesn't have to be a form of cultural pillaging. There can be reciprocity there, an exchange.

'Many people believe that one of the reasons this plant is exploding all over the world is that it's bringing us in so that we wake up before it's too late, changing perspectives to stop us destroying the Earth,' she says. 'So it depends on what kind of attitude you're showing up with. If you can show up with respect and humility and a willingness to work, that's the ground right there.'

Cooke has a different take on ayahuasca. Although far from dismissive about spiritual matters – he describes the Buddha as 'one of the most insightful psychologists who ever lived' – he thinks mystical trip experiences can be explained without deviating from our regular scientific frameworks.

I told him about my sense, so common in ayahuasca ceremonies, that an intelligent entity was guiding the process. He knew exactly what I was talking about and remarked that his own ceremony had featured a band of aliens conducting soul surgery.

'It's something that's incredibly striking and doesn't feel like it can be easily dismissed as a hallucination,' he says. 'Engaging with spirits is something that's found throughout cultures, and I actually want to see it respected and integrated into our understanding of what it means to be human.'

That said, while assuring me he is not 'aggressively wedded to the idea of it being a hallucination', he believes we can make sense of these experiences without invoking literal spirits. 'In terms of feeling like there's another intelligence there, I do think that's the kind of thing the human brain can do very easily – we're a social species, and a lot of our issues are interpersonal,' he says. 'So it could be that it taps into deep parts of us that need to reckon with interacting with others.'

Factor in the sense of ego dissolution we tend to experience through psychedelics – the loosening of our usual associations, the ousting of our inner puppeteer – and it may be that our sense of 'me' and 'not me' ends up going awry.

'I'm working on a theory of psychedelics, and the thing that launched it was thinking about why DMT has these particular properties, why its content is full of interactive, relational things happening,' he says. 'It's comparatively simple to explain ego dissolution, but there's something interesting going on with DMT. And my speculation is that DMT plays a role in the development of human psychology. Taking ayahuasca is like tripping a circuit, it's showing us our fundamental programming. I think this might be why it has such a vivid and "realer than real" feeling, because it's tapping into our deepest programming.'

Mystical experiences, he explains, tend to fall into two brackets. The first are unitive experiences, like his teenage ego death, in which concepts drop away and you're at one with all that is. There is no such thing as 'you' anymore. The second are relational experiences, in which you're still you, but you're engaging with another consciousness. The latter is something we see a lot within Judeo-Christian contexts – just think of Moses and the burning bush – and it's also likely to resonate with anyone who's taken ayahuasca or DMT.

'There's often a kind of encounter with some divine presence, and it absolutely feels realer than real,' says Cooke. 'If you come at it purely philosophically, it isn't a trivial thing to dismiss. You would have a hard time figuring out which level of reality is real, and you would run into problems in the same way that you can run into problems disproving solipsism.'

Nonetheless, he feels that if we grant ourselves a few assumptions – namely that this *is* the real world, and it will respond to our investigations scientifically – we can start to make progress in explaining what happens in a ceremony.

'I don't think we should be hostile to people who don't care for science, and who feel like it's taking away valuable experiences from them,' he says. 'But at the same time, I feel quite passionately that it's important we do make these cases. I've had a lot of experience of caring for a family member with schizophrenia, and seeing first-hand what it's like when someone's perception of reality falls apart.'

This point really grabbed me. If we hold that the spirit realm is real, and that we can literally encounter gods or aliens or angels or snake demons, then our ontology becomes frighteningly porous and unpredictable. Joseph Campbell, the theorist in comparative mythology, wrote: 'The mystic … enters the waters and finds he can swim; whereas the schizophrenic … has fallen or has intentionally plunged and is drowning.'[20] Maybe so, but if we validate the existence of those waters, do we actually help the person who's caught in the rapids?

While Cooke is about as science-minded as it gets, I was impressed by his clear respect for other viewpoints. 'There's a tendency in scientific circles to be quite dismissive of people who don't just take the line it's an hallucination,' he says. 'What I'm trying to do in my public-facing stuff is to be open to the philosophical discussions as well, and not have my mind closed to the idea that these things could show us something different about the world. Everyone acknowledges that there's a deep mystery here. There's no simple answer to what's going on.'

I'd concur with that entirely. My own ayahuasca experience had reinforced that I knew absolutely nothing about, well, anything.

Since then, I haven't had much patience for rhetoric, scientific or otherwise, that positions itself as superior or obviously true. And while I wouldn't say I've embraced a different framework exactly – there'll be no weird rants about awakening to the fifth dimension here – I do feel as though I've been through the looking glass. The world has become 'curiouser and curiouser', and the quest to make sense of it more thrilling.

I've also become much more open to the idea that there is a spiritual dimension to life. I now think that, when people talk about their mystical experiences, we should take their accounts somewhat seriously without immediately trying to rationalise them away. Sure, you might be able to frame them in terms of brain chemistry – just a bunch of neurons firing up – but that's true of *all* our experiences, and I've never heard anyone try to dismiss any other category of experience in this way.

I'm not alone in registering this kind of U-turn after taking a powerful plant medicine. A 2021 *Nature* paper found that psychedelic experiences were associated with 'significant shifts' in people's metaphysical beliefs. Post-use, people were more likely to reject physicalist or materialist views, the idea that reality is material in nature, and embrace positions such as panpsychism or idealism in which consciousness plays a more fundamental role. As the study authors pointed out, this doesn't constitute a philosophical argument against physicalism. But they did find a 'positive association between changes in metaphysical beliefs away from physicalism and increases in psychological well-being'.[21] This bolsters an argument I'll be making throughout this book: that there's a profound relationship between spirituality and mental health.

Another study involved over 2,500 DMT users who had encountered 'an autonomous entity' on their travels.* Eighty per cent reported that the experience had fundamentally altered their perception of reality, with the being typically described as

---

* I would place my own ayahuasca journey in this category: although I didn't meet a specific being, it absolutely felt like something other than me was pulling the strings.

'conscious, intelligent, benevolent, and sacred'. Prior to the encounter, 28 per cent of the sample identified as atheists, dipping to just 10 per cent afterwards. The proportion of those who expressed a belief in 'ultimate reality, higher power, God, or universal divinity' increased from 36 per cent to 58 per cent.[22]

Again, this is not a philosophical argument against atheism. We know that psychedelics heighten people's suggestibility, and I don't think drinking a magical cup of tea can turn you into a vessel for universal truths. But it is startling to consider that there are substances out there that can flip people's beliefs so radically; imagine if religious proselytising had that kind of hit rate. And without wanting to be starry-eyed about it, I suspect substances like DMT and psilocybin could play an important role in bridging the spirituality gap. They bring visionary experiences within the purview of the average person and can awaken a dormant sense of something magical, however you want to construe it.

At a time when pre-packaged belief systems no longer resonate with so many of us, I like the idea that psychedelics can bring us back to basics – revealing something profound at the very core of our consciousness, which each of us gets to decipher on our own terms.

Chapter 2

Yoga: Practice, Practice and All Is Coming

Ayahuasca may have shocked me into taking spirituality seriously, but the seeds of curiosity were planted long before I met 'God' on that grimy mattress. Rewind to 2013, and you'd have caught me beginning a tentative dalliance with yoga.

I say a 'dalliance' rather than a 'relationship' or 'love affair' because the dynamic was complicated from the start. It even felt a little furtive. Yoga wasn't exactly on-brand for me, a sardonic, smart-arse twenty-something who loved to mock the trappings of wellness culture. As far as I was concerned, chugging red wine and being sarcastic was great; sitting in a healing circle and chanting with cowbells was not.

So when I started skipping the pub to go to yoga classes, my journalist mates were bemused. I might have eased their concerns by telling them I was only there to get the 'scoop', some kind of investigative deep dive into the finer points of vinyasa flow. The reality, though, was simpler and more confounding. Something about the practice was calling to me, despite my aversion to all things hippie and the fact I was avowedly 'not spiritual'.

I'd happened upon my first class via a Groupon deal, which offered ten hot yoga sessions for £35. On first impression, the class confirmed my preconceptions, namely that this was the activity of choice for Earth Mother types too peaced out to move. Everyone was in corpse pose, lying flat on their backs. The air was thick with aromatherapy oil and Tibetan chanting. 'Bring on the carrot juice and be done with it,' I thought.

Once the instructor took charge, though, my complacency was smashed into little pieces. The poses ranged from the mildly strenuous to the seemingly impossible. It was a far cry from what I'd expected – the kind of gentle, reparative exercise your nan might do in a church hall.

Ten sessions in, I'd fallen in love. I loved feeling calm and strong and centred. I loved sweating out my purported toxins. I loved stretching my body into unlikely shapes, as though playing Twister in extra dimensions. I especially loved the instructor, who looked like he'd spent the past decade doing headstands in an ashram as opposed to eating KitKats in an office. I emerged from each class aglow with my own embodiment, alive to the fact I was not just some Cartesian brain in a vat, but had a beating heart and an under-utilised pair of lungs.

From that point on, I attended about three classes a week, thrilled by my rapid newbie gains. Before starting yoga, I had the upper body strength of a dishcloth. A few months down the line, I was pretzeling into arm balances and kicking up into handstands against the wall.

Would it be fair to say that I treated yoga as just another exercise class? Yes and no. Yes, in that exercise was my primary reason for being there. I assessed the quality of a class on whether they cued the hard poses, and whether I came out feeling like my muscles had been wrung through a meat tenderiser. If I got the wrong instructor – one who spent too long in the warm-up, say, or who cut out headstands to make time for a seated meditation – I'd feel anxious and restless, convinced they were deliberately trying to harsh my mellow. I was always relieved when the instructor had obvious muscle tone, was wearing gym kit rather than floaty harem pants, and preferred to play banging workout hits than whale music.

That said, you can't really practise yoga – even this neurotic gym-rat strain of 'yoga' – without noticing that there's more to it than that. 'There's no talk here about "getting shredded for summer",' I wrote in my journal. 'It's not about "blitzing your bingo wings", "melting your muffin top", "renouncing your sinful, Satanic flesh" or whatever cover lines *Women's Health* is running this month. Fundamentally it's a "moving meditation" – a meditation for people who are too bad at meditating to do so while sitting still.'

I think what appealed to me most was the idea of exercise without self-flagellation. As someone who lived very much in her head, I'd felt disconnected from my body for years. I saw my body (and, by extension, the squishy emotional part of me) as an unhelpful encumbrance that merited being punished or ignored. Normal fitness classes tended to reinforce the idea that my body was somehow extraneous to me, something unruly that needed to be controlled.

But yoga wasn't about controlling things. It was about noticing things. Notice how your body feels in that pose. Notice the in-breath and the out-breath. Notice any feelings that come up and observe them without judging them. While you might get stronger or slimmer or bendier, changing your physical form was beside the point.

What I was learning from yoga, then, was nothing less than a new way of configuring my sense of self. True, it was geared more around feeling the burn than immersing myself in the oneness of the cosmos. But something about my basic perception of the world was changing, and in that regard, I think you could call it 'yoga'. At a push, you might even call it 'spiritual'.

I'm being careful about my terminology here, because 'what is yoga?' turns out to be a surprisingly complicated question. If I do a quick stretching session via YouTube, is that yoga? What about goat yoga? Beer yoga? Trampoline yoga? Tantrum yoga? The fragile-masculinity-inspired 'broga'? Am I doing yoga if I'm beasting all the poses but am otherwise a terrible human being? What about if I post a really sexy, acrobatic picture of myself, and add an incongruous quote from the Dalai Lama with the hashtag #yoga?

More salient to me in the early days: can I claim to be doing yoga if I don't wholly buy into yogic philosophy? Let's say I'm reaping the benefits, the classes are improving my mental health, and I'm gradually becoming more mindful and less self-hating.

Is that yoga, even if I come at it from a Western standpoint and don't know the first thing about the Yoga Sutras? Also: can I practise yoga in good faith as a white European, or is that cultural appropriation?

I have my own answers to these questions (you may have others), but the fact I need to ask them at all speaks to a wider confusion around the subject. Yoga has become increasingly popular in recent years – nearly half a million Brits attend classes every week, generating revenues of nearly £1 billion.[1] It's billed as a way to calm our minds, strengthen our bodies and provide ourselves with a more palatable form of meditation.

At the same time, there is something truly weird about the position it occupies within our culture. How on earth did an ancient spiritual practice from South Asia turn into something akin to a bums-and-tums workout? Western yoga often seems entirely disconnected from its origins, its 'mystical' roots repurposed as marketing spiel or offered in cheap facsimile. At any given class, you might get sit-ups and a trip-hop playlist, or you might get ommmms and badly told Hindu fables.

For Dr Shreena Gandhi, a professor in the religious studies department at Michigan State University, sprinkling a bit of Sanskrit into a class doesn't serve to make it any more authentic.

'Some people don't want the spiritual aspect of yoga,' she tells me.[2] 'And oftentimes, the spiritual aspect is tied to a certain kind of orientalist construction of a spiritualist India, so I don't know that that's much better.'

In 2017, she and co-author Lillie Wolff wrote an essay expanding this argument.[3] Among other points, they remarked that the popularity of yoga is tied up with colonialism; that we've seen a widespread dilution of its depth and meaning; and that we need to understand the impetuses behind this cultural 'grabbing'.

'From my perspective as an academic, the basic ask is to understand why yoga has become so popular,' says Dr Gandhi. 'And in what ways has this been braided with the larger conversations about whiteness, white supremacy and cultural appropriation?'

I can't say that I'd thought about these questions in much depth when I embarked on my Ashtanga, vinyasa and Rocket teacher training in 2015. My story was a clichéd one: young white woman goes to a lot of power yoga classes and learns how to do a few party-trick poses. Along the way, she realises that yoga is helping her to manage her stress, that she feels more comfortable in her own skin, and that there might just be something to this whole mind–body business. 'Why don't I become a yoga teacher?' she thinks to herself, 'Why not introduce this practice to others like me?'

Where my story maybe diverges from the norm was my insistence on keeping the 'spiritual' bits at safe remove. As I wrote at the time: 'I find the woo stuff hard to reconcile. My approach is basically: yes to asanas, but no to energy fields. Yes to focusing on your breathing, but no to claiming a yoga pose cleanses your internal organs, releases the emotions stored in your hips, or unites you with the divine.'

I went in all guns blazing. 'Sceptics deserve yoga too!' I thought. So many people would love this practice if it weren't for the hippie-dippy packaging! I was a zealot, intent on converting my stressed-out brethren in the pub, who didn't know their chakras from their chimichangas. A few weeks into my training, however, I was worried I'd made a terrible mistake. Could I even claim to be doing yoga if I didn't draw from the associated traditions? Or would it show more integrity to roll up my mat and take up CrossFit instead?

Around this time, it was reported that a Canadian yoga teacher had seen her classes cancelled out of concern for cultural appropriation. When she suggested changing the name to 'mindful stretching', her compromise was rejected: as far as the University of Ottawa was concerned, this was a religious practice she was desecrating.[4]

Earlier that year, two Russian yoga studios had received letters from their local authorities, requesting they stop hosting classes to 'prevent the spread of religious cults and movements'.[5] And a church in Bristol evicted a yoga class from its hall, claiming that yoga is 'definitely a spiritual act whose roots are not Christ-centred'.[6]

I was starting to feel uneasy. The more I learned about yoga, the more I baulked at the thought of teaching it: it was like I'd discovered the True Meaning of Christmas and wasn't sure whether

I was entitled to celebrate. Did I get to have the turkey and sleigh bells if I didn't believe in baby Jesus? Or was the feel-good stuff reserved for the faithful few?

Based on what I was learning on the course, the True Meaning of Yoga was a bit of this and a bit of that – a mishmash of Hindu, Buddhist and New Age thinking. The teachers even wrote on the back of our coursebook: 'No theory is complete. All theories are valid. Explore.' But this didn't seem to leave much room for a science-based view of the world, in which theories are rendered more or less valid depending on what the evidence tells you. The existence of chakras and kundalini energy, or astral and causal bodies, required a leap of faith I wasn't sure I knew how to make. I could accept chakras as a metaphor for the mind, but not as literal 'energy nodes' that occupied a specific part of the 'subtle anatomy'.

Looking back now, I think that's something that often gets missed out of the cultural appropriation discussion. It's not just that Western yoga borrows the signifiers of another culture, it's also that it fails to integrate its concepts. Yoga becomes a kind of metaphysical grab-bag, from which you pull out, and are expected to make sense of, ideas belonging to a totally different paradigm.

The history of yoga is long and much disputed, and way beyond the scope of this book. However, to boil it down to some of the less controversial points: yoga has its roots in the Indus Valley civilisation of Northern India, probably around 5,000 years ago. The word itself, meaning something like 'yoke' or 'union', was first mentioned in the Rig Veda around 1,500–1,000 BCE, and over time, the associated practices were refined and systemised.[7] Patanjali's *Yoga Sutras*, written in the early centuries CE, describes an eight-fold path, in which the eight 'limbs' of yoga guide the practitioner towards higher states of consciousness. One of these limbs is asana – physical posture – although Patanjali doesn't then go on to choreograph a vinyasa class. He simply calls for yogis to maintain a 'steady and comfortable' posture that will help them meditate. Yoga, he said, is *citta vritti nirodha*, 'the stilling of the fluctuations of the mind'.[8]

Over the next few hundred years, more physical forms of yoga, known as hatha yoga, began to emerge, with a view to purifying the body and attaining deeper states of meditation. The *Hatha Yoga Pradipika*, written in the fifteenth century, describes several different asanas that can be deployed towards this aim.[9]

It wasn't till the late nineteenth century, though, that the physical sequences we might recognise as yoga really started to take hold. At this point, yoga masters like Swami Vivekananda began to travel to the West to spread the word.[10] Hatha yoga also experienced a revival in India, thanks in no small part to the work of Tirumalai Krishnamacharya, 'the Father of Modern Yoga', who incorporated a range of standing poses used in gymnastics. His pupils K. Pattabhi Jois and B.K.S. Iyengar pioneered Ashtanga and Iyengar yoga respectively, while his film star disciple Indra Devi helped popularise yoga among the American glitterati.[11]

Yoga's export to the West is often discussed as a benign cross-cultural exchange – if Indians themselves were offering up the practice, how problematic could it really be? However, this was a time in which India was under British colonial rule and anti-Hindu sentiment was rife. As Dr Shreena Gandhi explains, the likes of Vivekananda pandered to Western prejudice by selling yoga as universal and scientific – and actually not very spiritual at all.

'They were very savvy in that way – they said that it wasn't Hindu, and that it was a practice you could do while also being a Christian,' she says. 'In general, they really tried to de-Hinduise yoga while keeping to its South Asian roots. That's because they were selling a kind of mysticism to rich white women, who needed some form of empowerment beyond the doldrums of housewife life.'

From the mid-twentieth century onwards, yoga was touted as a way to get fitter and healthier. Indra Devi promised her followers that the poses would stave off ageing and illness, while Richard Hittleman introduced the practice to millions through his TV show *Yoga for Health*. During the 1960s and 1970s, the hippie counterculture took root and yoga experienced yet another boost, before becoming entrenched as a fitness movement in the 1980s and 1990s.

Since then, the commodification of yoga and its growth as an industry have been unstoppable. According to Statista, the number of Americans practising yoga climbed from 21 million in 2010 to 34.4 million in 2021 (around 10 per cent of the US population).

Worldwide, there are thought to be around 300 million practitioners, with a global market size in the tens of billions of dollars.[12] The yoga industry has splintered into dozens of different styles and lineages, such that one yoga aficionado, when using the term, might be talking about Rocket (the fast-paced progeny of Ashtanga) and another might be talking about a candlelit restorative gong bath.

Anecdotally, I'd say perceptions of yoga have shifted too. Sure, the thinking in some circles may still be that yoga is 'for hippies'. That was what I thought when I purchased my Groupon deal back in 2013 – I feared it might be a one-way ticket towards growing out my armpit hair and crocheting my own lentils. On the whole, though, its growing ubiquity means that yoga has lost those connotations. For many people, it's just another exercise class, no more or less remarkable than Pilates, barre, BodyPump, CrossFit, or any of the smorgasbord of options offered at your local Fitness First.

More troublingly, the social media age and the birth of influencer culture have brought a different set of stereotypes to the fore. If you went by what you saw on Instagram, you'd think yoga was the domain of slim, tanned, conventionally beautiful white women doing acrobatics on a beach. And while this kind of image fixation isn't exactly yogic, it's also the logical conclusion of a practice in thrall to market forces.

Dr Gandhi moved into yoga scholarship after noticing the absurdity of this trend. Having been introduced to yoga by her grandfather, she went on to study American religious history. During her PhD, she happened upon a TV show about something called 'yoga booty ballet'. 'Hmmm,' she thought, 'there's a story here.'

'Capitalism exploits everything – there are no exceptions,' she says. 'It's so encompassing, so pervasive, so much part of our daily lives. The good part of capitalism is it engenders all forms of creativity, like yoga booty ballet, right? But I think that when yoga is marketed as Western, or when academics say it was invented by white women or European wrestlers, my question is: why are you calling it yoga?'

In the years since my teacher training, a groundswell of South Asian yoga teachers have spoken out, explaining why they find the bastardisation of their heritage so painful.

Take Tejal Patel and Jesal Parikh, co-creators of the *Yoga Is Dead* podcast. In their first episode, 'White Women Killed Yoga', they take a broad-ranging look at white fragility, the links between racism and spiritual bypassing, why representation matters, and why yoga is innately political. As Jesal puts it, many white yoga teachers are 'super-liberal women who claim to be all about social justice and equality and intersectional feminism'. And yet when yogis of colour bring up issues, they 'deflect by demanding unity ... [saying] we're just a positive space, we're all about love and light ... we are all one. You hear that all the time – it's just another way of saying shut up and maintain the status quo.'[13]

Nadia Gilani, London-based author of *The Yoga Manifesto: How Yoga Helped Me and Why It Needs to Save Itself* (2022), has talked in depth about the problems with modern yoga – and why she loves the practice anyway.

'Teaching yoga has made me question whether I'm wrong to feel conflicted about what's happened to it,' she wrote in a viral article called 'Why I'm No Longer Talking To White People About Yoga'. 'I can't help feeling that what's going on is in fact a perverse form of 21st Century colonialism. Here I am, a South Asian yoga teacher, feeling forced to distort a tradition that is a part of my own ancestral heritage. This paradox is exhausting to exist within.'[14]

It's a conversation that resurfaces every few months or so, amid a flurry of media articles with titles like 'How the West Ruined Yoga'.[15] The sheer churn rate of these think pieces made me wonder whether the situation has moved on at all. Over the past ten years, has Western yoga culture become more cognisant of why its Lululemon-leggings-and-butchered-Sanskrit schtick might be a bad idea?

'The conversation is starting to happen, but more conversations need to happen,' says Rina Deshpande, an Indian-American yoga teacher, writer and researcher.[16] 'It would be nice if it were an easy fix, but it's not always that way. For instance, I wish not to feel offended when I walk into a trendy store and see Sanskrit printed on T-shirts. But yoga shows us it's a process, we need to stay in practice with it, opening our eyes to the meaning of yoga, and over time we will see things evolve.'

Deshpande agreed to talk to me on the proviso that she could check how her quotes were used. At times, she says, journalism puts an inflammatory spin on the issue: Indian people versus white people, gatekeeping who gets to pick up a yoga mat.

'I don't know of any person from my culture who is versed in true yoga saying others cannot practice it,' points out Deshpande. 'There's a generosity of heart there; it is intended to be shared and is helpful to many.'

However, she does take umbrage against the way yoga is packaged and presented, from marketing it as a weight-loss tool to misusing Sanskrit terminology. There's also the issue of access. Yoga classes can be expensive and its image exclusionary, placing it beyond the reach of many of the communities who could benefit.

'It has become monetised, often by people who might not be grounded in the depths of the practice by having lived and studied and embraced it,' says Deshpande. 'Yoga is becoming another packaged thing that is, ironically, a bit disconnected from what it really is.'

Growing up as a first-generation Indian American, Deshpande was raised to practice yoga as a way of being. That meant following the teachings of gurus, overcoming negative patterns of behaviour, and maintaining a connection to ancestry. 'When I talk about practice, I'm talking about life – it's not just about seeing yourself on a mat,' she tells me.

This isn't the place to delve too deeply into yogic philosophy. However, to take a quick look at the eight limbs of yoga, as outlined in the Yoga Sutras: we begin with *yama* (moral disciplines) and *niyama* (positive observances); before moving into *asana* (physical posture) and *pranayama* (breathing techniques). Next we go deeper into *pratyahara* (sense withdrawal), *dharana* (focused concentration) and *dhyana* (meditative absorption); before eventually reaching *samadhi* (enlightenment or bliss).

You'll note that the *yamas* and *niyamas* – Patanjali's ethical code – come first, and that you're supposed to be observing principles like *ahimsa* (non-violence) and *santosha* (contentment) before you even think about busting out a down dog. From there, the physical posture and breathing techniques are meant to help you prepare the body for meditation. The next three limbs focus on aspects of meditation itself: directing our attention internally, quietening down the chattering mind and sharpening our concentration. The logical endpoint on this journey, promises Patanjali, is a state of merging with one's point of focus, transcending the individual self and realising the oneness of all that is.

It's hard to see how anyone could take issue with any of this. But Deshpande's childhood experience of yoga was often sullied by xenophobic bullying.

'I used to get made fun of for yoga – if I was saying a mantra, or had anything with turmeric in it, I would be consistently put down and teased about it,' she says. 'I thought, "This is embarrassing, and I shouldn't be doing it." To grow up and see it gain traction is very validating, but it's disheartening when it's publicised mainly as an elite and Western thing. To have people not even realise that yoga comes from India.'

She returned to her practice in early adulthood, at a time when she was burnt out from teaching public school in New York City. It proved immensely healing, helping her assuage her depression and anxiety and restore a sense of pride in her heritage. She went on to train as a yoga teacher, along with creating yoga-based interventions for clinical research.

'For instance, I was involved with designing a yoga research app that the Marines were using,' she says. 'We're exploring how mind–body practices can support resilience, anxiety management and stress, which comes with these high-intensity experiences.'

Deshpande's approach to yoga struck me as an interesting bridge between East and West. Ever since yoga was first exported here, Westerners have wanted to understand the practice in relation to measurable benefits. Whether that's tapping into the elixir of youth, looking sexy in a bikini, or improving our physical and mental health, there has to be some kind of endgame that informs why we're practising in the first place. It's a mindset that's hard to shake, even though it may not be entirely yogic.

In the Yoga Sutras, the final *yama* (ethical guideline) is *aparigraha*, which often translates to 'non-attachment' but can also be interpreted as 'non-grasping'. Chasing after a benefit, as capitalism insists we do, is essentially a form of grasping – it posits that there's something that we don't already have, that we need in order to reach wholeness or completion. Yoga, by contrast, asks you to sit with things as they are – observing and accepting, while resisting the urge to seek something different.

For instance, if you turn up at a class called 'yoga for weight loss', and approach your practice through that prism, you're doing something that our twisted culture applauds, but you're not abiding by *aparigraha*. A more yogic approach would involve holding space for yourself and your sensations, including the discomfort you may feel around your weight. If you can succeed in doing that (which to my mind is much harder than burning calories), you might just reach a place of peacefulness that helps you recalibrate your relationship with your body.* In other words, the benefits will come to fruition precisely because they aren't aggressively pursued. As Deshpande has argued in an essay for *Yoga Journal*, this chimes with another central tenet of the Yoga Sutras, the principle of *Vibhūti Pāda* – 'the accomplishments that come as a byproduct of yoga practice'.[17]

In that regard, it isn't entirely misguided to argue the case for yoga's health benefits. The practice has been shown to improve flexibility and muscular strength,[18] manage pain,[19] stimulate brain function[20] and reduce risk factors for heart disease,[21] among other physical payoffs. On the mental health side, it is associated with stress management, improved body image,[22] and reductions in anxiety and depression.[23] One 2017 meta-analysis concluded that yoga can be considered an effective treatment for major depressive disorder.[24]

Deshpande believes that for the most part, yoga philosophy can be compatible with Western approaches. 'There's definitely a connection, and I feel like what we're doing in modern research is giving names to a lot of things that have existed for thousands of years in this practice,' she says. 'So, for example, *samskaras* – we're talking about these habits that we've formed that we get stuck in, which are hard to transform. But is it possible? Absolutely. And with brain research, we see there are actually shifts that happen in the brain when we start to change our thought patterns.'

---

* This may or may not lead to weight loss, but it's an important end in its own right.

To unpack this a little – a *samskara* in yoga philosophy is a 'subtle impression of past actions', which eventually starts to colour our thinking process. It's a habit of mind, which gets stronger through reinforcement. To go back to that 'yoga for weight loss' example, maybe one of your *samskaras* is a tendency to view your body with disgust, or a fixation on 'improving' it. Yoga promises that you can start to dissolve these *samskaras*, largely by generating insight into their illusory nature.

And as Deshpande was saying, you can view this process from a scientific perspective too. Neuroscience shows us that every time we repeat a behaviour or thought process, we're strengthening the associated neural pathways, increasing the likelihood that we'll fall into the same mental rut next time round. Changing these patterns is tricky, but not impossible. Think about the ski slope analogy discussed in the previous chapter, in which the psychedelic 'snowstorm' serves to cover up our existing tracks and allows us to forge new pathways.

On a similar note, *samadhi* – the eighth limb of yoga, in which you blissfully transcend the self – sounds a lot like Dr James Cooke's unitive mystical experience, which, in scientific terms, translates to reduced activity in the default mode network of the brain.

In both these examples, we can see how ancient yogic philosophy and modern research take us back to a similar place, even if the terminology is different. The distinction between what counts as 'mental health' and what counts as 'spiritual' starts to get rather blurry.

I put a similar line of questioning to Dr Gandhi. Like Deshpande, she has no qualms about viewing yoga through a mental health lens, and thinks that, overall, this kind of perspective can be very positive.

'Anything that makes a practice better, more accessible and more thoughtful when it comes to people's various triggers or traumas, I don't think is a bad thing,' she says.

That said, she believes that if your sole aim is to feel good, then you've missed the point. Yoga was never meant to be about 'good vibes only', 'love and light', or any of the other toxically positive states that might masquerade as robust mental health. Rather, it's about an honest reckoning with reality – which will mean contending with the 'bad vibes' for long enough to challenge systems of oppression.

'The skills you learn when you practise yoga – like observation of self, sitting with discomfort – those are skills that you can use to become antiracist,' says Dr Gandhi. 'If you turn those observational skills outward, you can sit with the discomfort that you may or may not feel because of things like white supremacy, colonialism, and, especially in the British context, imperialism.'

Although the Western pursuit of wellness isn't incompatible with yoga, she thinks it's too narrowly focused on the self. She advocates for a form of yoga that gives back, not least by donating some of its profits to the parts of the world it originally came from.

'A lot of spirituality today is very singular and unaccountable. So, if you want to transform your practice in any way, how do you make it less about you and more about others?' she says.

Talking to Rina Deshpande and Shreena Gandhi, I felt I gained some clarity on issues that had vexed me for years. You'll recall that during my teacher training, I wasn't sure to what extent yoga had to be 'spiritual'. If I came at it from a purely secular standpoint – for instance, treating the practice as a mental health booster – was I divesting it of its true essence?

This question seemed pertinent because, to me, the word 'spiritual' carried baggage. It meant believing things without evidence that they were true. When you leave a fundamentalist religion, you become pretty damn resistant to the 'because I said so' line of reasoning; you don't trust the assertions of gurus, sages, holy men or 200-hour yoga teacher trainers, unless they've given you exceptionally good cause. On top of that, I wasn't sure whether it was even admissible for me to believe in things like chakras, or whether buying into these terms was some heinous form of appropriation.

As the course went on, I began to understand that what I believed was mostly beside the point. Yoga isn't supposed to be an intellectual exercise, or a collection of dogmas to swallow: it's about stilling the fluctuations of the mind, rather than frantically theorising. However you choose to define spirituality, memorising what your course tutors tell you about astral bodies probably isn't it.

The version of yoga I was coming to love, and would end up teaching, was predominantly physical. But it was meditative too. It was about linking the movement with the breath, calming down my 'monkey mind', finding a peace that had, up till that point, eluded me. Sure, I only seemed able to reach this place if I was also breaking a sweat and choreographing my movements to an electronica playlist, but it was at least an entry point into something deeper.

'In Ashtanga, there's this idea of "practice, practice and all is coming", or "yoga is 99 per cent practice and 1 per cent theory" – both of these are Pattabhi Jois quotes,' says Laura Harvey-Collins, a yoga teacher and studio owner based in Croydon.[25] 'The idea is that you can leave the body by going into the body, and that if you do that enough alongside the other limbs of yoga, you'll be able to reach enlightenment. So, when people look at a purely physical practice and say, "Oh, that's not real yoga," I think that's a very complicated question.'

Harvey-Collins, who has a master's degree in Consciousness, Spirituality and Transpersonal Psychology, is a close friend and someone I've always been able to rely upon for clarity in this discussion. Like me, she tends towards quite physical styles of practice, and she shares my reservations about classes that feel like workouts with a 'spiritual' bit awkwardly tacked on.

'In the class, you've got an hour, you need to get everyone warmed up,' she says. 'You need to talk safely about the anatomy. People expect a physical class. And between leading that, teachers are trying to sprinkle in "Open up your chakra! And three, and four, and quick, realise your oneness with the universe!" Coming from me, it sounds absolutely ridiculous. That's why my teaching is very focused on what you're doing with your body. I recognise that this isn't yoga necessarily, but I try to bring in a sense that it's different from other forms of exercise and you're doing it from a mindful, non-grasping place.'

What she has seen is that, among people who start doing yoga for fitness, there often seems to be a trajectory. The process of learning the poses, and the discipline of focusing on the breath, may open up new ways of seeing the world that are congruent with Eastern philosophies.

'I think what yoga is saying is that your perception of the world is a product of your filters,' says Harvey-Collins. 'You can move beyond them and experience what reality really is, which is that we're all connected.'

Admittedly, this is not the kind of thing you'd glean from a quick lunchtime vinyasa class at Virgin Active. But it is a remarkably consistent finding among seasoned meditators, not to mention a view that is supported by mainstream science. What's more, the idea of yoga as a connector (remember the word means 'yoke' or 'union') works on multiple levels. The practice connects mind and body. It connects movement and breath. If you attend a given class regularly, it can connect you with others in your community. There is something about moving in sync with other people that reminds me of the better parts of church.

I look back at my younger self and I see someone who felt perpetually alienated and broken – someone who didn't feel quite at home anywhere, someone who thought there was something defective at her core. I was always running from something, jumping from one chaotic situation to the next to distract myself from what I dubbed 'the terrifying existential void'. I saw this void as an honest reckoning with reality, rather than as an indication there was something amiss with my filters.

It wasn't as if I tried a few yoga classes and instantly felt better. But I was drawn to the practice because, deep down, I knew it was what I needed.

I'm hardly the only person in Western society to have felt like this, nor to have found something healing within yoga. Looking past the ways it's been hijacked by consumerism, Rina Deshpande reckons this may be why the practice has taken off in the West.

'If I were to look at it from a very compassionate perspective, I think that people are feeling a disconnection from self and from meaning,' she says. 'Friends of mine don't really know their roots or history; I wonder what that must be like. It makes sense to me that a practice that I believe is so powerful to connect you back to self, back to greater meaning, would be desired by people who are feeling disconnected.'

Dr Shreena Gandhi goes further, arguing in her essay that this sense of disconnection is no accident. For her, it's the inevitable upshot of white supremacy – in itself a 'process of exchanging cultural grounding from the unearned power and privilege of whiteness'. White people are taught to be ahistorical, she says. And they 'are grasping for something to belong and connect to outside of the empty and shallow societal anchors of materialism and consumerism, which do not nourish or empower people in any sort of meaningful or sustainable way'.[26] (As a white person, this is hard to hear, but it strikes me as being on the nose.) She is currently working on a manuscript exploring the cultural history of yoga in the US, which will flesh out these arguments in greater depth.

'My whole argument about yoga [in the West] is that, yeah, it's cultural appropriation, but I'm never going to tell anyone to stop doing it,' she tells me. 'It's a practice that can work for people. And so why would anyone want to take that away?'

According to a 2021 review paper that looked at the connection between yoga and spirituality, newfound insights and the 'development of an integrative worldview' are two frequent outcomes of a regular physical practice.[27] Others include 'a more positive outlook on life', 'a sense of meaning and peace', and 'lower levels of existential anxieties'. The paper found that 'even yoga practice without explicit spiritual teachings can affect spirituality', and that while 'the initial aim is often to achieve the "perfect yoga body,"' subsequently, 'more profound mental and spiritual intentions appear'. This suggests to me that the West has not in fact ruined yoga, even if it might seem that way at first blush.

After finishing my training, I taught yoga part-time for about a year. But I had to stop when I moved abroad, and when I came back to the UK, my attempts to resume teaching were repeatedly thwarted. First came a pandemic, and then a pregnancy. It was as though every time I tried to get back in the saddle, the yoga gods threw me off like a bucking bronco. Not for the first time, my own practice had fallen by the wayside, and it struck me that I had fallen into a common trap of mine – intellectualising something 'spiritual' at the expense of doing it.

In the discombobulating months after giving birth to my daughter, I hadn't wanted to slow down long enough to look at the changes my life had undergone. It was with some apprehension, then, that, three months postpartum, I set up my mat and closed the door. I had opted for a mandala class on YouTube, a form of vinyasa flow in which you move in circles round your mat, holding most of the poses for one breath only. This class was taught by an instructor I knew, working in a style I loved, and I had a whole hour to myself without interruption. It was the distillation of 'me time'. Yet I wasn't sure I felt good about this new 'me' I'd be meeting here. It wasn't the 'me' I'd brought to the mat a year previously, who'd had a flat stomach, a sense of ease in her physicality and could comfortably kick up into a forearm stand. Sure, I hadn't lost my fitness altogether. But my body didn't feel like my own.

As my practice got underway, I realised how tense my muscles were. I sensed it wasn't only from holding my baby in awkward positions, it was also as though they were braced against my new reality. I took deep, diaphragmatic breaths, and gave my permanently sucked-in belly the latitude it needed to expand. I felt the safety of the ground beneath me. The thawing of my tension as I stretched out. I attempted flamingo pose and remembered that yoga could be playful; I got lost in a sense of ritual as the flow repeated on the left-hand side.

I felt other things too. A knee pain I'd been ignoring, my diminished strength in dolphin pose, a fatigue that set in more quickly than I'd have liked. But within the framework of this practice, these sensations felt safe. Not something to be spurned, angrily, as I yearned for a former version of myself, but neutral sensations I could hold space for. Just part of the flux of being alive.

Is this kind of yoga truly spiritual, as opposed to just self-help? Again, it comes down to definitions – but if someone like me gets to use the word 'spiritual' at all, I can't think of a more appropriate context.

What I simultaneously love and retreat from is that yoga asks me to meet myself where I am. I might be meeting someone strong and flexible with an Instagram-worthy 'yoga body', or I might not. I might be meeting someone emotionally, mentally and spiritually balanced who looks like she belongs in a spa brochure, or – understatement of the century – I might not. Often, if I'm totally honest with myself, I'm meeting someone who is scared of looking inward; who's using her intellectual confusion around yoga as an excuse not to get on the mat.

None of these versions of me has mastered yoga, but if the practice has taught me nothing else, it has taught me that mastery is a mirage. And every time, it comes with a promise attached: what you bring to the mat is enough.

Chapter 3

Tarot: The Fool's Journey

In the summer of 2018, smarting from a bad breakup, I did something that would have appalled my former self: I visited a tarot reader. Up until that point, my knowledge of tarot had been cursory at best. I saw it as a type of divination, something to be bracketed with palm-reading, crystal balls and Zoltar the animatronic fortune-telling machine. Tarot cards were the kind of thing you might deploy as a prop if you needed a fancy-dress costume in a hurry and you had a headscarf to hand. Or if you were a hammy filmmaker who wanted to throw in some clunky foreshadowing: what could be more ominous than a visit to a tarot reader, who inevitably pulls the Hanged Man or Death?

I had consulted the odd fairground psychic in the past, purely because I was curious about how I came across on a cold reading. One had told me I'd work with animals, while another said I'd meet a man with a distinctive nose at a salsa-dancing class. Suffice it to say, this didn't happen (though that's my bad; I never got round to attending a salsa-dancing class). Tarot was much the same to me. It was just for fun – a colourful bit of esoterica one step removed from a Magic 8 Ball.

What would have horrified me, then, wasn't the tarot reading per se. It was my intent. Rather than going there for a laugh, or out of curiosity, or with some smart-arse mission statement about debunking the paranormal, I was searching for answers. And Larissa the mythic tarot reader seemed like she might be the person to provide them.

The past couple of months had been rough, especially since the breakup had occasioned leaving our cat behind. Archie was scrappy, tiny and troubled, the feline embodiment of a Dickensian street urchin. We'd adopted him the previous autumn, and he was starting to trust me. He'd sit with me on the sofa – not on me, or even that close to me, but beside me and, crucially, not punching me – and I felt maternally protective.

Archie was staying with my ex, though, and our final goodbye had been harrowing. Two weeks after the breakup, having left with only a suitcase, I returned to our beautiful apartment on Amsterdam's Prinsengracht to collect the rest of my belongings. Archie emerged from under the sofa, looking even smaller and scrawnier than I remembered. A big patch of fur on his back was missing, presumably scratched off. He came up to sniff me. I stroked him, and he hesitated. 'I'm so sorry, Archie,' I said, before hauling my boxes out the door and sticking the knife right into his formative abandonment wounds.

By the time I came to visit Larissa the mythic tarot reader – so-called because her tarot deck uses scenes from Greek mythology – I had mostly reconciled myself to the breakup, but less so to the cat desertion. Oh, and I still didn't have a place to live. I'd spent the past month crashing with a friend's ex-partner in a small Dutch town, which was as odd as it sounds. I didn't know whether I wanted to return to Amsterdam, move back to London, or continue the travelling I'd been doing before I'd met my ex. I also didn't quite know who I was in the wake of the breakup, nor what I wanted to write in this terrifyingly blank new chapter of my life.

Larissa didn't exactly give me any answers, but she did introduce me to a practice far removed from what I was expecting. She guided me through a Celtic Cross reading, in which you pull ten cards to illuminate different aspects of your situation. I quickly saw how it worked – each card was rich with symbolism, allowing the reader to draw out salient meanings. For instance, my first card (representing my perception of the situation) was Eight of Wands and my second (representing my principal challenge) was

The Moon. Eight of Wands is a card about movement. As the only card in the deck devoid of figures, it has an abstract, impersonal quality, with a suggestion that events have their own momentum outside of your control. The Moon can be read as a card about confusion and illusions, an intimation that all is not as it seems. Placed together, the cards suggest the beginnings of a narrative: you don't have the full picture yet, so trust the flow of events and don't be afraid of rapid change.

That narrative might be different if you were approaching the cards with a different question. Intuitively, you'll settle on the meanings that most resonate and, in doing so, hold up a mirror on what's going on deep down. Like a good therapy session, a tarot reading reflects you back to yourself, placing you back in touch with the gut feelings you may have obscured. In this case, the cards reflected a person who'd made the right call by leaving, who was more exhilarated by the unknowns ahead than scared. I can't say I wasn't a little thrown by getting the Death card in the 'outcome' position (was my flat-hunting going to take a morbid turn?) but Larissa reassured me that this was mostly a card of transformation; the need to start over by severing a link with the past.

As I gathered my things to leave, I decided that tarot was more sensible than I'd first thought. This was just storytelling, I told myself. You took the raw, unprocessed matter of your life and translated it into the language of archetypes. There was nothing woo-woo about it, and certainly nothing spooky: no one was gazing into a crystal ball and telling me I was about to meet a handsome stranger on the double-decker Intercity train.

Then I saw something that made my stomach leap into my throat. On Larissa's wall was a poster of a cat. Underneath it, the name Archie.

In Carl Jung's 1952 book *Synchronicity: An Acausal Connecting Principle*, the eminent psychologist recalls an incident in which his patient dreamed about a scarab beetle. Just as she was recounting this dream, a scarab beetle tapped on the window and flew into the room. Jung presented the beetle to his patient, saying, 'Here is your scarab.' It was at this point that the patient was able to make progress in therapy: her 'highly polished Cartesian rationalism' began to break down, allowing a 'somewhat more human understanding' to shine through.[1]

Prior to this incident, Jung had been hoping that 'something unexpected and irrational would turn up, something which would burst the intellectual retort into which she had sealed herself'. The scarab incident fulfilled his desire, not least because the beetle itself was 'a classical rebirth symbol'. For Jung, and for those who have followed him, this was a powerful example of synchronicity, a meaningful coincidence in which an internal mental state somehow attracts a real-world parallel.

This idea, like so many of the spiritual concepts explored in this book, emerged from a worldview in which psyche and matter are not separate from each other. While the scientific mainstream places matter front and centre – mind relegated to a by-product of brain function – Jung believed in a universe of mysterious connections. In this view, the recounting of the dream didn't *cause* the scarab to appear, but the two incidents, the dream and the physical apparition, were indeed linked. According to the philosopher Herbert van Erkelens, Jung saw base reality as a 'unitary domain outside the human categories of space and time, and beyond our division of reality into matter and spirit'.[2]

When I saw that poster of Archie, I didn't exactly think: 'Whew, time to overturn the materialist paradigm of reality.' If pressed, I'd have said that it was just a weird coincidence, and that my reaction was part of the brain's deep-rooted tendency to see patterns in random noise.*

But much like the patient with the scarab beetle, it did allow me to allay my rationalism for a minute. Rather than saying to myself, 'Well, that means nothing,' I took it as a sign that all would be well with Archie. It was like a wink from a wiser being, a hug from a higher power; the feeling was one of warmth and reassurance. I wasn't going to spoil all that by second-guessing it.

Jung's idea of synchronicity is interesting in that it doesn't claim that anything supernatural is at play. It also doesn't say that coincidence is just coincidence. Uncanny coincidences, for Jung,

---

* The word for that, I later learned, is 'apophenia', and it's why we can't help but see a man on the moon or shapes in the clouds.

are the result of neither spooky witchy woo, nor of the brain's pattern recognition system going into overdrive. They're more like a structural feature of how the world works – with causality being one way in which events are connected, and synchronicity being another.

As the academic Bethany Butzer has put it: 'If we live in a materialist universe in which physical matter is the only reality, then it makes sense to conceive of synchronicity ... as being the result of random error or mental meaning-making. But if we consider post-materialist perspectives that suggest that consciousness might be more fundamental than matter, then synchronicity ... [becomes a component] of a universe in which mind and matter are deeply interconnected.'[3]

Personally, I have no idea whether the Jungians are onto something, but I can see why this perspective appeals to so many tarot readers. Sure, you can construct a helpful narrative from whichever cards you pull. But in many cases, the cards drawn seem too uncanny, the wisdom too on-point, as though they were the only ones that could possibly have fitted the situation. As I've gained more experience with tarot, I've encountered many further synchronicities, in which the reflection held up by the cards appears freakishly accurate. Whatever is going on, I get the most out of the experience if I allow myself to suspend my disbelief and surrender to the cards' strange magic.

While the history of tarot is a little murky, it appears it was invented in the fourteenth century, when Italian noblemen used their custom-painted decks for parlour games. Around 200 years after that, people started using their decks for divinatory purposes, and around 200 years after *that* people started assigning specific meanings to each card. Increasingly, the practice became associated with esoteric knowledge, hermeticism, Kabbalah, and other fringe spiritualities that were trendy in the Victorian era. At this time people devoted a lot of energy towards photographing ghosts, so it's not surprising that they also sought to tell the future with their playing cards.[4]

A key moment came in the early twentieth century, with the meeting of Arthur Waite and Pamela Colman-Smith. He was an American-born mystic living in London, while she was a British-born, New York-educated illustrator who had written books about Jamaican folklore. Both were members of the Hermetic Order of the Golden Dawn, a secret occult society that had a fair bit in common with the Freemasons.

In 1908, Waite paid a visit to the British Museum, which had acquired photographs of the Sola Busca deck, the world's oldest existing tarot cards, dating to 1490. Inspired to design his own version, he teamed up with Colman-Smith to produce what would become the Rider–Waite deck. I use the name Rider–Waite with some reservations – Waite supplied design instructions and wrote an accompanying guide, while Rider was the original publisher – but it was Colman-Smith's unmistakable artwork that would ensure the deck became a classic. Each of the 78 cards contains an allegorical illustration, as notable for its visual brilliance as it is for its symbolic richness. Her style reminds me a little of William Blake's, run through an Art Nouveau filter.[5]

The 22 cards of the Major Arcana tell a story about life's main themes, a kind of big, archetypal hero's journey. Our protagonist in this journey is The Fool – an everyman character who, in the first card, is about to step off a cliff. Clearly not deterred by this experience, he goes on to meet a colourful band of characters. Each has some hard-won secrets to share with him, from the grisly, hermaphroditic Devil, to the horse-riding naked baby beneath The Sun. By the time he reaches the end of his journey, our man (or in some decks, our non-binary character) is a fool no more. He re-enters The World (card 22) for the cycle to begin again.

The 56 cards of the Minor Arcana depict more day-to-day issues. This part of the deck is divided into four suits, Cups, Swords, Wands and Pentacles, which roughly correspond with emotions, the intellect, personal drive and material concerns. Each suit in turn contains cards numbered Ace to Ten, and court cards – a Page, a Knight, a Queen and a King – in a nod to the tarot's origins as playing cards.

As Carl Jung himself put it: 'They are psychological images, symbols with which one plays, as the unconscious seems to play with its contents. They combine in certain ways, and the different combinations correspond to the playful development of events in the history of mankind ... It is applicable for an intuitive method that has the purpose of understanding the flow of life.'[6]

The Rider–Waite deck stayed in print throughout the early twentieth century, but never found runaway success. Colman-Smith died little-known and penniless, while Waite's obituary didn't so much as allude to his tarot deck. It wasn't until the 1970s, when US Games Systems began selling the deck, that its popularity began to take off. Today, there are over 100 million copies in circulation.[7]

Since then, tarot has become vastly more widespread, and in a way that goes far beyond end-of-the-pier entertainment.[8] There are thousands of decks available on Amazon and Etsy, ranging from my personal favourite, the LGBT+ friendly Modern Witch Tarot Deck, to Tattoo Tarot: Ink and Intuition. More gimmicky options include zombie- or mermaid-themed decks, or one based on the characters from *Friends* (with the tagline, 'a look into your future from Central Perk'). In 2021, US Games Systems told the *Financial Times*: 'Sales of our decks have been steadily increasing over the past few years ... We've had to double many of our print runs because they sell out so fast.'[9]

In fashionable circles, tarot has shed its kooky reputation. You can have your cards read at swanky Selfridges, paying £150 for a half-hour session with The Psychic Sisters.[10] There are glossy coffee-table books about tarot, and tarot-related art installations. Tarot has even made inroads into couture, with Dior's Spring–Summer 2021 collection alluding to tarot motifs.

However, the internet has had the greatest impact on democratising tarot. Given the visual nature of the cards, it is no surprise that tarot-related accounts are big on Instagram and TikTok, where the likes of @thehoodwitch, @tatiannatarot and @themoontarot have amassed hundreds of thousands of followers. Some of these readers take a divinatory perspective, holding that tarot can indeed show us the future, whereas others are more introspective. Jessica Dore, a tarot reader-cum-social worker, has made a name for herself with her cerebral blend of cognitive psychology and mythology. 'Tarot is often considered more a spiritual practice than a psychological one, but it is inherently psychological, and psychology is inherently spiritual,' she writes in her fascinating book, *Tarot for Change: Using the Cards for Self-Care, Acceptance and Growth* (2021).[11] These words have rung true for me as I've developed my own relationship with the cards.

On top of that, there are a bunch of free resources online, teaching you to interpret the cards yourself. A quick look at Google Trends suggests that's exactly what people are doing – while searches for 'tarot' itself have remained flat or even declined,[12] searches for any given card (say, 'Nine of Cups') have been steadily rising since about 2009.[13] This isn't so much about esoteric spirituality as it is about therapeutic spirituality, the intersection of meaning-making and self-care.

Perhaps the internet's leading tarot resource is Biddy Tarot, which offers free card meanings, online tarot courses and masterclasses and tarot business coaching. I used Biddy Tarot extensively myself when I was in the early stages of learning to read the cards. Unlike some tarot explainers, which can lean towards quite doomy interpretations ('Seven of Swords means someone's trying to trick you!', 'Three of Swords means someone's going to break your heart!'), Biddy Tarot is never less than constructive. Yes, Seven of Swords *can* indicate 'theft, betrayal, deception and trickery', but it can also suggest you need to be strategic about your priorities. Sure, Three of Swords *can* signal that 'you are feeling deeply hurt and disappointed', but it can also speak to the need for emotional release.

I spoke to Brigit Esselmont, the driving force behind Biddy Tarot, on what was a cold winter's evening in the UK and a glorious summer's morning in Australia. A hot water bottle clutched to my lap, I dialled into Zoom, where I was met by a vision of radiance – Brigit herself. It struck me that there was something very 'tarot' about this juxtaposition. The deck is meant to encompass the totality of human experience, all aspects of this world of opposites. Some readers even hold that each card contains its converse, with the shadow side of any given archetype coming to the fore when the card is reversed.

'Tarot is allowing more people to have a voice, and without having to be validated within the traditional structure of things,' Esselmont told me.[14] 'If you look at TikTok right now, there are people with a million followers sharing their thoughts about tarot.

Pre-internet, you couldn't have done that because it would have been seen as weird and woo-woo. But now we're able to come out and be true to our voice.'

Biddy Tarot began as a hobby – a fun project in the early days of the internet, which sat alongside Esselmont's career in management consultancy and HR. By 2012, though, her online takings were exceeding what she earned in her day job. She decided to quit the corporate world and pursue a career as a tarot reader (a better term these days, she says, would be 'tarot *leader*').

'Here we are now in 2023, with a team of fifteen people,' she says. 'At last count, I think we have over 10,000 students who have taken our programmes. People always go, "Oh tarot, isn't that lovely – what does your husband do?" And I say, "Well, actually, he works with us." People think it's [so] niche, but we have 15 million people visiting our site each year. That's more than [the population of] most countries.'

Since Esselmont went full-time with Biddy Tarot, she has noticed a real upsurge in interest – a trend she attributes not only to the rise of social media, but also to the decline of traditional religion. People, she says, are finding new ways to connect to their spirituality, ways that are more flexible, fluid, and inclusive than those offered by established faiths.

'As humans, we're always searching for meaning and purpose,' says Esselmont. 'And I think tarot is one of those tools that really helps us connect to that deeper meaning and deeper purpose within ourselves. We can get to that point through any which way, with different sorts of vehicles.'

Perhaps unsurprisingly, organised religion has tended to frown on tarot, as it has on most forms of self-directed spirituality. According to Deuteronomy 18:10–11: 'There shall not be found among you any ... that useth divination, or an observer of times, or an enchanter, or a witch, or a charmer, or a consulter with familiar spirits, or a wizard, or a necromancer.' Or, more succinctly and charmingly, there's Exodus 22:18: 'Thou shalt not suffer a witch to live.'

I doubt that many churches these days would interpret those verses literally, but the church I attended as a kid did take a hard stance against the occult. This included tarot, astrology, Ouija boards, heavy metal music, horror movies, pentagram necklaces, heptagram tables and the Harry Potter books. Apparently, these practices allowed demons to infiltrate your brain, which is a far more generous assessment of tarot's powers than you'd find among most tarot readers.

If you ask readers how their practice works, you're likely to get a variety of answers. Unusually for a practice with such New Age connotations, the tarot community is a broad church; readers are just as likely to be found posting on the SecularTarot subreddit ('a space to discuss the cards without the mysticism, pseudoscience or woo') as they are to be pontificating about their spirit guides.

Esselmont herself thinks about tarot on a few different levels, tailoring her explanation to her audience. 'When I'm talking to people who may be a little sceptical, I talk about how imagery and symbolism help to bypass our conscious mind,' she says. 'Tarot cards are just reflecting back to us what our subconscious mind is experiencing. I've had many times where I've led people through this process, and what starts to be revealed to them is so profound.'

For those who are more mystically inclined, she will talk about a 'matrix', a universal field of energy that tarot cards help us access.

'Tarot cards are simply one vehicle that will help us tap into that greater matrix, that collective wisdom,' she says. 'When I'm doing a reading for someone, and I'm seeing that they've got this hot, passionate young lover that no one ever knew about, that comes from tapping into the matrix as well. I think tarot can tap into information that really no one [else] knows.'

While not averse to the more mystical side of things, Brigit doesn't see herself as psychic and doesn't believe our future is set in stone. For her, tarot cards are more of a spur to action – helping us determine how we want our futures to be – than they are a portent. In other words, don't freak out if you pull Death.

'When you look at the more subtle energies that are at play in the subconscious, that might give us clues about where we're heading,' she remarks.

Above all, she sees the cards as tools for introspection, for drawing on an inner wisdom we may, in our exaggerated rationalism, have obscured. Going deeper still, she thinks we can move beyond self-reflection and access something more ineffable – something she calls the 'essence of spirituality'. These days, she doesn't read professionally, preferring to teach people how to interpret the cards themselves.

'You haven't really experienced tarot until you learn how to use it for yourself,' she says. 'If we rely on having a reading done, we're putting all our power outside of ourselves, but when we read for ourselves, we bring that power back in. We're saying, "Actually, I have all the answers within, I just need a tool."'

Following my visit to Larissa the mythic tarot reader, I put my own interest in tarot on the back burner for a while. It wasn't till after my dad died later that year that I was ready to follow this path where it might lead.

On my thirty-third birthday, a couple of friends gifted me my first deck, a classic Rider–Waite. I spent half of my birthday party doing mock 'readings' for people, based on wilful misunderstandings of Coleman-Smith's illustrations. Before too long, though, I was on websites like Biddy Tarot, learning to read the cards in earnest. It was a little unsettling to find myself going down this road; I had long prided myself on my rationalism and, along with my other new proclivities (ayahuasca retreats, veganism, haphazard attempts at meditation), this seemed like one heck of an identity shift. On the other hand, people notoriously respond to grief in strange ways. If I wanted to respond to mine by turning into a bargain bin Mystic Meg, well, that was my prerogative.

Of course, I wasn't soothsaying, just introspecting. And throughout this difficult period, the cards reliably seemed to offer nuggets of wisdom. They called me out on my shit (Eight of Swords) as much as they commended me on my resilience (Strength). Pulling the cards was like chatting with a no-nonsense mate, who was able to cast a light on things I hadn't noticed and reframe my perception of the situation.

You'll recall that during my ayahuasca ceremony it felt uncannily as though I was conversing with something beyond my own psyche. Reading tarot can feel similar, as if I'm encountering an astute and often tricksy psychospiritual 'other'.

To give an example of how this works: as I was writing the lines above, I stalled for a while. It felt too cringey. 'Anyone who reads this', I thought, 'will think I'm a credulous loser.' Then came another thought: where does that knee-jerk sense of shame come from? Perhaps my deck can help me probe it.

I drew two cards – the first to represent my inner critic, the second to show me what to do about it. For the inner critic, I pulled The Hanged Man, which, for me, is a card all about stasis. In some scenarios, it can be a positive stasis, as when you surrender to a situation that's outside your control, but the feelings that came up in this context were all negative. The Hanged Man just looks uncomfortable, doesn't he? He's hanging upside down from a tree by one ankle, his hands tied behind his back. And though his big shiny halo may go some way towards redeeming his situation, he isn't going anywhere any time soon. 'My inner critic', I thought, 'is so busy overthinking everything that she's rendered herself immobile. If she had her way, I'd never write another word.'

For 'what to do' I pulled the Two of Cups, which is a card about reciprocity and exchange. It's an innocent, optimistic card, featuring two figures swapping cups (cups being a symbol for the emotions). It's often read as a promising omen for romantic relationships, but here it served to remind me about what writing can be. If I hold back my true feelings and thoughts, I'll end up writing anaemic prose that fails to connect with anyone at all.

Now these were just my own personal snap assessments of the cards, thoughts that came to me after having played around with tarot for a while. Tarot is far from an exact science – although each card has certain conventional meanings, your personal associations are just as important. Under this approach, you're working less with arcane symbolism, and more with your own feelings. The deck becomes a highly accessible means of self-interrogation.

Reading for other people isn't something I've mastered yet. But when I do try, it works in the same way: asking the other person what the cards elicit for them, while tuning into my own hunches. Sometimes, the reading resonates deeply and other times not. Perhaps that has to do with the cards themselves; if you hold that the card choice is random, it makes sense that they wouldn't always fit the question. Or perhaps the card choice is not random at all, and it's my reading skills that need some work.

Victoria Smith-Murphy, a London-based leadership coach who works with tarot, is far more seasoned in this art. As a proud Jungian, who's studying for an MSc in Consciousness and Spirituality, she sees synchronicity as key to how the cards work.

'I was coaching a client a couple of years ago, over the phone, and we pulled the cards towards the end,' she says when we talk over Zoom.[15] 'In this deck, [the card we drew was] a picture of a woman standing on a rock, looking out at a lake with green forest in the background, and a cloudy blue sky. And my client sent me a picture of where she was in that moment. She was standing on a rock in front of a lake, overlooking forest with blue sky. I've got the pictures side by side, and I don't believe that that is coincidence.'

Smith-Murphy is far from the stereotypical tarot reader. Having started out in data marketing, she was a self-described 'bull in a china shop' who favoured facts over feelings and earned the nickname 'Red Vikki' because of her fearsome drive. In 2015, she retrained as a coach, and has developed a niche in working with senior leaders. Many of her clients, she says, are experiencing a crisis of meaning – they have money and status, but lack a sense of purpose, or struggle to balance their personal and professional lives.

'They're at a point of spiritual emergence, where they're moving from a certain set of values and anchors, to exploring something that goes beyond our material experience,' she says. 'And they're figuring out how to integrate that into the life they've built, which tends to be quite successful [and] high achieving. There's often a bit of conflict there.'

Smith-Murphy discovered tarot in 2016. As she recalls, she was wandering around the Strand bookstore in New York, when she found herself drawn to Jessa Crispin's *The Creative Tarot*. She read the book cover to cover, then started teaching herself to decipher the cards. Very quickly, she saw how it could help people access their intuition and resolve confusion. Today, while tarot is only one of many coaching tools she uses, it is perhaps the one that most entices clients.

'I think tarot has become a bit of an anchor point for contemporary spirituality,' she tells me. 'There's something about the archetypes on the cards, particularly when you use a couple together and they seem to interact, that brings a clarity you don't get when you're trying to resolve something within your own cognitive space.'

A big part of what she does with clients is tarot-based 'shadow' work. Our shadow is the part of ourselves we don't feel comfortable looking at – and, according to Jung, the easiest way to bring it into the light is to notice what we don't like about other people. 'Everything that irritates us about others can lead us to an understanding of ourselves,'[16] he wrote, which is fighting talk if ever I heard it. Tarot cards too can illuminate the things we're keeping hidden from ourselves.

'For instance, when I pull The Hierophant,* that reveals to me a really uncomfortable part of my own shadow,' says Smith-Murphy. 'For me, it's associated with superiority and restriction and judgementalism. I know all that stuff is in my shadow. I am quite intellectually superior. I tend to think I'm right about most things.'

This was an eye-opening exchange for me, as I also hate The Hierophant card with a passion. I'd always assumed that this had to do with my feelings about organised religion, as the guy in the card has some heavy papal energy. Perhaps, though, it goes deeper than that. If I'm honest with myself, I often don't want to engage with authority because I think that I know better. And if I didn't have a latent intellectual superiority complex, why the hell would I be writing this book?

While tarot evidently lends itself well to a depth psychology angle, it hasn't yet made huge inroads within psychotherapy. According to a 2019 *Cosmopolitan* article: 'Finding therapists who incorporate tarot isn't as easy as signing in to Zocdoc. Recommendations often come by word of mouth.'[17] Perhaps that's unsurprising, given the rather stuffy mores of licensing boards, and the ethical standards to which the practice is rightly held.

That said, you wouldn't be stretching the bounds of orthodoxy to suggest the cards might have therapeutic uses. Recently, Smith-Murphy participated in a wellness day in partnership with the

---

* A priest figure, counterpart to The High Priestess card.

mental health charity Mind, in which she did readings for people who were facing extensive mental health challenges. This was far removed from her usual fare of midlife crises and professional ennui. What came up was intensely powerful, though it felt more important than ever to hold the space safely for each client.

'We need to be treating stuff like this with respect,' says Smith-Murphy. 'Any time we're dealing with someone's psyche, whether they're mentally well or unwell, we need to be very careful.'

Smith-Murphy comes across as forthright and fiercely intelligent. She's warm too – which I imagine makes her very good at her job – but unlike many in the New Age world, she positions herself as very matter-of-fact. 'I don't like things that don't make sense,' she asserts. She also doesn't seem like the type to embrace a practice like tarot without first sussing out the mechanism.

'Tarot works within a post-materialist view, which holds that mind and matter are two halves of the same whole,' she explains. 'We're using an external stimulus to access an internal experience.'

Intriguingly, she thinks this also speaks to the question of whether tarot can tell the future. Although she doesn't use it for such purposes herself, she doesn't think this capability is completely out of the question.

'The only reason we're really asking about the future is because we believe that the future is separate to the present,' she points out. 'But if you're working within a post-materialist paradigm, you're moving slightly out of the classical physics view of time and space. How you use tarot depends on the worldview that you are able and prepared to entertain.'

As someone whose own view on the subject is far from settled, I was intrigued to meet someone who had not only considered these questions seriously but had also found some answers – and some quite 'out there' answers at that. Smith-Murphy feels that standard explanations like apophenia simply aren't satisfying, which should prompt us to consider alternatives.

'The two main perspectives on synchronicity are: it's either a psychological phenomenon or a metaphysical phenomenon,' she says. 'If it's a psychological phenomenon, synchronous experiences are our psyche's way of resolving inner conflict, which is what Jung tended to. I think that is going on, but I also think there is something [else] that is beyond us. This comes back to that question about: are we even separate to everything else?'

In other words, if you think there's a hard line between you and the rest of the universe, then synchronicity – and by extension, tarot – can only be explained in psychological terms. If you want to add anything else into the mix – for instance 'spirit' or collective consciousness – you need also to countenance that separation is an illusion. In this view, meaning-making doesn't just happen in the mind, it's inherent to the cosmic order.

By now we have come a long way from the idea that tarot is 'just storytelling' – and these kinds of perspectives may seem frankly absurd to some. The good news is that a more psychological, therapeutic angle on the cards is always available, even for those who wouldn't dream of countenancing 'post-materialist paradigms' – still less a universal energy matrix full of secrets about your passionate young lover.

Recently, Smith-Murphy used the cards in a workshop with sixty Mastercard executives, and found the vast majority were receptive. It struck me as a sign of the times that you can stick a load of corporate high-flyers in a room, present them with a series of esoteric images vaguely connected to Kabbalah, and not have a mutiny on your hands. Perhaps the corporate world is softening around the edges – or perhaps, as Smith-Murphy reminded me, 'it's just people'. And most people are seeking a form of meaning-making that goes beyond barking about the bottom line.

'I honestly think we've completely fucked the world up,' says Smith-Murphy. 'We don't know how to relate to each other, and people aren't finding purpose in things that used to hold purpose. The structures that held society together fifty years ago aren't holding it together anymore. People are looking for something different.'

So, how exactly does tarot satisfy our craving for meaning and relationship? Smith-Murphy's take is that, as a society, we're becoming more interested in 'the energy of the feminine' – which has less to do with women, and more to do with traits seen as feminine, such as receptivity, wisdom and intuition. By contrast, the corporate world is archetypally very masculine. It is fuelled by competition, ambition, energy, domination and drive; forces that can be dangerous if left to grow unchecked.

If you buy into this idea, then many of the world's wider issues can be framed as the 'masculine' run out of control. On a societal level, an excess of 'masculine energy' entrenches oppressive hierarchies and stirs up wars. On a planetary level, it is fuelling the climate crisis. On an individual level, it leads to burn-out. Smith-Murphy thinks people are looking for ways to create some balance, and that introspective practices like tarot can supply a yin to match the yang.

That's true at a macro scale too. In fact, she suspects the interlocking crises we're experiencing right now are a kind of 'collective spiritual emergence'. The term comes from the Czech transpersonal psychologists Stanislav and Christina Grof, who are also known as early pioneers of psychedelics and meditation. Their view was that some people experiencing a mental health crisis, or emergency, might in fact be undergoing a spiritual awakening, or emergence – a kind of dark night of the soul from which they wake up radically altered.

While it's easy to see how our current juncture in history represents a state of collective *emergency*, calling it an 'emergence' requires more of an imaginative leap. That said, if Smith-Murphy is right, society will emerge from this dark period with a revised set of values. Possibly it's no accident that new forms of spirituality are flourishing at a time of permacrisis, when many of our institutions, systems and cherished worldviews are breaking down.

Now, it may sound a bit overblown to situate tarot in such a grand narrative. We're talking about a souped-up pack of playing cards, after all. However, like the other practices discussed in this book, tarot clearly has an outsize potential for meaning-making. Much like Jung's scarab, the cards can function as a tool for dismantling our 'highly polished Cartesian rationalism', allowing a 'somewhat more human understanding' to shine through.[18]

I decided to conclude this chapter by posing the same question to my tarot cards: why, in their own view, are they having a resurgence? I pulled The Tower, one of the darkest and most dramatic cards in the deck, in which people are leaping out of a burning building that's been struck by lightning. The Tower suggests that something needs to be destroyed in order for something better to take its place. It might not be fun – in fact, it'll probably be chaotic, painful and disorientating – but it offers the chance to rebuild on firmer foundations.

Make of this daft experiment what you will, but to me the message seems fitting. As Biddy Tarot puts it in her reading of The Tower card: 'The best way forward is to let this structure [social structures, in this case] self-destruct so you can re-build and re-focus.' And with any luck, 'you may be able to see the cracks forming and take action before the whole structure comes tumbling down.'[19]

Chapter 4
Astrology: Star Stuff

Back when I was at university, I remember taking great relish in a meme that roasted people based on their star signs. It wasn't exactly the cleverest meme of all time (this was the mid-2000s, and the internet was a very different place), but each zodiac sign had its own cartoon, with a list of unflattering adjectives around it. There are few things more satisfying than telling your little sister, a Taurus, that she's bull-headed and exasperatingly self-righteous. I also strongly identified with my own Piscean roast, which told me I was impractical, overly sensitive, escapist and absent-minded.

It wasn't that I believed in astrology. In fact, I'd have taken pains to tell you that I didn't. But I was of the age when your identity is up for the taking, and that central question – who *am* I? – needs probing from any angle you can find. I was obsessed with the quizzes on a website called The Spark, which quantified my purity percentage and analysed my main 'personality defect'. I was equally fascinated by the Myers-Briggs test, which purported to be more scientific. As an out-and-proud ENFP (Extroverted, Intuitive, Feeling and Perceiving), shading into INFP depending on the day, I was supposed to be 'a true free spirit – outgoing, open-hearted and open-minded'. According to the website 16personalities.com, I share this personality type with the likes of Kelly Clarkson, Spiderman, Ellen DeGeneres and Willy Wonka.[1] An illustrious roll call if ever I saw one.

Of course, there's a lot that could be said about the rise of the personality test and why society in general, and navel-gazing undergraduates in particular, crave this kind of image-crafting. You could link it to our rampant individualism, or to a mass-scale identity crisis. After all, with social roles in flux, who among us knows who they're meant to be? In her book *What's Your Type? The Strange History of Myers-Briggs and the Birth of Personality Testing* (2018), the academic Merve Emre highlights how passionately people embrace their Myers-Briggs type, often defending 'its inviolability with the kind of ardor usually reserved for matters of the deepest faith'. She describes it as a 'modern technology of the self: a system of personal interrogation that is as committed to self-discovery as it is to self-care'.[2]

Zodiac signs struck me as part and parcel of that mania for self-analysis. Knowing I was a Pisces was no more or less edifying than knowing I was 60 per cent pure, or that I was a Gryffindor with Ravenclaw leanings, or that I was a Miranda with a touch of Carrie. I knew these constructs were probably nonsense, but as an endlessly confused twenty-year-old, they helped me feel seen.

Fast forward to the present day, and astrology is having a moment. It's hard to find precise statistics on how many people engage with their zodiac signs, but it appears to be on the rise. In a Pew Research study from 2018, 29 per cent of American adults said they believed in astrology, including 26 per cent of Christians and 47 per cent of those who defined themselves as 'nothing in particular'.[3] However, if you were to ask how many people read their horoscopes or know their sun signs, the figure would doubtless be much higher.

There have been think pieces analysing the resurgence of astrology since at least 2017, when forecasting agency WGSN declared 'new spirituality is the new norm'.[4] Two years later, a *New Yorker* article noted that we are seeing a new generation of practitioners: 'people who aren't kooks or climate-change deniers, who see no contradiction between using astrology and believing in science.'[5] The engagement is surely very casual for some. But for others, astrology offers a connection with something greater and a source of guidance that might once have been the province of religion.

These days, the astrology memes don't just allude to your zodiac sign, be that an absent-minded Pisces or an exasperatingly self-righteous Taurus. They talk about, for instance, 'Libra sun, with Aquarius moon and Cancer rising' – the idea being that a whole host of celestial bodies were doing meaningful things at the moment you were born.

Horoscopes have levelled up too. Rather than turning to a column in the *Metro*, today's astrology fans might download Co–Star, an AI-driven app that describes itself as a 'legitimate tool for self-care'. This app, which creates forecasts based on a person's specific time, date and place of birth, is downloaded every three to four seconds in the US and is one of a cluster of astrology apps to have raised some serious funding.[6]

Today, Co–Star tells me, 'You feel torn between the pressure to concentrate on the project in hand and your desire to wander.' It recommends 'pondering, blank page and serifs', while proscribing 'browsing, assumptions and speakerphone'. A different Pisces, with a different date and place of birth, would be given a different, though no doubt similarly oblique, daily forecast. Perhaps some of them would be actively encouraged to put their phone on speaker.

I'm not twenty anymore and the 'who am I?' question doesn't occupy as much headspace as it used to: I'm just a person in the world muddling along. But, as I was to discover, the art of birth chart analysis, also called natal astrology, can soon become deeply seductive.

'When I looked at your chart, what was really exciting is that I almost see the proposal for your book in it,' says astrology coach Chloe Smart.[7] 'This is because you have a lot of planets in Pisces. And then you have a very strong Sagittarian signature as well. Those two energies are kind of conflicting. But it shows two aspects of what you were describing.'

Smart and I had met seven years previously on our yoga teacher training and had stayed connected through social media. I knew that she had two little boys, and that in recent years she'd established herself as both a doula and an astrologer. Lately, she'd been posting at @themoonwitchesclub about a service she offered to new mums, helping them understand their birth story by exploring the themes in their own birth chart. I wasn't planning to take advantage of the service myself because it didn't seem germane to this book, but I loved the idea of such a debrief. With long dark hair, and a deep knowledge of all things esoteric, she is every bit what you'd expect from a self-styled 'moon witch'.

'It was like coming out of the closet – the first posts on Instagram where I was saying these things,' she says of her path towards becoming a pro astrologer. 'It was really scary, but liberating at the same time.'

Prior to our call, I'd given Chloe my date, time and place of birth, which she'd used to craft my personal birth chart. It looked intimidating in the same way that a calculus textbook looks intimidating: an impenetrable patchwork of numbers, symbols, lines and angles. Aside from resembling something a wizard might use in their dark arts, it also reminded me slightly of a Spirograph.

'Your chart is a picture of where the planets were at the time of your birth,' explains Chloe. 'Each of the planets live in houses. So you can see the chart is divided into twelve parts, which are the different areas of our lives. For instance, the first house is the self, [our] identity and what we look like, while the second house is about values and possessions, what brings us security. When a planet is in a particular house, it will express itself more in that part of your life.'

The interlinking lines, she told me, have to do with the relationships between the planets; blue lines are relationships of support, while red lines indicate a conflict. When the planets are directly across from each other, that's known as an 'opposition', while overlapping ones are a 'conjunction', and the ones that sit at a 90-degree angle are a 'square'. Overall, the chart creates a map of the psyche, in which our many sub-personas find expression, sometimes singing in harmony, sometimes creating a note of discord.

'When you just know your sun sign, can you see how small that is?' asks Chloe. 'Some people really relate to their sun sign, and some people don't. But we are so much more than that. We are very nuanced.'

I thought of Walt Whitman's famous lines: 'Do I contradict myself? / Very well then I contradict myself. / (I am large, I contain multitudes.)'[8] It certainly seemed applicable to a birth chart analysis, according to which each of us contains a sun, a moon, eight planets, a bunch of asteroids, two lunar nodes, a 'black moon Lilith' and something called 'Chiron the wounded healer'.

Of all these cosmic bodies, my own 'big three' are a Pisces sun, Sagittarius rising and Leo moon. Sun, moon and rising are the trio you'll find in astrology memes and on apps like Co–Star. For those who find a single zodiac sign too simplistic, and a full birth chart too complex, this tripartite model may hold an intuitive appeal, with shades of Freud's superego, ego and id.

'If I look at your chart on an elemental level – earth, fire, air and water – you've got a very big layer of water, but it's fiery water, which is quite an interesting mix,' Chloe says.

As for this book lurking in my birth chart, when Chloe broke it down, I could just about see what she meant. Pisces, apparently, is all about boundlessness and oneness, the mystical sense that separation is an illusion. Conversely, Sagittarius wants to find intelligible forms for all that ineffable energy. I suppose you could frame this book as an argument between my Piscean spiritualist tendencies and my Sagittarian scepticism, or even between the intuition and the intellect.

As Chloe was doing my reading, I found myself identifying with much of what she had to say. And when things weren't so clear-cut, I was seized by a desire to investigate further, riffing on what they might mean.

'People express their charts, they can't help it,' says Chloe. 'It's almost like I meet the person through those lines and squiggles.'

I got the sense that her sessions were as helpful as you wanted them to be. You could keep the focus on the big picture, as I did, or you could go in deeper and use your birth chart as a spur to explore your inner conflicts. In this regard, she is one of a growing wave of psychological astrologers, who treats astrology more as a form of therapy than a predictive tool. She has a compassionate, open-ended approach, using the zodiac signs as a lens to reflect whatever comes up.

'I'm not here to tell you you're this and you're that,' she says. 'I'm going to say this planet is placed here and tell you a few key words, and ask you how that shows up for you. What am I to tell you who you are? It's about you gaining self-understanding.'

It struck me that, while you could treat this as merely a bit of fun, the more arcane aspects of what Chloe does are never too far from the surface. With some of her clients, the conversation will turn to their 'soul purpose' – a potential latent within their birth chart, which they have come to this world to express. If that doesn't match what they're doing with their life, she says it can manifest as a profound sense of unfulfilment.

'In astrology, there's this idea of past lives that you can adhere to or not,' she explains. 'It implies the soul chooses to incarnate at a certain point. It's almost [as if] the chart is a map of the lessons you're going to learn, of the different energies that you are made up of.'

For her at least, birth chart analysis isn't just therapeutic, it's spiritual too. In Chloe's understanding of the term, that means recognising that we are cyclical beings who are deeply connected to nature, our psyches linked to the patterns of the planets and stars.

'Our cycles mirror the cycles of the moon, they mirror the seasons,' she says. 'We are one with nature and the world, and through connecting to these practices, we can connect to our higher self or purpose.'

While the Pisces in me lights up at this idea, I'd be doing my inner Sagittarius a disservice if I didn't ask some tougher questions. Clearly, each of us *does* contain multitudes: a cast of inner characters that hold court in different ways depending on the day or the circumstance. Might it not be the case that any birth chart could be spun to tell any story? If I'd been given your birth chart, instead of mine, would I still be feeling like it resonated, or would I be rejecting it out of hand?

My guess is that something in your chart would have rung true for me, no matter what, and I'd have been inclined to latch on to that and ignore the rest. Psychologists call this 'the Barnum effect'; named for the notorious showman P.T. Barnum, this term describes our tendency to take generalised personality descriptions and believe they apply to us specifically.[9]

As far as I can tell, if natal astrology really does work – if there is, in fact, something uniquely mine about the archetypes on my birth chart – then that says something big and startling about the nature of reality. It suggests that the various bodies in our solar system somehow imprint on a baby's psyche at the moment of their birth. And it means that those lumps of rock and balls of gas, millions of miles away, have a bearing on our day-to-day psychodramas. If that's true, the paradigm most of us are operating under is bust wide open.

'Astrology does raise philosophical or cosmological questions about the world and about what we're doing here and what this means,' says Chris Brennan, the Denver-based host of *The Astrology Podcast*.[10] 'You know – does fate exist, or destiny? To that extent it does start getting into an area of spirituality, which is how we contextualise what our meaning and purpose is here.'

Brennan was happy to talk so long as we recorded our conversation for his podcast, which we did under the title 'Explaining Astrology to a Skeptic'. I have edited his quotes for length, but the whole podcast is easy to find online.[11]

'Part of my goal as an astrologer has always been trying to figure out how to explain what I do to people who aren't familiar with this subject,' he says. 'There are science educators, like Neil deGrasse Tyson or Bill Nye, who try to explain science to the public. And I always felt we needed something like that in the astrological community, so I've tried to a certain extent to play that role.'

Brennan was a fascinating interviewee. Highly intelligent and articulate, he is a history buff who has written a book called *Hellenistic Astrology: The Study of Fate and Fortune* (2017). He's also what I'd describe as an astrology apologist, willing to mount a passionate argument in service of views outside the intellectual mainstream. His listeners love him. Of the 200-odd comments that appeared beneath our podcast on YouTube, the vast majority sang his praises, with several commending me for having picked the right person to talk to and one calling me out for being 'aggressively blind'.

Despite being introduced as a sceptic, I wasn't too interested in having a sparring match with Brennan. What I wanted to know was how astrologers understand their own discipline. Do they believe in it as one might believe in a religion, or – given that astrology makes specific and often falsifiable predictions – is it more akin to a science? After all, if it's treated as a science, rather than as an article of faith, then Carl Sagan's aphorism 'extraordinary claims require extraordinary evidence' surely applies. Has astrology ever tried to generate anything of that kind? And if not, is it happy to accept its widespread designation as a pseudoscience?

'The problem with astrology is that it really has a foot in both fields,' says Brennan. 'It has elements of science to the extent that it has this empirical component, but then it also has these religious and philosophical components at the same time.'

To begin with those religious and philosophical components, a phrase I kept coming across in my research was 'as above, so below'. This alludes to the idea that cosmos and psyche are subject to the same archetypal patterns.

This principle, known as the Law of Correspondence, supposedly derives from the lost teachings of a philosophical system originating in ancient Alexandria, known as Hermeticism. These were first collected in a 1912 book called *The Kybalion*, although the book's authenticity has been disputed, with the writer Nicholas E. Chapel remarking that, while '*The Kybalion* pretends antiquity, it is decidedly a product of modernity'. He asserts that it owes more to the nineteenth-century New Thought movement than it does to actual Hermetic philosophy.[12]

Whether or not that's true, the Law of Correspondence itself seems to go back a long way. As Chapel explains, it echoes a Hermetic treatise called the Asclepius, which claims that 'All earthly things are images, reflections, of their eternal forms within God, and in this sense the world is an image of God.' Underpinning this view is a strain of philosophical idealism, common to both Hermeticism and the New Age movement, which holds that everything in the universe exists within mind. As we've already seen, this is an inversion of our usual metaphysics, in which minds emerge from certain arrangements of matter, and the movement of the planets has little bearing on your day.

Carl Jung was a big fan of astrology, as well as tarot. 'Everything without is within, everything above is below. Between all things ... reigns "correspondence" (*correspondentia*),'[13] he wrote in 1929, in a direct reference to *The Kybalion*. Jung suggested that astrology represents the 'sum of all the psychological knowledge of antiquity', and often used horoscopes as a diagnostic tool in his work with clients.[14]

Tarot and astrology are routinely bracketed together, and with good reason. Either practice can be used for introspective purposes; even if you don't believe there's anything inherently special about the cards you pull, or the planetary placements on your birth chart, you might see them as a storyboarding tool. You can treat them almost as a Rorschach test, asking yourself, 'What does the Nine of Cups or a Moon in Taurus mean to me today?'

Alternatively, you can use them as a jumping-off point for some much bigger claims about the cosmos, for instance the idea that base reality is a 'unitary domain outside the human categories of space and time',[15] or that there exists a matrix of collective wisdom that we can tap into, or just that 'there are more things in heaven and earth, Horatio / Than are dreamt of in your philosophy'.[16]

However, tarot and astrology diverge in an interesting way, which has to do with what Brennan calls 'the empirical component'. As far as I know, nobody has ever made the case that tarot is 'scientific' in any meaningful way. For astrologers like Brennan, however, astrology fits the bill not only for an esoteric tradition, but also for a hard science. And here, he and I disagree.

Brennan himself discovered astrology, along with many other New Age practices, in his early teens. While the other practices fell by the wayside, his interest in astrology persisted, thanks to its having aspects 'that I could validate through repeated observations'. Today, he remains convinced by the basic premise: that there's a persistent correlation between celestial movements and events on Earth.

'Realistically, as a normal, Western person, we grow up in a cultural circumstance where astrology is not really something that we think should work,' he tells me. 'So there was something very fascinating to me about that, that something like that *could* work and what that says about the nature of the world.'

Now, as someone who has never studied astrology in much depth, my knowledge of how it came to be is derived mostly from Carl Sagan's magnificent book *Cosmos: The Story of Cosmic Evolution, Science and Civilisation* (1983). In the early section,

Sagan discusses the age-old human tendency to sit in front of a campfire, watching the night sky. The stars would have looked vivid to ancestral humans, and many people would have noticed patterns. They would have spotted different constellations arising in different seasons, as well as the sun rising and setting on a different spot on the horizon every day. The skies, says Sagan, became a 'great calendar'. Depending on where the various celestial bodies appeared, you could determine when to go hunting, for instance. As Sagan asserts, it was a small step from there to wondering about the influence of the planets – if the sun and moon and stars had a real connection with human affairs, then surely the same applied to those 'vagabond stars' too?[17]

The same idea emerged in many different parts of the world: that these mysterious moving stars exerted an influence over nations and empires. If something bad had befallen the king the last time Mars entered Aquarius, then perhaps he ought to watch his back next time round. This branch of astrology is known as 'mundane astrology', despite being anything but humdrum. It was a short step from there to the idea that the planets could affect your personal destiny, and from there to the genesis of the birth chart.

For Westerners, much of what we understand as astrology today can be traced back to Ptolemy, a polymath living in Roman Alexandria around the second century CE, who was as much an astronomer as he was an astrologer.*

I asked Brennan for his thoughts on how astronomy and astrology diverged, the one cementing its scientific credibility while the other retreated to the no-man's land between science and religion.

'There's a common presumption that astrology and astronomy used to be one and the same in the ancient world,' he tells me. 'But I think there has always been somewhat of a distinction, where astronomy has been about the observation and measurement of the heavens, while astrology is about the study of the correlations

---

* There is also much to say about Vedic astrology, but I fear that including both practices would be too ambitious a goal for this book. Chris Brennan has some podcasts on the subject at https://theastrologypodcast.com/tag/vedic-astrology/.

between celestial movements and earthly events. The fall of astrology had to do with a paradigm shift that occurred in the Renaissance, which rendered the cosmology that had been used up to that point obsolete.'

He is talking about the 'Copernican Revolution', the discovery that the sun, not the Earth, is at the centre of the solar system. Astrology, says Brennan, 'was an incidental casualty of that in some ways', because it was associated with the earlier geocentric model.

'It's not like all of a sudden people did a bunch of scientific studies in the 1700s that showed that astrology was statistically not valid,' he remarks. 'Instead, there was this shift in worldview. Astrologers had been taking that worldview for granted for centuries, as part of their assumption about why astrology works.'

As Brennan explained by way of analogy, let's say a modern-day Ptolemy were to concoct an explanation for astrology, one that most educated people found plausible. They might invoke quantum theory or general relativity or some other aspect of current science. Several hundred years from now, those scientific paradigms might shift, and astrology would be discarded too: the starry-eyed baby thrown out with the quantum bathwater.

I wasn't quite sold on this idea; were the great enlightenment thinkers motivated solely by intellectual fashions, rather than by the pursuit of truth? But following Brennan's thread to the end, I asked him whether that was an argument for accepting astrology regardless of the causal mechanism. He seemed to be saying that, if we tether our belief to a particular explanatory framework, then the whole edifice is liable to crumble as soon as that explanation no longer serves us.

'To a certain extent I think it's important that we come up with an overall justification and cosmology for astrology but it's not the main thing; the primary thing is just to establish whether it works and what you can do with it,' he says. 'In the same way, I can use a microwave to heat up food without necessarily knowing the scientific details of how microwaves work.'

I wasn't too sure about this either. Sure, I don't know exactly how microwaves work but I know for a fact that they *do* work and that someone smarter than me would be able to explain the process. In fact, I can google 'how do microwaves work' right now and learn all about the principles of electromagnetic radiation. Where Brennan and I part ways is that he thinks astrology is equally, evidentially, as reliable: turn the timer, set to high, and *ping*! Accurate predictions are all warmed through.

I put it to him that any birth chart might work for any person, seeing as they speak a language of very rich and multivalent archetypes, but he was quick to dismiss that theory.

'As anybody who does consulting astrology on a regular basis can tell you, if you sit down with a person and you start talking to them about their life, the vast majority of people will be very quick to tell you if something doesn't resonate,' he says.

He suggested that my reaction to my own birth chart – essentially, that I had been suckered in by the Barnum effect – indicated that I might not be as open-minded as one might hope.

'At least in your perception, it seemed like it was working, despite your initial preconceptions,' he says. 'There's an assumption that your perception must be faulty and this is still wrong, and therefore, you should reject it despite having [had] that experience. There's an element of, almost, faith there, ironically, that's leading you to reject it despite having seen some evidence to the contrary.'

This gave me pause for thought. If I was honest with myself, there was a big part of me that was rejecting the empirical aspects of astrology out of hand. It was easier for me to accept that I was being seduced by my own psychological biases, than that my personality and fate were indeed written in the stars and that something very strange was afoot with reality.

But Brennan and I weren't going to settle this one by arguing about whose belief system was more rigid. It was time to roll out the big guns – the question of the randomised controlled trial. Had anyone ever conducted thorough scientific research to this effect? For instance, had people been given a random selection of birth chart analyses and asked to guess which one was theirs?

'Some small-scale, haphazard studies were done in the eighties,' says Brennan. 'One of the issues you run into with studies like that is that they need to be replicable under a very controlled set of circumstances, but there's a huge degree of variability in terms of the training and skills amongst different astrologers.'

On a similar note, mundane astrology claims to be inherently predictive. It should be easy enough to test its powers by taking a retrospective look at past predictions. Did anyone see Covid-19 coming, for instance?

'Yeah, there was a French astrologer named André Barbault, who had made a specific study about the astrology of the pandemics,' says Brennan. 'He went back and studied a bunch of planetary alignments in the past. In 2012, he wrote an article saying, 'We may ... be in serious danger of a new pandemic at the 2020–2021 mark.'[18] On my podcast, we did our year ahead forecast in November 2019, and we made a joke about that time that ended up being weirdly prescient. We said, "There will be no hugging in the third week of March of 2020."'[19]

It seems that 2020 was marred by a conjunction of Saturn and Pluto, last seen in the early 1980s during the AIDS epidemic. Brennan told me that many astrologers had been concerned about the planetary placements for 2020, but that, given the ethics around making negative predictions, few had been sure how to broach it.

As for what may be coming down the road, there is a lot of chatter around the movement of Uranus into Gemini, which begins in 2025 and will persist till 2032. The last two times when Uranus was in Gemini coincided with the Second World War and the American Civil War. Many astrologers believe the planet's forthcoming appearance in this sign will presage another turning point in US history.

'We could expect that there would be another major defining conflict that would take place between 2025 and 2032,' says Brennan. 'A question is: if there does end up being some major war, will that be sufficient as a demonstration?'

These kinds of predictions apply at a more personal level too. Brennan thinks that, if people are curious about astrology and want to see if it has any validity, they should start by looking into the concept of 'transits', the relationship between your birth chart and the planets currently moving in the sky. Transits are supposed to reflect the energy patterns unfolding in your life. After all, the birth chart was classically used more for predicting a person's life path than it was for analysing their personality.

'You take your birth chart, and then you see what happens during different planetary alignments in your life,' says Brennan. 'Have major planetary alignments at important turning points lined up in a way that symbolically spoke to that situation? Like when a person had their first child or got married – the planets should be showing that. From the perspective of astrologers, they do.'

After the podcast aired, a British astrologer called Chris Odle got in touch with quite a different take on how astrology functions. He pointed me to a trove of empirical data that, in his view, sound the death knell for astrology as a science – at least in relation to its day-to-day practice by consulting astrologers.

'The truth is, there have been many hundreds of experiments over the years, many of them very well thought out and with large sample sizes, and the overwhelming majority of them have proved negative for astrology,' he wrote. 'You may wonder why, as an astrologer, I'm pointing this out. My only concern is for astrologers to see the truth of what they are doing, which the practice of it will point to.'

He sent me a link to an open-access book called *Understanding Astrology: A Critical Review of a Thousand Empirical Studies 1900-2020*. The book summarises its findings as 'remarkably consistent', stating that: 'Factual truth is not part of the deal … Personal meaning is provided by birth charts including wrong birth charts. But it comes from seeing faces in the ambiguous clouds of chart symbolism, not from some mysterious property of astrology.'[20]

Skimming the book, I was particularly taken by the story of Verle Muhrer and Tim Allen, psychologists working in the early 1980s. They arranged for volunteers to visit top astrologers for a reading, only with a twist – they used the birth data of notorious serial killer John Wayne Gacy. As Allen writes: 'Verle had picked Gacy for the experiment because Gacy's chart should portray a clear picture of a sadistic sexually motivated killer … If astrologers are able to spot personality traits and destinies in birth charts, then they should have no trouble with this one.'[21] Unfortunately for astrology (although fortunately for their own peace of mind), the astrologers failed spectacularly, describing Gacy variously as 'a very, very sensitive person'; 'kind, generous and considerate', and 'a good role model'. In a further blow to their professional credibility, all five astrologers agreed that the client should go into youth work.

This is clearly one of the 'small-scale, haphazard studies' Brennan was talking about, and I doubt its finding would put many people off astrology if they were inclined that way in the first place. The book quotes the late UK astrologer Dennis Elwell as saying: 'If some piece of research proves [to be] a dead end, I do not question the authenticity of my experience, I question the competence of the research or its underlying assumptions.'[22]

There is evidently a great deal of mudslinging on both sides of this debate, with astrologers and sceptics alike quick to discredit each other. As the book points out: 'From its early days astrology has been the focus of arguments for and against, a never-ending shouting match in which each side shouts from entrenched positions.'[23]

I felt this somewhat during my chat with Brennan. To me, his approach seemed to come from quite a defensive place, as though what he held sacred were under threat, and intellectual argument were the only means of safeguarding it.* Despite conceding that astrology wasn't entirely scientific, Brennan seemed intent on convincing me of its veracity through this lens.

For instance, he asked whether a new American war starting in 2025 would be sufficient for 'someone like me' to be persuaded. With my science journalist hat on, the answer to that would have to be no. The whole point of science is that you can't cherry-pick data points and use them to draw sweeping conclusions. However compelling the visible patterns are (such as American conflicts taking place every time Uranus pops up in Gemini), you'd have to find ways to investigate those patterns dispassionately, using controls. As the *Understanding Astrology* book records, a lot of researchers have already tried this, and astrology hasn't come out of it well.

On the other hand, I don't think something has to be scientifically verifiable to be personally significant, spiritually sustaining or even (if you want to be postmodernist about it) subjectively

---

* For what it's worth, some of the YouTube commenters said something similar about me.

The Spirituality Gap

true. I got a lot out of my birth chart reading, and I have no doubt that astrology often 'works' – I just don't know that it can thrive under the icy glare of scientific scrutiny. For a lot of people who enjoy astrology, or astrology-adjacent practices, the question is less 'What does the data say?' and more 'Does it help me? Is this a source of guidance? Does it make me feel like part of something greater than myself?'

Odle, for his part, views astrology more as a form of divination, which functions like a collective mythos. He thinks a lot of what astrologers do is storytelling, pure and simple, and is currently writing a book to this effect.[24]

'In a way, it is like a religion or spiritual practice, and it's time for astrologers to be honest about that,' he says.[25] 'It's not something they need to be scared of – it can be embraced. But it can be terrifying for male astrologers, in particular, to go there – they love charts and diagrams, and you'll see very sophisticated lines and models attempting to rationalise what they do.'

He adds that some astrologers are paranoid about being bracketed together with fortune tellers. In their view, astrology is a data-driven discipline, and therefore different from other divination. For instance, they use a book called an ephemeris, which shows where the planets are – much like a celestial train timetable.

'There's a real arrogance and hubris that some astrologers have, that they think they can access the mind of God at will, as opposed to moments of grace when things are revealed to us,' says Odle.

Whether or not this is specifically a male viewpoint, I'd concur that the intuitive parts of our mind are generally coded as lesser than the rational parts. Perhaps that is what needs to change if astrology wants to broaden its appeal, rather than making an intellectual case for its convictions. Maybe there is a leap of faith involved – and that might be no bad thing.

'I'm trying to say, "Look, it's a mystery tradition,"' explains Odle. 'There's nothing wrong with that. There's something ineffable at the heart of it, and that's OK, because the heart of life is ineffable. We can't approach it with our minds.'

The absent-minded Pisces in me would be inclined to agree.

Chapter 5

Manifestation: Magnetic Thoughts and Vision Boards

It's a Sunday morning in Alexandra Palace, North London, and a long queue of mostly twenty-something women is snaking out of the East Court entrance. The majority of them are flawlessly put together, with coiffed blow-dries and outfits straight out of an influencer's playbook. Some have come in small groups, bringing a mild hen-party energy, while others are solitary go-getters. Just past the ticket scanners and bag check is a sign, reading: 'Manifest. Someone once told you that you couldn't have it all. I'm here to tell you that you can. Roxie Nafousi.'

What I want more than anything at that moment is a coffee, so I join yet another queue inside and soak up the ambience as I attempt to manifest my brew. There's a wall just to the left, plastered in posts from Roxie Nafousi's Instagram feed: 'Just remember, as one chapter closes another always begins', and 'When you have a nice thought about someone, don't keep it to yourself, say it to them'. Uncontroversial enough. People are being photographed against the wall, presumably so they can post it to their own Instagram feeds, while others are clutching copies of the *Manifest Daily*. There's an impressive selection of manifesting merch – £35 for a journal, £13 for some pens, £65 for a hoodie – and a QR code you can scan in the hope of winning a year's supply of collagen.

Coffee manifested, I pick up my own copy of the *Manifest Daily* and am disappointed to find it's not a full-blown newspaper, just a folded-up A3 sheet hawking more of Roxie's products. It has a wordsearch too, and some mantras – 'I am worthy of abundance', 'I am vibrating at a high frequency' – the latter of which seems true for me as the caffeine kicks in. I follow the excited throng into the theatre and examine the freebies on my seat. These include a sample collagen supplement and 30 per cent off more collagen.

Roxie Nafousi is a self-development coach, inspirational speaker and much-lauded 'queen of manifesting'. She's also a double *Sunday Times*-bestselling author, with her two books *Manifest: 7 Steps to Living Your Best Life* (2022) and *Manifest: Dive Deeper* (2023) having soared to prime positions in the non-fiction charts. I skim-read the first *Manifest* book on the train here, and found it to be a peppy, motivational read, heavy on the therapy-speak and disarming personal anecdotes, while light on oddball claims about the universe.

Why would I be expecting oddball claims about the universe? you ask. Well, Roxie's style of manifestation may be uber-fashionable, but when you dive into the history of manifestation you quickly run into some fringe spiritual beliefs. There's Abraham-Hicks, aka the inspirational speaker Esther Hicks who channels a group of entities called Abraham.[1] There's the nineteenth-century clockmaker Phineas Quimby, pioneer of the New Thought spiritual movement, who claimed to have rediscovered the healing methods of Jesus.[2] There's Noel Edmonds, the gameshow host who notoriously used 'cosmic ordering' to manifest a new TV show, a helicopter, a powerboat and a wife.[3]

Then there's the defining tome of manifesting, *The Secret*, a now-infamous 2006 book written by Rhonda Byrne that emphasises using your thoughts to attract 'all manner of things – from a specific feather to ten million dollars'.[4] For reasons I'll go into shortly, I'm not sure it's trendy these days to say you admire *The Secret*.

Roxie Nafousi's brand is more of the moment. She's a life coach and pop psychology pundit in equal measure, advising her followers to heal their inner child while working hard to build their businesses. ('I didn't manifest a book deal sitting on my arse,' she tells the audience.) Her social media feed is tastefully curated, mostly inspirational slogans on neutral backdrops. It doesn't hurt that she is extremely beautiful, in the mould of the Kardashian and Jenner sisters. Today she is wearing a royal-blue trouser suit, like a Renaissance Madonna reimagined for the girlboss era.

'My first great love is manifesting, but my second great love is Instagram,' she tells the audience, before showing us a trick for taking the most grid-worthy photos of the event. I put my phone away and, not for the first time today, feel about 600 years old. Thank goodness the event is sponsored by collagen.

I must admit that, more than any other topic explored in this book, I felt uneasy about delving into manifestation. It might be different for those significantly younger than me – in fact, I'm sure it is, given that '#manifesting' has 7.1 billion (yes, BILLION) views on TikTok.[5] But for those of us old enough to remember *The Secret*, it can be hard to shake the icky connotations.

I was at university when *The Secret* came out, and while I didn't exactly rush off to buy a copy, I read enough snarky articles to get the gist. It wasn't just silly, it was also predicated on something downright offensive. In his essay 'The Staggering Bullshit of *The Secret*', blogger and bestselling author Mark Manson makes the case that the self-help movement has always brought 'its own generational edge' to the basic concept. But whereas other books of its ilk offer 'quite good advice for stretches', he says *The Secret* 'brings a harrowing narcissism and an "I'm the center of the universe" angle to the same old ideas'. He concludes that 'books like *The Secret* are like McDonald's for the mind. They're easy and make you feel good, but they also make you mentally fat and lazy – and emotionally, you die a much more painful death.'[6]

Having finally purchased a copy of the source material, I can testify that 'dying a painful death' isn't too bad a summary of the reading experience. I don't think I've ever seen so many wild ideas conveyed with such unflinching self-confidence. According to Rhonda Byrne, the author, 'whatever is going on in your mind you are attracting to you'. That's not too controversial a take, if you're simply talking about the power of positive thinking. You need a dollop of self-respect to attract a healthy relationship, a spoonful of self-belief to chase your dreams, and a spicy pinch of self-advocacy to push for more in your career. Clearly, a negative mindset can keep people entrenched in negative situations, deepening a groove of learned helplessness even when there's a way out.

But *The Secret* holds that you can magic things into existence simply by believing in them; it actually uses the analogy of a genie. Why? Well, 'Thoughts are magnetic, and thoughts have a frequency. As you think, those thoughts are sent out into the Universe, and they magnetically attract all like things that are on the same frequency.'[7] This is as bad a description of magnets (which famously repel like things) as it is of the philosophical problem of mental causation.

Byrne writes that the great poets and artists of the last 2,000 years were all proponents of the Law of Attraction, and that every major world religion conveys its message in some capacity. Those with more of a science bent will be pleased to know the 'discoveries of quantum physics and new science are in total harmony with the teachings of *The Secret*', and that Byrne is qualified to say so because 'when I read complex books on quantum physics I understood them perfectly'.[8] Would it be unsporting to dispute this claim given the previously mentioned misunderstanding of magnets?

As far as I can tell, Byrne believes in an idealist universe, in which mind creates matter rather than the other way round. This is a recurring theme of modern spirituality, and it's as valid a philosophical position as any other. More startlingly, she believes in an ungrammatical universe, which 'doesn't compute … words of negation'. Apparently if you think to yourself 'I don't want a bad haircut', the universe translates this as 'I want a bad haircut' and gives you exactly what you've asked for. You need to think about *good* haircuts, and picture yourself sashaying out of the salon with movie star tresses, if you want to avoid inadvertently manifesting a bowl cut.[9]

I won't waste too much more time on Byrne, as ripping into the book quickly starts to feel like a blood sport. But a few more points explain why it gets my hackles up. First, her version of the Law of Attraction involves some serious victim blaming. Let's say you're still down on your luck despite having made a vision board and performed a bunch of 'scripting' exercises. Was that your own fault somehow? Are the one-percenters of this world somehow more spiritually aligned than the rest of us?

To look at the issue from another angle, what about if you're anxious or depressed, or prone to intrusive thoughts? Are you doomed to create the circumstances you're afraid of? As far as *The Secret* is concerned, the answer is, explicitly, yes. There's an unsettling passage in which Byrne talks about 'events in history where masses of lives were lost'.[10] Apparently, the victims attracted these events through their own negative mentation.

The obnoxiously wealthy, too, are only getting their just desserts. Byrne has no complaint with their disproportionate hoarding of resources – she maintains they simply understand *The Secret* better than the rest of us. You too can join their bloated ranks if you shake off any thinking to the contrary!

Mark Manson attributes the book's uncomfortable message to the fact it was 'launched amid the social media/smartphone age'. I'd be more inclined to link it with the precarious economic boom that preceded the 2008 crash. The idea that we should all be chasing more money, more resources, more opulence, might once have seemed aspirational. But today it looks very much like the kind of toxic growth mentality that leads to planetary crisis.

At Alexandra Palace, Roxie Nafousi is telling the audience how manifesting changed her life. She'd hit rock bottom, she says. She was twenty-eight years old and addicted to cocaine, bouncing from one toxic relationship to the next. She lived for partying because she didn't have a job. Having just returned from yoga teacher training, which she'd seen as a path to sorting her shit out, she crashed back into her old coke-fuelled lifestyle. It was only once a friend sent her a podcast about manifesting that she managed to turn things round. She quit the drugs, met the future father of her child on a dating app, and set up her manifesting business. Since then, her upward trajectory has been dizzying.

One might scoff that hers was a privileged form of rock bottom – Roxie is from a wealthy background, and one of those toxic relationships was with the UK's richest living artist, Damien Hirst. But pain is pain, and she seems authentic; I'm totally willing to buy that she was in a dark place. I also suspect if you had found unconditional love via your son and a sense of purpose via your work, your manifestation journey would feel like a dramatic arc to you even if it isn't exactly a case of rags to riches. There is something endearingly unguarded about her, which is of course all part of what she's selling. If Roxie had insecurities, hangups and fuckups just like you, then maybe you can be just like Roxie.

Since her book came out, she says, hundreds of thousands of people have followed her seven steps to 'living your best life'. These steps are outlined in her book, described in today's workshop, and plastered all over her merch. And they seem uncontentious: you are supposed to be clear about what you want and 'align your behaviour' to achieve it. In other words, you can't just stick your dream house on a vision board and visualise it into existence; you also must spend some time on property websites. There is stuff about 'overcoming tests from the universe', which means sticking to your guns and not settling for less. Further, you need to embrace gratitude while reframing envy as inspiration.[11]

She invites us to do an inner child exercise in which we visualise our younger selves and tell them we're sorry for everything that's happened to them. We're also encouraged to say to ourselves, 'I love the person that I am' and, 'my friends and family are lucky to have me'. This isn't *The Secret*-style narcissism so much as it is a sorely needed corrective. In this room of young, 'together'-seeming women, there is a presumption that you might not value yourself very highly. This much is deeply sad.

Perhaps the only element that could be dubbed 'spiritual' is the seventh step, 'trust in the universe', which isn't too far removed from the old-fashioned enjoinder to trust in God. You are supposed to believe that the cosmic forces have your back, that the universe is an ultimately benevolent place in which the flow of events is orchestrated by divine timing. While *The Secret* alleges that said universe works like a genie – 'who is there to serve you and never questions your commands' – *Manifest* offers a more toned-down version. Here, you are encouraged to let go, surrender, and let things come to you in the way they're meant to. There's something almost pious about the sentiment.

If, as Mark Manson would have it, every generation gets the version of manifestation that most befits them, I think this speaks well of Gen Z. Rather than treating the cosmos like a pizza delivery app, they'll take their magical thinking with a side order of hard graft and inner healing.

Nick Trumble is as passionate an advocate of manifestation as any, telling me: 'I feel like this is my chosen subject on *Mastermind*.' A serial entrepreneur and filmmaker, he has used this technique across multiple business ventures, not least an air toy called Volleybird, for which he managed to manifest an appearance on *Blue Peter*.

'All of my accomplishments and probably important moments in my life have come from manifestation, which for me just means visualisation of what that end goal or experience looks and feels like,' he explains.[12] 'It's about creation, and maybe the key to tapping into it is avoiding limiting beliefs.'

When he's feeling down and depressed (a state Law of Attraction fans call 'vibrating at a low frequency'), it tends to be the case that the proverbial doors slam in his face. But when he's feeling lighter on his feet and open to ideas, that's when opportunities arise.

'That's also when these weird synchronistic things pop up,' he says. 'I'm an atheist, I believe in science. But when I'm in the groove, as it were, and I'm not facing the world as though people and things are against me, I find I can turn challenges to my favour.'

A fellow new parent, Nick rhapsodised about the way babies see the world; in the absence of any limiting beliefs, they are free to appreciate the magic all around them. For him, manifestation is a way of stripping back our accumulated layers of jadedness and recapturing the natural joy of life.

'All these remarkable magical things had to fall into place for us even to be here right now,' he points out. 'Our constraints come from society; race, religion, gender, politics are all thrown at us, and we're shoved into this thing and instructed not to be part of this joyous world. But the fact that we live in these buildings, that I'm [taking the interview from] this car, just shows that we are on this path of creation – we can create and build unlike any other mammal before us.'

The Spirituality Gap

I don't think Nick, whom I've known for some time, would mind me describing him as a deeply uncynical person. I picked up on this trait among the attendees at Roxie's workshop too. Everyone I spoke to took pains to distinguish the Law of Attraction from positive thinking. Yet there was something unwaveringly buoyant about their tone. For them, manifestation is first and foremost a way to wring the possibilities out of life, and who can argue with that? In this regard, inveighing against it feels a bit like kicking a puppy.

That positivity has been integral to the Law of Attraction since the outset. Despite proclaiming itself as very ancient, the practice has its roots in the American New Thought movement of the nineteenth century. I mentioned the New Thought movement in the previous chapter in relation to *The Kybalion*, which seems to be the starting point for several different strands of New Age thinking. According to the philosopher William James, New Thought is not just 'an optimistic scheme of life', but a 'genuine religious power' involving 'an intuitive belief in the all-saving power of healthy-minded attitudes'.[13]

In 1886, the author Prentice Mulford wrote an essay called 'The Law of Success' that outlined the principles of the Law of Attraction. 'Your prevailing mood, or frame of mind, has more to do than anything else with your success or failure in any undertaking … The mind is a magnet … What kind of thought you most charge that magnet (your mind) with, or set it open to receive, it will attract most of that kind to you,'[14] he wrote, beating Byrne to the punch in his misunderstanding of magnets.

Over the course of the twentieth century, the concept recurred in books such as Napoleon Hill's *Think and Grow Rich* (1937) and Norman Vincent Peale's *The Power of Positive Thinking* (1952). If many of these books appear to involve a peculiar intersection of spirituality and business, that's no accident: in contrast with other, more ascetic forms of spirituality, the Law of Attraction holds that money is not bad, and there is no reason why our divinity shouldn't express itself in worldly success.

From the mid-1980s onwards, Esther Hicks and her (now deceased) husband Jerry began to channel 'Abraham', 'a group consciousness from the non-physical dimension'. Among other teachings, Abraham-Hicks posit that 'you are a creator; you create with your every thought', 'anything you can imagine is yours to be or do or have', and 'relax into your natural wellbeing. All is well. (Really it is!).'[15] Esther Hicks appeared in the original film version of *The Secret*, although her part was eventually cut following contractual disputes.

Some modern manifesters use explicitly spiritual lingo, whereas others are keen to distance themselves from it and stick to sciencey jargon instead. Take the Swedish YouTuber Carl Runefelt, who goes by the alias The Moon. A high-school dropout and former cashier, Runefelt used the Law of Attraction to become a cryptocurrency billionaire.[16] He believes that nothing in the universe is real, other than vibrational energy, and therefore we can use the power of our minds to rearrange reality. 'This is quantum physics by the way, this is mainstream quantum physics, I'm not making this up,' he says in a TikTok video.[17]

The overall message here is one of relentless optimism: prosperity can be yours, save for the beliefs holding you back! It strikes me as an obvious counterpart to the American Dream: How to Succeed Under Capitalism 101.

In that broadcast of personal agency and optimism, though, something gets drowned out. You have to trawl really hard through the writings and social media postings to find any reference to wider society, or any discussion around whether promoting individual prosperity might come at the expense of the collective. If there is an underlying economic theory, it's the idea that there is always and invariably enough. There is also a widespread reluctance to acknowledge the practice's shadow side.

'Can we manifest crappy things happening to us?' ponders Nick. 'That's been a huge concern for me as well, but I think it falls into the category of limiting beliefs. Our experience on this planet is going to come with challenges and difficult times, because we are these biological creatures, and we go through so many things in these decades of life. So I always have faith that if something bad happens, something else will come along [that's] better, and that [the bad event] had to occur.'

Evie Sparkes is a Law of Attraction coach, who offers a range of manifestation and mindset coaching packages. For £350, you can embark on '4 weeks to the best version of you', a programme comprising four Zoom sessions and email support, which is supposed to help you get yourself out of a rut. Then there's the 'Relationship Package' at £365 – three Zoom calls helping you get to the root of your relationship issues. 'Is there someone in particular you want to manifest a relationship with or is it someone you haven't yet met?' writes Evie. 'What's holding you back?'

A former marketing professional and content writer, and the author of five books, Evie came to coaching almost accidentally. Since starting out, though, she has encountered an astonishing level of demand.

'It's gone crazy,' she tells me.[18] 'I had to rein it in, actually, because it was taking over my life. I was having no time to write or do anything else.'

Evie speaks quickly and loquaciously, in a lovely West Country burr. She strikes me as a genuine, caring person, in a field that I imagine attracts its fair share of charlatans (for instance, she'll refuse to work with people who are too hung up on manifesting a specific person). And despite building a life around the Law of Attraction, she handles the subject with an admirably light touch.

'Mostly my coaching is around *not* trying to manifest everything,' she says. 'In the past, I took it too seriously, and nothing was moving, I felt stuck. So I'm very mindful of other people not feeling like that. It's about how best to make it work for you while still enjoying life.'

When Evie first read *The Secret*, she treated it as 'all a bit of fun': using it to manifest a bit of money here, a fortuitous meeting there. What she really wanted, though, was to be a published writer, so she doubled down on her practice, trying to follow Law of Attraction doctrine to the letter. As she now maintains, her attachment to this outcome became an obstruction to getting it.

'I was going into try-hard mode,' she says. 'You'd hear from people, "You've just got to keep persisting until it shows up in your life," and I didn't know any different at the time. Eventually I decided, "Forget all this nonsense – it isn't about persisting, there's something else." I just set an intention to be a writer and thought, "Let's see what happens." A few days later, I met someone who asked me to do all his business writing. This gave me the confidence to self-publish a book.'

As she sees it, manifestation involves a delicate balance between setting a goal and then leaving it alone. It's as though you've written the script, and the universe is the director. Jumping onto the set, and meddling around with what goes where, will only serve to stave off your chosen outcome.

'People want certainty, and sometimes when people are manifesting something they want to break it down into all its parts,' she tells me. 'But this isn't like that. You have to embrace the uncertainty. I just know that if I have a feeling about something in the moment, almost as though it's happening, and then I go about my business, then at some point it's going to show up in my life.'

Since Evie's goal is to help people, not write a treatise, her engagement with the subject is more practical than theoretical. She remains agnostic about the way that the Law of Attraction works, preferring to attribute it to 'all a bit of magic'. 'If we were to suddenly see how it worked, I don't think our pea brains could fathom it,' she tells me.

That said, she suspects that manifesting is a by-product of the subconscious mind. 'It makes sense to me that the internal and external are all one big thing – so we're feeling good, we manifest on the inside, and then the outside just catches up because it's all part of the bigger picture,' she says.

In practice, it means that if you're fixating on the thing you want, your whole energy becomes prohibitive. You're putting out a 'lack energy', and the universe returns your signal by giving you more of that. Release this lack energy, and the desired outcome finally has space to come in.

The best way to test this out, says Evie, is to look at your own experiences. What were you doing at the times your long-held dreams truly did fall into your lap?

'I bet in 90 per cent of cases you weren't doing anything and that's when it happened,' she says. 'I know, it's such a paradox. You can want it, but you can't want it too much.'

My plan had been to try to manifest something myself, but my conversation with Evie made it clear that this might be a lost cause. According to her interpretation of the Law of Attraction, the actual techniques are secondary to the kind of feeling or 'vibe' you put out. Put out a happy, trusting vibe, and you'll attract more of the things that make you happy. Put out a sceptical vibe, and you'll attract more of the things that make you sceptical. Since my vibe was mostly quizzical, I suspected I was going to manifest a lot more questions than answers.

The Law of Attraction, then, is probably not something that lends itself well to facetious experiments. Instead, following Evie's advice, I decided to do a retrospective analysis and look back at times in my life when I'd attained something I really did want. Had I done the Law of Attraction without realising it?

The most obvious contender here would be meeting my husband. Now, if you want to manifest a life partner – a phrase that sounds so creepy I'm squirming just typing it – the internet, unsurprisingly, has suggestions. One website advises writing mantras about this imagined paramour, describing their value system, journalling about the memories you wish to create together, and writing a letter of gratitude to the universe for having met them. You then seal the letter and put it away, to be opened after they manifest in your life.

If I wanted to be snarky, I'd say there's a missing final step: 'What to do when the person you manifested serves you a restraining order.' I suspect my partner will be relieved to hear that I don't have any letters to share with him. If I wanted to be more generous, however, I'd say there's something in all this that does chime with my experience.

Throughout my twenties and some way beyond, my approach to dating was haphazard. I didn't know what I wanted, which was hardly surprising given that I didn't know who I was. I may have thought I was being selective, but the selection mechanism does not seem obvious in retrospect. What I remember is that I didn't hugely like myself. I wouldn't have known where to begin with the manifesting instruction about using 'self-love to become their energetic match'. In fact, I was so fixated on male validation I probably came across as a walking beacon of 'lack energy'.

By my early thirties, I was determined to break these negative patterns, and after one bad date too many, I *did* write a list of things I was looking for in a partner. While this had nothing to do with the Law of Attraction – it was more about blocking my ears against the siren song of wildly unsuitable men – it did help me clarify what I wanted. I also decided to set aside dating for a while to focus on my writing and (if you'll forgive a rather barf-worthy turn of phrase) 'personal development'.

About a year later, during a momentary lapse in my pact with myself, I reactivated an old dating profile and swiped on someone who seemed intriguing. There was an instant spark. Before long we were co-habiting, and then married, and then became parents. Dusting off that list of things I was looking for, I find that he not only meets it but exceeds it (why did I put 'OK with me being vegan' when I could have gone one better and manifested a fellow member of the tofu-eating wokerati?).

Now, you might say there's some crossover here with the Law of Attraction. I was clear about what I wanted, I'd made a bit of progress with the whole self-love thing, and I was relatively relaxed about the outcome (at least to the extent that I wasn't boiling bunnies and mood-boarding wedding dresses). To an extent, this pattern has applied across other areas of my life too. It's not quite 'it'll happen when you least expect it' – it's more 'things have tended to happen when I let go', 'chasing something too hard makes it less likely', or 'buried feelings of personal inadequacy have a sneaky way of expressing themselves in outer circumstances'.

I wouldn't say I've trusted the universe to provide, though. And I certainly haven't driven myself mad by visualising something that may or may not happen. On the contrary, I think my big wins in life have come with a hearty element of fluke. After all, if it really is our own 'energy' that's responsible, shouldn't we also be holding ourselves culpable for the times when things haven't worked out so well?

As I journalled during a time when everything seemed bleak: 'I firmly endorse the right to be negative, the right to be angry, the right to feel the full spectrum of human emotions instead of clinging desperately to the "good" ones. I want to welcome my shadow side rather than running away from it. I want to feel whatever I bloody well feel, without having to worry that my negative thoughts are somehow going to manifest negative circumstances.

Surely it would do far more damage if the thoughts are repressed, the feelings bolted down, the disappointment clogging my gut rather than being properly metabolised.'

To go back to that obvious objection: if our thoughts really do have the power to create reality, then presumably that applies to our negative or intrusive thoughts as much as it does our positive ones. Am I truly at risk of manifesting my fears each time I succumb to dark imaginings? And as for those people who *do* end up living the worst-case scenario – was that their very own nightmare creation?

Evie tells me I'm not the first person to have made the jump from 'our thoughts create our reality' to 'woe betide anyone who gets themselves stuck in gnarly thought spirals'.

'I speak to a lot of people with anxiety over this, and if I can help anyone with that I will,' she says. 'I say to them, "Think of all the things you've worried about in the past that haven't happened. Well, it's no different than that – only now you know what you know about Law of Attraction, you're more scared of your feelings. But you're not conjuring up the actual energetic version of an event within yourself."'

She adds that if you do suffer with OCD or anxious thoughts, getting too hung up on manifesting can exacerbate those thought patterns.

'This is why we should take it with a light touch,' she says. 'There's something going on here that we don't understand. I can set a light intention for what I'd like in my life, and not go any further than that.'

At its simplest level, manifestation strikes me as a bid for control, an attractive prospect for anyone who's lived through, say, a pandemic or a cost-of-living crisis or a climate breakdown fuelled by complacent petrostates. Its cosmology is appealing too. Rather than being a discrete individual in an empty universe, the Law of Attraction holds that you're fully enmeshed with cosmic forces, and that through wanting something hard enough, you can make those forces do your bidding.

'Sometimes I'll call it God, even though I'm not religious, and sometimes I'll call it source and the universe,' says Evie. 'It depends how I feel. There can't be a rule because we don't understand it.'

More importantly, I have no doubt that the Law of Attraction really can be a tool for living your best life. I'd imagine that the average holidaymaker, picking up a copy of Roxie Nafousi's *Manifest* at the airport, is happy to use the book for self-improvement without dorkily fleshing out its metaphysics. There's nothing wrong with harnessing the parts that make life better, while discarding the rest.

That said, I feel manifestation does take you into some very questionable territory if taken to its logical extremes. I'd be interested to see where future versions of the concept lead, as the flaws in capitalism become ever more apparent. Will we manage to manifest our way out of the climate crisis for instance, or will the philosophy be forever tethered to a blithely optimistic, ruggedly individualistic model of society? Is it possible to believe in the Law of Attraction without also believing that the world is innately meritocratic and that personal 'vibrational energy' is what distinguishes the haves from the have-nots?

Beset by such questions, I must admit I skulked out of Roxie's event early to join some similarly cynical friends in the pub. I didn't manifest much that day, other than a hangover. But in the interests of balance, I'll let the last word go to Evie, who has noticed a real uptick in many of her clients' happiness levels since starting out down this path.

'If people can have a bit of coaching with me and go away knowing they can do this – "I don't know how it's going happen, but I get the feeling that it's possible" – then, to me, that's my job done,' she says.

Chapter 6

Reiki: A Spoonful of Wellness

So far, I've made the case that tarot, astrology, manifestation and the rest can function as legitimate spiritual practices. That said, I do think there's one aspect that differentiates them from more traditional spiritualities – and that's their focus on self-care. Many of these types of practice sit at the intersection of something rather mystical or transpersonal, and something more healing or therapeutic.

A yogi might say that through casting off your negative *samskaras* (therapeutic), you're more clearly able to see the ways in which everything is connected (spiritual). A psychonaut might say that with reduced activity in the default mode network, you'll both dislodge unhelpful thoughts about yourself (therapeutic) and come to understand the very nature of the self (spiritual). A tarot reader might seek guidance and insights (therapeutic) by tapping into a source of collective wisdom (spiritual), while an astrologer might use the stars to trace someone's central conflicts (therapeutic) or uncover their soul purpose (spiritual). A manifester might say you need to work on releasing your limiting beliefs (therapeutic) in order to receive from the universe (spiritual). I'm not sure it makes sense to consider one part of the equation without knowing where you stand on the other.

Organised religion is not entirely lacking a focus on health and wellbeing. Evangelical Christianity has some tendrils in the nineteenth-century New Thought movement that also spawned the Law of Attraction[1] – and the church I grew up in made faith healings a regular part of the repertoire. C. Pierce Salguero, a Buddhism scholar whom we will meet later in this book, told me that physical and mental health alike have been a focus of Buddhist texts for millennia, and that this has often been one of the religion's main selling points during periods of cultural collision.

In general, though, traditional religion hasn't exactly sold itself as being 'therapeutic'. For instance, some research suggests that Mormons experience lower rates of depression, anxiety and suicidal thoughts than irreligious people.[2] If the Church of Jesus Christ of Latter-day Saints marketed itself in the same way yoga does, that'd be the first thing its missionaries would tell you. And yet 'positive mental health' is not even slightly part of the sales pitch, which focuses much more on God's commandments and Jesus's atonement.

Modern wellness culture represents a particular confluence of spirituality and health that, if you were to unpick it, would tell us a lot about the fixations and neuroses of our times. That doesn't mean the spiritual component is illusory. But it does seem to mean that, as a secular culture, we struggle to make sense of our spiritual impulses unless they are couched in the language of mental health.

In some cases, I'd say the wellness part is – intentionally or otherwise – a kind of Trojan horse. Push past the palatable exterior, spruced up for easy marketing on social media, and you might end up somewhere much more 'out there'. A prime example is reiki, otherwise known as energy medicine. The selling point for many clients is physical healing. Underpinning this, though, is a decidedly spiritual worldview, which, depending on how deep you go, involves infinite energy, mysterious attunement rituals and ancestral spirit guides.

'Take a deep breath in through the nose, then out through the mouth,' says Sushma Sagar, when I visit her for an energy healing session in February 2023. 'And again, in through the nose and out through the mouth. Now be present in your body. All the different parts of you – on the phone, on your emails, at home, with your baby – allow each of them to arrive in your body.'

I'm lying on a massage table in Sagar's front room, eyes closed. As I picture myself in each of these scenarios, it hits me how incredibly scattered I am. I'm researching and writing this book, my daughter (three months old at the time) is temporarily unwell, and I'm so very tired. I wonder briefly whether the double espresso I've just necked was a no-no, and whether Sagar can tell. Still, if I'm ever going to embark on energy healing, it might as well be in a moment when my energy is all over the place.

My exhaustion, I think, has made me more porous and suggestible. As Sagar starts laying her hands on, or over, various parts of my body, I enter an almost trip-like state. First comes the heaviness in my torso, as though I'm made of concrete. The whirlwind that's been my life lately suddenly stops whirring, all that kinetic energy distilled to a point. Then comes the sense of having something to release. Sagar has warned me that this might happen. She has told me to go with it, and not to be alarmed by anything that might come up. I'm not too surprised to find myself crying. But I am surprised to find my muscles shuddering, especially my shoulders and glutes. It's involuntary, and I'm a little weirded out.

'Soften into it, don't resist it,' Sagar advises me, after maybe ten minutes of rigid jolts. I do as requested and the shudders become continuous. Something particularly intense starts to happen when she hovers her hands over my pelvic region. It occurs to me that I pushed a human out of here not too long ago and, while I haven't had much time to dwell on that experience, the body, notoriously, keeps the score.

At one point, she places a hand under my sacrum and another under my shoulders and asks me to lean my whole weight into her, as though I'm being held. It's a surprisingly hard thing to do. During our post-session debrief, she notes that I have problems receiving, a common issue among her clients. I think it's a bit of that, mixed with the strangeness of the situation and my own conflicted feelings about energy medicine. How can I best equip myself to receive something I don't understand?

That said, I can't deny something has happened here. If nothing else, the session has tuned me into my feelings of overwhelm, turning up the volume on the physiological feedback I've been muting just to get through the day.

'You're really sensitive to energy,' Sagar informs me. 'It's as though you're a seismometer for energy. Have you heard the term highly sensitive person – HSP?'

Sushma Sagar is a reiki master healer and teacher, author of *Find Your Flow: Essential Chakras* (2020), and founder of the London-based energy healing clinic The Calmery. I'm trying one of her hour-long reiki energy healing sessions, which she offers from her clinic in Harley Street or by invitation at her home. She also provides sessions over Zoom, and hosts an online group called the Healing Club once a week. From the branding, marketing and (let's be honest) price-point perspectives, The Calmery is a long way from the kooky reiki stereotype. Sagar founded the clinic with a view to demystifying energy healing, or as she puts it, 'taking it out of the weird and into the weekday'; her typical client wouldn't be caught dead brushing the room with sage or joining a moon circle in Glastonbury's Healing Fields.

'I came from a fashion background, and I knew how to create a desirable brand for a certain kind of woman,' Sagar tells me when we speak the following week.[3] 'I knew what this woman was like. I knew how particular she was about her skincare, about her clothing, her nightwear, her underwear, her handbag, and I knew she needed a wellness brand that talked to her in the same language. Up until that point, there was nothing out there that communicated in a very clear, non-spiritual, non-unicorny type way.'

Prior to founding The Calmery, Sagar was the UK marketing director for fashion brand Kate Spade. She had been passionate about reiki for a while, having practised it on the sly since her mid-twenties, but struggled to form a bridge between her two lives.

'I would secretly connect with the energy medicine world, but I didn't want anyone to know,' she tells me. 'I felt ashamed to be associated with that kind of rainbow, witchy, butterfly-wing thing. Coming from fashion, it really bothered me. But I realised I had all this experience in brands and communicating to this woman, and then I had this hobby that needed a rebrand like I've never known in my life.'

The Calmery was born out of a desire to 'make reiki beautiful' – to disencumber it from the off-putting stereotypes and create something that would resonate with her own demographic. Sagar founded the clinic in 2017, stepping out of the spiritual closet and helping propel reiki into the mainstream.

'Even in the Wirral, where my parents live, there's this tiny beauty salon and on the board it says we do nails, we do hair, we do this, we do that, we do reiki,' she says. 'To me, that is as mainstream as it's ever going to get – in this tiny suburban town in Birkenhead next to Tranmere Rovers Football Club, the market there is open to the word "reiki".'

It's difficult to get a handle on how many people have tried reiki, but anecdotally it is becoming more popular. In 2015, 16 per cent of English adults accessed a complementary or alternative medicine – a broad category including reiki, acupuncture, homeopathy, massage and chiropractic. That was up from 12 per cent in 2005,[4] and is likely even higher now in a country racked by a healthcare crisis. In the US, around 20–30 per cent of the population is thought to use some form of alternative medicine, not including prayer.[5]

Just as importantly, a high proportion of Brits are open to reiki-adjacent concepts. In a 2021 YouGov survey, 46 per cent of those surveyed said they believed 'humans can emit "negative" and "positive" energy or vibrations', while 34 per cent agreed that 'humans have energy points (chakras) across the body that can impact wellbeing if they get blocked or misaligned'.[6] This means energy medicine as a wellness business is ripe for the taking.

'I wanted it to be cool, to be more lifestyle,' said Sagar. 'Back then I was the only brand out there doing that, but now everyone's doing it. In a way, my work is done, let's say.'

Certainly, nobody looking at The Calmery's website would start thinking about rainbows and witches and unicorns. They'd be more inclined to think, 'Let's fit in some reiki in between my latest round of microdermabrasion and a trip to the organic juice bar.' This is wellness for high-flying go-getters; it isn't overtly spiritual, and it certainly isn't whimsical.

But once you start digging into what reiki actually is, you're bound to run up against some questions. What exactly is going on when a reiki master hovers her hands over your chakras? How does this practice achieve its touted benefits: healing heartbreak, easing stress, kickstarting the body's own healing mechanisms? And to really get back to basics, what is 'energy'? A seismometer for energy I may be, but what does that even mean?

The legend of reiki starts with a man on a mountain: a Japanese headteacher called Dr Mikao Usui (1865–1926), who had climbed the sacred Mount Kuruma in pursuit of enlightenment. After three weeks of fasting and meditation, a great light entered through the top of his head, attuning him to a 'spiritual life force' with a wealth of healing benefits.*

On descending the mountain, Usui is said to have performed a succession of minor miracles. He cured a young woman's toothache, a monk's arthritis, and – underwhelmingly – his own stubbed toe. A few years later, Japan was rocked by a devastating earthquake, and Usui began treating up to five victims at any one time. With so many people in need of healing, Usui initiated hundreds of new reiki practitioners.[7]

Although reiki-like practices have existed for millennia, most modern teachers can trace their lineage back to Usui, via his student Hawayo Takata (1900–1980), who brought reiki to the USA after the Second World War. The practice spread slowly to begin with, before gathering momentum and splintering into an array of different systems. What they share, though, is the belief in the human entity as an energy system. Maladies of various kinds, whether physical or emotional, are believed to stem from blockages in that system.[8]

'The person who is doing the reiki healing is channelling a universal healing energy, that is everywhere, and is infinite,' says Sagar. 'They have been taught how to allow that energy to pass through them and through their hands. You become hollow, and you allow this beautiful healing force [to flow] through you. It guides you where to put your hands, and that energy then will connect with the person's own energy and find where the blockages are.'

---

* *Rei* means 'universal soul or universal consciousness', while *ki*, like *qi* in Mandarin or *prana* in Sanskrit, means 'life force' or 'vital energy'.

She uses the analogy of a plumber, who has come to fix the radiators in a clogged system. 'They pump new water through, in order to bust through the blocks and get the water flowing again,' she says.

Following the yogic tradition, this energy is allegedly mediated by spinning energy centres known as chakras ('wheel' in Sanskrit). The chakras hold together the physical and energetic bodies, like buttons fastening your psyche to your meat suit. Some traditions count as many as 88,000 chakras,[9] but for the purposes of a reiki treatment there are seven, connected through a network of energy channels that correspond with the spinal cord. Each relates to certain physiological functions, as well as to aspects of our emotional health. For instance, the solar plexus chakra maps onto the adrenal glands and stomach, but also onto our 'gut feelings' about a situation. The heart chakra maps onto all the sappy stuff a heart symbol denotes, as well as the actual physical heart.

As Sagar writes in her book *Find the Flow*: 'Think of the chakras as wheels. When they are healthy, they spin clockwise and draw energy into our bodies to be used as needed, just like water being sucked into a plughole. When they are imbalanced, they will spin slowly or not at all. They may even spin backwards when they are really clogged.'[10]

In a reiki session, the practitioner holds their hands over each chakra for a few minutes, sometimes touching the person but at other times not. Following their intuition, they may notice that certain parts of the energy field feel heavier or more 'stuck'. As Sagar explained it to me, she will sometimes notice sympathy sensations in her own body that guide her towards where she should go. She doesn't need to know *why* that spot demands attention, just that it does. After all, when you're sweeping the kitchen floor, you're going to find all kinds of detritus – crumbs, hairs, dust, rubber bands, bits of old popcorn. You wouldn't construct an elaborate backstory for each bit of gunk. You'd simply sweep it up and chuck it out.

'When I prepare a room, I'm calling in the lineage of master healers and guides who I want to support me on an invisible basis,' says Sagar. 'They're there, putting ideas into my head, moving my hands without me even knowing … I go into a space and I just allow whatever to happen. And I trust that when I enter that space and I open myself up to this work, I am a conduit for the highest form of healing to flow through.'

At this point in the conversation, I realised we had veered some way from the 'weekday' image The Calmery seeks to cultivate. Rainbows, witches and unicorns there may not be, but I can imagine some of Sagar's clients baulking at this talk of spirit guides. Sagar told me that she's careful to lead with the wellness angle – helping you feel better, helping you feel energised, helping you get over your ex. Her website is full of glowing testimonials of this nature. 'I felt like I was in a state of both total presence and bliss, and as relaxed as if I'd woken up from the perfect nap,' said one client; 'I'm lit inside again. I'm so happy I could cry,' said another.[11]

After a while, though, Sagar maintains there's magic to be had. 'I'm not going to start [by] saying, "Do you want to connect with a deceased ancestor? Do you want to connect with your spirit guide or animal?"' she told me. 'But you may end up doing that if you work with the power of reiki.'

In other words, this is a definitively spiritual practice, no matter how many spoonfuls of wellness you take to help the medicine go down. Sagar herself has ventured far down this road, having graduated as a shamanic energy medicine woman in a Peruvian Incan tradition. Over the course of our conversation, she spoke passionately about such topics as clairsentience, Western shamanism, and how the essence of most religions is the same when you strip away the trappings of power and control.

'I want to be a threshold to help people take the first step into the world of alternative techniques,' she tells me. 'I say alternative, but these were the original techniques before Western medicine – Western medicine isn't even 200 years old. If you look at ayurvedic medicine, [those practitioners] were working with energy thousands of years ago. The Egyptian pyramids are just big sound-healing chambers. All shamanic cultures have been doing it in some way or form – that's how they heal. And so the idea of working with energy for healing, for wellbeing, for spiritual purposes, has been around since the beginning of time.'

Against the backdrop of such big ideas, it almost seemed petty-minded to turn the conversation to scientific evidence. But it felt important too. Unlike most of the practices covered in this book, energy medicine is geared around physical as much as spiritual health. If you're going to sell your clients on what reiki can achieve, you do need some evidence-based grounding for your claims.

In 2011, the British Advertising Standards Agency (ASA) upheld a complaint about an online reiki marketing campaign, which declared that reiki could be effective for a huge range of conditions ranging from ADHD to back pain to cancer. More dangerously, the website's messaging also discouraged patients from seeking conventional medical treatment.[12] This is the realm of quackery and snake oil salesmen, peddling a miracle all-purpose cure without heed for truth or accuracy.

Of course, a reputable practitioner would be unlikely to promise they could blast your back pain. The International Association of Reiki Professionals (IARP) explicitly states that reiki isn't a cure-all for anything. It says that, rather than curing your ailments, reiki healing helps 'get to the root cause of a condition, get back on track and create an optimum environment for the body to heal'.[13] In other words, it's indirect and holistic, rather than targeted and symptom-focused. Sagar's own website includes the caveat that 'Energy medicine is not a substitute for conventional medicine and works best as a complementary therapy, in conjunction with any treatment you may be receiving from your doctor.'

For reiki's detractors, though, that isn't enough to warrant its integration into conventional medical settings. In 2022, the NHS posted an advert for a 'spiritual healer/reiki therapist', who would earn £26,000 a year working with cancer patients at Manchester Royal Infirmary. The job posting was roundly condemned. 'That the NHS should [endorse] such quackery in the midst of a funding crisis is frankly appalling,' Professor Edzard Ernst at the University of Exeter told *MailOnline*.[14]* A similar backlash has arisen in the US, following reiki's introduction into numerous prestigious hospitals. 'I've been bemoaning this development a long time,' wrote the oncologist Dr David Gorski, on the website *Science-Based Medicine*.[15]

---

* It should be noted that the funding came from a private charity, the Sam Buxton Sunflower Healing Trust, rather than from the taxpayer.

After all, as far as mainstream medicine is concerned, reiki is a textbook example – if not *the* textbook example – of a pseudo-science. You need only glance at its Wikipedia page to see this message aggressively hammered home. Sceptics have taken pains to point out that many reiki concepts can't be empirically verified, not least the spiritual life force it purports to manipulate. And for anyone schooled in typical Western systems of thought, ancient ideas like chakras and meridians might be challenging to get your head around.

Many attempts to explain reiki involve a misappropriation of scientific terms, or a spiritual interpretation of scientific terms that few actual scientists would recognise. Of course energy exists: we all learned about potential and kinetic energy at school. However, the kind of energy that reiki practitioners are talking about has so far eluded detection. At least, that's the orthodoxy. Some reiki practitioners are pinning their hopes on an instrument called a SQUID – a superconducting quantum interference device – which measures extremely small magnetic fields;[16] while Sagar told me about a technique called Kirlian photography that some say takes an image of your aura.

As for the idea that distance reiki – in other words, reiki performed over Zoom – works via quantum entanglement, I suspect this contention did not originate from someone trained in quantum entanglement.

If you'll allow me a quick digression, any appeal to 'quantum' in New Age spaces tends to set off my bullshit alarm. I've heard it a lot in relation to manifestation; remember Rhonda Byrne and her perfect understanding of quantum physics? The phenomenon is common enough to have its own name, 'quantum mysticism', which the physicist Philip Moriarty describes as the 'misappropriation of physics terminology in a wider, every-day context'. As Moriarty has explained, the 'defining problem at the heart of quantum mysticism [is] the assumption that the colloquial and formal meanings of a term from physics – "energy", "frequency", "resonance", etc. – are equivalent.'[17]

Quantum mechanics is especially ripe for the picking because the science is ridiculously complicated and its jargon easily

Reiki: A Spoonful of Wellness

misconstrued. For instance, the 'observer effect', in which the introduction of a measurement apparatus changes what's being measured, is often taken as 'proof' for an idealist metaphysics. According to the writer Morten Tolboll, 'the claim that *quantum mechanics proves that consciousness creates reality* is one of the biggest lies in the last century'.[18] That might be an overstatement, but when I hear spiritual leaders proselytising about quantum mechanics, I can't help but feel that their message loses, rather than gains, legitimacy.*

My sense is that, in their attempts to sound sciencey, New Age types risk alienating the very people they are trying to attract. I get it, they want to build a bridge between science and spirituality, harnessing some of the respect that is normally accorded to disciplines like physics. But to my mind, this kind of talk just serves to widen the chasm between the two ways of thinking. (If their science isn't accurate, does that discredit the spiritual aspect too?) As for a device like the superconducting quantum interference device measuring extremely small magnetic fields, it reminds me of the medieval scholastics and their obsession with how many angels could dance on a pinhead. Historically speaking, attempts to quantify the ineffable haven't gone very well.

The fact remains that under scientific scrutiny reiki has shown mixed results. In one classic study, a nine-year-old girl named Emily Rosa devised a clever experiment to see whether 'therapeutic touch' practitioners could sense their clients' energy field. Under tightly controlled conditions, they performed no better than a coin toss.[19]

There are plenty of studies out there that *do* show benefits for reiki over placebo, particularly when it comes to metrics like pain, stress, anxiety and overall wellbeing.[20] However, there are no large and conclusive trials, and many of the positive studies have been subject to methodological flaws. According to the US National Center for Complementary and Integrative Health: 'Reiki hasn't been clearly shown to be effective for any health-related purpose.

---

* With books called *Quantum Healing* and *Quantum Body*, the author and New Age guru Deepak Chopra exemplifies what I'm talking here.

It has been studied for a variety of conditions ... but most of the research has not been of high quality, and the results have been inconsistent.'[21]

Some academics have even suggested we ought to stop researching reiki altogether. 'Studying highly implausible treatments is a losing proposition,' said Steven Novella of Yale University in 2014. 'Such research only serves to lend legitimacy to otherwise dubious practices.'[22]

So what would Sagar say to sceptics who argue reiki has no evidence base, or who dismiss it as a pseudoscience?

'Number one, it's not a science,' she says pointedly, echoing my own thoughts on the subject. 'Number two, it's an experience and the only way to prove it is to have your own experience with it. No one can say, "Oh no, you're not feeling the benefit." You have to try it, and only then will you be able to have an opinion on whether it's real.'

It may seem as if these two ways of understanding reiki – the scientific and the spiritual – are incompatible. However, I don't think the two have to be at loggerheads, and since reiki is so helpful for many people, it's worth trying to find some points of connection.

One question we could ask is whether the research community is using the right investigative tools. I wouldn't be the first person to argue that the randomised controlled trial (RCT) is a blunt instrument for assessing holistic practices of this kind. RCTs determine whether a given treatment performs better than placebo. You're looking for a measurable effect that's divorced from context, mindset, expectation, attitude, the relationship between patient and practitioner – something above and beyond what is endowed by the overall setup. That's exactly how it should be when you're testing a pharmaceutical. But with treatments like reiki, it's not obvious how you would separate the 'active ingredient' from everything else. There's a powerful social ritual at play that is surely integral to its mechanism.

Am I suggesting that reiki's benefits are mostly – maybe entirely – down to the placebo effect? Well, that's what the research seems to show. There are plenty of trials out there that find benefits for reiki *and* for the placebo group, not least a 2011 study on 200 cancer patients who were receiving chemotherapy. In both wings of the trial, the patients felt better. As the authors wrote: 'The findings indicate that the presence of a RN providing one-on-one support during chemotherapy was influential in raising comfort and well-being levels, with or without an attempted healing energy field.'[23]

In trials like this, the control group receives 'sham reiki', in which the person performing the treatment is an actor. They're doing the same things as their reiki-trained counterpart, from welcoming the client, to placing their hands in the same spots; it's just that they haven't received an 'attunement'. Colour me shocked if the attunement, a brief ritual that takes place during training, is not in fact the most therapeutic component of reiki.

All this said, 'the placebo effect' strikes me as an imprecise and dismissive turn of phrase, indicative of a whole set of phenomena that conventional Western medicine has historically glossed over. It is into this category that we bracket a lot of things we don't much understand, from the healing potential of trusting your doctor to the medicinal power of being cared for. There is an increasing body of research that suggests the placebo effect involves measurable physiological changes but, perhaps because it's such a diffuse concept, we haven't tended to take it seriously. Perhaps a lot of spiritual phenomena wind up in this bracket too.

In the words of Professor Ted Kaptchuk of the Beth Israel Deaconess Medical Center, one of the world's leading placebo researchers: 'The placebo effect is a way for your brain to tell the body that it can feel better.'[24] To my mind, this sounds very similar to the stuff about holistic healing on the IARP website.

In thinking about this subject, I am indebted to Jo Marchant's book *Cure: A Journey into the Science of Mind Over Body* (2016). She makes a compelling case for the ways in which we've underestimated the role of the mind in healing.

'In many situations, we have the capacity to influence our own health, by harnessing the power of the (conscious and unconscious) mind,' she writes. 'It's not necessarily the potions or needles or hand waving that make you feel better. Consider the possibility that these are just a clever way of pushing your buttons, enabling you to influence your own physiology in a way that eases your symptoms and protects you from disease.'[25]

This isn't to say that reiki is all in your head, or that it can't possibly work via the mechanisms its practitioners say it does. Colloquially, we all know what's being referred to when you mention the 'vibe' or the 'energy' in the room. It's just to say that, if we want to translate this kind of practice into Western scientific language, we may have to enquire more deeply into the ways in which mind and body interact, and what it would mean to harness these interactions more fully.

After my own treatment with Sagar, I can't say that I felt vastly different, but there were lots of confounding variables in the mix, not least the fact that my baby had started waking each night at hourly intervals, a phase that lasted for the next four months. I lurched through some days like a zombie, and ricocheted through others in a frenzy, feeling suspiciously full of beans. A lot of the time, I felt as though I'd taken an ill-advised concoction of party drugs. If chakras are real, mine were presumably spinning madly.

My interest in reiki had been piqued, however, and Sagar had recommended I do a training. There are three levels of reiki training: level one, which enables you to perform reiki on yourself and family and friends; level two, which confers the ability to practise professionally; and level three, master level, which permits you to initiate others into reiki. Level one typically only takes a day, and there were spaces available on Michael Kaufmann's London course the following month.

Michael Kaufmann is a meditation and reiki teacher, who has introduced around 5,000 people to the practice since 1997. He has a spry build, a curly moustache and a mischievous, puckish energy. He also has a way of bouncing round the zaniest concepts that makes you feel there's something to them. I tried making notes but couldn't jot them down fast enough – no sooner had I written 'death as a way to reshuffle and refresh' than he'd be off again, rhapsodising on how the body is your pet and how hunching over your computer all day is animal abuse.

It started early in the day. 'Why did I choose to incarnate as this upgraded ape?' he said, I presume rhetorically, as we introduced ourselves.

He talked about reiki energy as an endlessly creative life force, pulsing through a world in continuous flux and retaining a deep memory of where it's been. The physical body arises out of this energy: 'like throwing iron filings into a magnetic field'. When two people meet, their energetic bodies fuse and one fleetingly *becomes* the other – that's why first impressions are so often on point. Nobody really understands reiki energy, but nobody understands gravity either. The chakras resent being confined to the physical body, just as a genie resents being confined to a lamp.

I wasn't too sure about some of this (I mean, wasn't understanding gravity Einstein's whole deal?) but I let his words wash over me, almost in the manner of spoken word poetry. After all, this is a man for whom the purpose of reiki is 'to inspire people to fall in love with life again'. His passion for the subject was infectious. I decided that I would dampen down my inner Ben Goldacre* and just enjoy the day.

There were around twenty of us there for the training, which took place at the Light Centre in Moorgate, Central London. All but two were women, which didn't surprise me; women are the demographic most drawn to alternative, decentralised spiritualities. Let's leave the rant about why that might be (*cough* *the patriarchy* *cough*) for another time.

Kaufmann asked each of us to explain why we were there; for most people it was a natural progression after having had their own powerful reiki experiences. One person credited reiki with unblocking her third eye chakra, which in turn had allowed her to 'feel more' with her massage clients. Another attendee described how, post-reiki, she'd skipped around high on life, eating lollipops and telling a fairground worker she loved him. 'It allowed you to connect with your inner child,' said Kaufmann, approvingly. Another had had what sounded like a full-blown psychedelic experience, complete with visits from a kundalini serpent and her ancestral spirit guides.

'Did anyone feel *worse* after their reiki treat?' asked Kaufmann. (He made a point of referring to reiki sessions as 'treats', as the

---

* Author of *Bad Science* and noted anti-woo-woo grouch.

connotations of 'treatment' are too clinical.) One lady mentioned her stomach aches, and Kaufmann talked us through the concept of the 'healing crisis'. As the thinking goes, reiki brings all kinds of repressed baggage to the surface, and you may feel worse before you feel better. This made me wonder about an issue pervasive in complementary therapies: how are practitioners, whose training may only have amounted to a few days, supposed to behave when more difficult issues come to light?

But reiki practitioners don't profess to be psychotherapists. What they can do is hold space, safely and gently, for whomever comes through their door. Kaufmann emphasised that the real skill for a practitioner is being egoless; they need to trust the universal energy, abandon their personal will, and get out of the way. 'When you want to be a knight in shining armour, that's a dark cloud pushing between your energy and the source,' he said.

Just before the lunch break, we received our attunement, the ritual that distinguishes reiki from sham reiki. What this ritual involved, I'll never know, as Kaufmann instructed us to keep our eyes shut. But whatever happened during that half-hour – be it a goat sacrifice or just a few symbolic hand movements – it meant we were ready to practise reiki on each other. Now initiated into the ways of energy medicine, we got into pairs and took turns hovering our hands over our partner's chakras. I was ready, my inner sceptic muzzled, my energetic pathways open to receive.

Sadly, this was a damp squib of an exercise that, two hours later, had very much stopped feeling like a treat. Lovely as my partner was, she was terrible at manipulating my energy field, and I struggled to manipulate hers too. I stood there sheepishly, one hand near her chest and the other near her back, trying to discern whether the occasional tingle in my hands was anything other than what hands normally feel like. I was tired. I was bored. I needed to express some milk. I wondered what kind of mother I was, that I'd chosen to spend the day suspending my hands over a random data analyst's heart chakra rather than hanging out with my baby. 'Set and setting?' I wrote in my notes, borrowing a phrase from the world of psychedelics. In other words, was it simply my mindset and environment that determined the effectiveness of a treatment? Was that why I'd experienced all-body tremors first time round, and this time nothing at all?

'I think your mindset very much flavours the experience – a mindset is like a filtering system,' Kaufmann said to me after the class.[26] 'Someone who takes on a particular mindset will look out for certain things and magnify them in their experience, and discredit other things that don't fit. If somebody really disliked reiki and said, "No, this is all nonsense," then obviously they would block the energy. They would make sure that their experience confirms their beliefs.'

This made a certain kind of sense. During my experiences with reiki, my own level of openness had oscillated wildly. In my treatment with Sagar, I felt trusting and safe, not to mention in need of emotional release. While I didn't know what I thought about reiki intellectually, I knew it was OK to let the less guarded, more 'spiritual' part of me take over and follow that animal sense wherever it led.

On the training, though, I just felt awkward. There were a lot of us in the room, and there was no way I was going to sit on that chair shuddering and convulsing in front of everyone. I was blocking the energy either literally or figuratively, less through my limiting beliefs and more through sheer embarrassment. Besides, my partner and I didn't know each other or have any reason to trust each other. There were clearly some prohibitive interpersonal dynamics at play.

According to Kaufmann, the most important skill in reiki is establishing rapport with the client. Apparently, the person can feel your intention in your micro-movements, which means your true feelings about what's happening can't help but come to light.

'We talked about chakras during the reiki course and how chakras are organs of perception,' he noted. 'And we also talked about how people's energies fields connect before the first word has been spoken. So it's important to be genuinely welcoming. And the setting, of course – it's got to feel safe for the receiver to enter a receptive state and let that guard come down.'

I told him about the shudders I'd experienced with Sagar. He suggested they might have to do with releasing stress in a self-protective way.

'Tension can be integrated into the body really well without the person even noticing,' he said. 'When we relax deeply, through reiki but also massage or deep meditation, sometimes our protective tensing is missed for a moment, so we let go. Then we go "Oh my God, I'm opening, but I'm not ready, not safe." It's a jerky movement. I've had people almost coming off the table with a full body release. Once the person realises what it is and trusts it, it becomes a little softer, a more conscious letting-go.'

Kaufmann maintains that this isn't faith healing, despite its glaring overlaps with the Christian practice of 'laying on hands'. While you do have to be open and curious about reiki, you don't have to buy into the theory for it to work. This struck me as counterintuitive to begin with. But then I started thinking about the equally weird, yet scientifically robust, idea that placebos work even when you know you're getting a placebo.[27] In both cases, there's something going on that transcends your intellectual suppositions about the process. You could probably go into a reiki treatment, resolute that nothing would budge your Enlightenment-informed scientific materialist worldview, and still receive some benefits if you were open to it.

It rang true to me on a personal level too. I still don't know whether I believe in universal reiki energy, at least as anything other than a psychological construct. But I do suspect that what we call the placebo effect is bigger and more mysterious than we give it credit for, and that you don't need to buy into the surrounding mythology to use reiki as a tool for healing.

'Where does it come from, Abi, this underlying aggressiveness towards these kinds of practices?' mused Kaufmann. 'But I do think the general attitude is becoming more receptive, as more and more people say it makes a real, positive difference. Most people who come to see me have tried every other avenue and are still looking. So that shows there's a need for healing beyond managing symptoms, which other modalities haven't yet been able to address.'

As we've seen, there's another part of the equation too, and that's the more spiritual side. While many people come to reiki to heal a particular ailment, probably just as many are attracted to the underlying cosmology. After all, there are a lot of people out there who believe in *something*, but who find the idea of God off-putting. They're not interested in worshipping some patriarchal power who knows your business and wants to control you.

'Spiritual life force', as a central anchor for belief or ritual, lacks that baggage. Whether or not it is the basis of how reiki 'works', it undoubtedly taps into some deeply rooted spiritual intuitions, which the more science-minded among us shouldn't be too hasty to dismiss.

Chapter 7
Atheist Churches: Pentecostalism for the Godless

After wading into tarot, astrology, manifestation and reiki, I must admit I was feeling a little burnt out. In all these cases, I'd been trying to balance the logical part of my mind with the part that secretly believed in magic. I wanted to enact some diplomacy between the two sides. But in practice I'd found myself flip-flopping between the two, sometimes feeling like a classic 'spiritual but not religious' hippie and sometimes like an angry atheist grouch.

I was grateful, then, to have a reprieve in sight – a topic that was unlikely to give my rational mind anything to complain about. Perhaps I would find that atheist spirituality was a bit watered down emotionally, or that hardcore rationalists had their own blind spots. But I wouldn't find myself getting riled by theories like 'thoughts are magnetic' or 'astrology is mysterious like a microwave' or 'distance reiki works through quantum entanglement'. Whatever you want to say about atheists, and people like to say a lot of things about atheists, their critical thinking skills are rarely in contention.

You may well wonder whether a chapter on atheist spirituality strictly belongs in this book. Any self-respecting 'free thinker' is going to pull me up on my definitions, asking me first what I mean by 'atheist' and second what I mean by 'spirituality'.

The Spirituality Gap

To address the atheist part first, many secular people are atheist in the technical sense that they don't believe in a god or gods. They reject traditional religion and all the baggage that comes with it, they don't go to a place of worship, and they don't believe any single faith has a monopoly on all the answers. When you enquire further, though, this group of people might say there's a bigger purpose at play in the world or that 'everything happens for a reason'. You might catch them talking about 'energy' or 'spirit' or 'source', or participating in some of the New Age practices covered in this book.

According to a 2022 study from the Christian think-tank Theos, 32 per cent of non-religious Brits fall into the bracket of 'Spiritual Nones'. Although religiously unaffiliated, Spiritual Nones are spiritually open, and don't believe that science has all the answers. They often believe in some form of higher power, even if they wouldn't call it God.[1] It's the same story on the other side of the Atlantic, with almost half of American nones describing themselves as spiritual in a 2024 Pew Research Center survey. Sixteen per cent said they kept crystals for spiritual purposes, and 25 per cent said they felt 'the presence of something beyond this world at least several times a year'.[2]

In this chapter, I won't concern myself with that kind of atheism. I'm more interested in those who espouse a purely naturalistic worldview, however they self-define.

For some in this bracket, the word 'spirituality' is just as loaded as the word 'God', and just as ripe for renunciation. Take the prominent atheist firebrand Greta Christina, whom I interviewed in 2020. She told me that she hated the word 'spirituality' 'with the fire of a thousand suns'.

'The word [is] used to mean belief in the supernatural, belief in souls, belief in gods – and then it [is also] used to mean a sense of awe and a deep connection with the universe,' she remarked. 'Those two meanings [are] confused in a way that gets weaponised against atheists, even in the current progressive movements. People will say, "Well, are you spiritual?" And if you say no, because you don't believe in spirits, they assume you don't have the other meaning of spirituality, and there's no seat for you at the interfaith organising table.'[3]

I heard something similar from Jack Thompson of Seattle Atheist Church, who relayed a frustrating anecdote about Oprah Winfrey. 'Oprah was interviewing an atheist back in 2013,' Thompson told me.[4] 'She said she didn't believe that atheists can experience awe and, in fact, because the atheist was experiencing awe, that means that she's not an atheist.'

Evidently, it needs to be stated out loud that atheists can experience awe and wonder, and embrace 'the other meaning of spirituality'. This was the whole point of Richard Dawkins' book *Unweaving the Rainbow*, which explains how science can unlock the door to more of that good stuff, rather than less. Its title is a riposte to the Romantic poet John Keats, who accused Isaac Newton of destroying the poetry of the rainbow by 'reducing it to the prismatic colours'. Not so, countered Dawkins – poetry is inherent within the laws of nature, and the 'deep connection with the universe' that some would term spirituality can exist without a supernatural realm.

As Thompson recalls, he started one of his talks with the Oprah anecdote, before moving on to read out passages from Richard Dawkins and Carl Sagan, and rhapsodising about the dizzying realities of the natural world.

'Just consider how the stars had to go supernova in several cycles in order to get just the elements that we need for life,' he says by way of example. 'And then how long it took evolution to get to here, and what plethora of life forms came up alongside of us and before us. We find ourselves just thrown into this life, and we don't need to take anything on insufficient evidence in order to really appreciate the wonder that surrounds us.'

Dr Phil Zuckerman, professor of sociology and secular studies at Pitzer College in California, devoted a whole chapter to 'Aweism' in his book *Living the Secular Life: New Answers to Old Questions* (2014). Here, 'aweism' is a somewhat tongue-in-cheek word for naturalistic spirituality.

'I didn't really expect people to suddenly start calling themselves aweists,' he tells me.[5] 'I was just saying that for many secular people we lack the vocabulary to express deep meaning, existential wonder, transcendence, deep tranquillity, deep affinity, deep mystery, all of that. In a purely naturalistic worldview, there is this idea that we don't experience that. But we do, we just don't say it's something magical.'

Clearly, there are people out there who do imagine that a world without gods or spirits or 'source' is somehow colourless, the dimension of the sacred entirely blanched out in the absence of religious mythologies. I don't know what it is they think atheists are experiencing when they look up at a starry night sky, or down from the summit of a mountain, or into the eyes of their newborn child, but presumably they imagine something robotic and clinical. Something less than fully human. Or, like Oprah, they surmise that anyone experiencing transcendence is in fact a secret believer.

To me at least, this perception is very wide of the mark. I decided that, rather than hammering home a message that should be obvious, I'd take a different tack and look at how atheists are channelling their sense of 'spirituality', for want of a better word. Is there a case for doing so in an organised, church-like setting? If not, why not? Do the things that people get out of religion – community, a sense of meaning, ritual, a set of ethical precepts, 'aweism' – need to be grouped together? Or does the growing tide of secularism suggest that for many people, these elements don't need to come as a package deal?

I've been curious about these questions since 2013, when a spate of headlines proclaimed the launch of 'Britain's first atheist church'. This was the Sunday Assembly, a gathering for the non-religious with the tagline: 'Live better, help often, wonder more.'

As lore would have it, the Assembly was founded by comedians Pippa Evans and Sanderson Jones, who started chatting about their backgrounds on the way to a gig. Both had grown up religious, and while they no longer bought into the God bit, they missed everything else that came with it.

'There didn't seem to be a space for people who didn't believe in God, but did want to work in the community, did want to live a full and happy life, did want to be a part of something bigger than themselves,' said Evans in a 2017 TED Talk. 'I tried atheist meetups but a lot of them seemed to be about campaigning against religion and finding ways to mock religious people. Having been mocked a lot when I was religious, and not really being sure where I was with the whole God thing, there wasn't a space for me.'[6]

On that long car journey, they hit on an idea: why not create something that was like a church, but was totally secular and inclusive? It would be non-religious instead of anti-religious (no booming out Dawkins' *The God Delusion* from the pulpit); there'd be pop songs instead of hymns; and the talks would 'inject a touch of transcendence into the everyday'. They wanted people to gather, sing, and think about the deeper issues in life. Sanderson Jones described the basic premise as 'Pentecostalism for the godless'.[7]

The first Sunday Assembly took place in January 2013 in a deconsecrated church in Islington. Around 200 people showed up, and the numbers continued to grow week on week. Soon they moved to Conway Hall in Holborn, attracting 600 people at their peak.[8] In the flurry of media attention that followed, chapters sprung up around the world. At one point, there were around ninety separate assemblies, as far afield as Germany and New Zealand, Hungary and LA.

'We were centrally organised, which made sense at the time. There were so many new assemblies popping up that, even without having any kind of doctrine, "Sunday Assembly" could have ended up meaning anything,' recalls Matt Lockwood, one of the organisers of Sunday Assembly London, when I ask him about his memories of this time.[9]

In the years since then, many chapters have dissolved, and the congregation sizes are down. A typical Sunday Assembly London meeting now attracts around seventy people, rising to around 200 at peak times of the year like Christmas.

That said, the chapters that have gone the distance are well established, stable and self-organising. There are six in the UK, a handful in continental Europe, quite a few in the US, along with prospective chapters in Africa and Asia. Sunday Assembly London successfully weathered the pandemic, and despite pivoting to digital assemblies throughout the lockdowns, was back at Conway Hall in time to celebrate its tenth anniversary.

'The first time back was rather emotional,' says Lockwood. 'That we still had over 100 attendees seemed rather beautiful.

The Spirituality Gap

The fun part was trying to remember how everything worked and which wires plugged into which holes.'

Stephanie Pollard, the former producer and booker for Sunday Assembly London, remarks that growing the community isn't their dominant focus.

'We're not going to be taking to the streets and saying you should join us,' she says.[10] 'Our numbers have shrunk since those early days of being in the press all the time. But if we can touch the lives of 100 people every time we get together, that's worth all the time and effort we put into it.'

Smiley and warm, with purple hair, Pollard is about as far from the tub-thumping atheist stereotype as you can get. While she used to be 'atheist with a capital A', she has moved towards a softer version of secularity, and is even happy to use the word 'spiritual'.

'We're all made out of stardust,' she points out, 'and it makes sense that if you pull a string here it unravels somewhere else. I think the difference between your average Sunday Assembler and your old-school New Atheist anti-theist is that the Sunday Assemblers are just more open to the idea of us all being in it together.'

I'd asked Pollard her thoughts on how atheism had changed; the strident New Atheism of the 2000s having morphed into something so much gentler. After all, in the years immediately post-9/11, atheism had seemed like a force to be reckoned with. A series of tomes were published that railed against the harms of religion in all its guises. These included *The End of Faith* (2004) and *Letter to a Christian Nation* (2006) by Sam Harris; *Breaking the Spell* (2006) by Daniel Dennett; *The God Delusion* (2006) by Richard Dawkins; *God Is Not Great* (2007) by Christopher Hitchens; and *Infidel* (2007) by Ayaan Hirsi Ali.

The Four Horsemen, as Harris, Dennett, Dawkins and Hitchens became known (Hirsi Ali is sometimes added as an honorary fifth member) didn't agree on everything. But they shared the conviction that, as Harris put it, 'religious dogmatism hinders the growth of honest knowledge and divides humanity to no necessary purpose'.[11] In this, they were massively influential.

Twenty years later, anti-religious invective is no longer trendy. Hitchens died in 2011, Harris has become enmeshed in the so-called 'Intellectual Dark Web'[12]; Dawkins has made some enemies via spats on Twitter; Dennett has returned to writing about philosophy and evolution; Hirsi Ali, rather startlingly, has converted to Christianity;[13] and the group has struggled to shake its association with Islamophobia and the alt-right pipeline. For many former New Atheists, their memories of that time carry a bitter aftertaste. Many non-white, non-male members were subject to vile online abuse – Greta Christina told me she 'spent many years being actively harassed, threatened, libelled, slandered … The email conversation list on our blogging network got hacked.' Since then, the original New Atheism appears to have split along political lines, splintering into a progressive left and a reactionary alt-right.

At the same time, the urgency is no longer there, at least not in quite the same way. In 2000s America, not only did the religiously unaffiliated comprise a tiny slice of the population, but they were up against a powerful taboo. For many Americans, believing in the Christian God was synonymous with having a moral compass. Lose what tethers you to civility, and you're left with someone menacing and anarchistic: not someone you'd want teaching your children, holding public office, or disseminating their dangerous ideas.

Cut to the present day, and non-belief has almost become a non-story. As we saw in the introduction, organised religion is massively on the wane in the US, the UK and many other places, with significant portions of the population self-identifying as having no religion.[14] According to the Pew Research Center: 'The core population of "nones" … is gaining a lot more people than it is shedding, in a dynamic that has a kind of demographic momentum.'[15]

To an extent, then, the New Atheists have become a victim of their own success. They have been followed by a swathe of even *newer* atheists (and agnostics, secular humanists and 'nones'), for whom belief or lack thereof is no longer such a defining issue. This is a group who might, in principle, be open to Sunday Assembly-style gatherings.

As the philosopher Alain de Botton wrote in his 2012 book *Religion for Atheists: A Non-Believer's Guide to the Uses of Religion*: 'In a world beset by fundamentalists of both believing and secular varieties, it must be possible to balance a rejection of religious faith with a selective reverence for religious rituals and concepts.'[16] His solution, to construct a series of 'Temples for Atheists', was widely derided, but it was easy to understand the rationale.[17]

'I feel like the anti-theist era has passed,' agrees Sunday Assembly's Pollard. 'A huge proportion of people would probably benefit greatly from being part of a community without hating on other communities. People still listen to Dawkins and Hitchens, but not in the same way as they did before.'

She adds that, in Sunday Assembly's early days, the branding did include the phrase 'atheist church', but it was quickly removed. Atheism vs theism, naturalism vs supernaturalism, simply isn't a subject that rears its head.

'We don't really mention religion much at all in either a positive or a negative way,' concurs Lockwood. 'We're all about community, not division. One of the organisers of Sunday Assembly Brighton is a Christian believer and doesn't see any conflict between the two.'

What unifies the Sunday Assemblers, then, is less a worldview, and more the desire to be part of a tribe. On top of the meetings themselves, which are held on the first and third Sundays of the month, members can join special interest groups ranging from a rock-climbing club to board game nights to a choir. There's a peer support group called Live Better, and, in a nod to what religion would give you, there are even attempts to create new rituals.

'One time, the guy who ran [the now dormant] Sunday Assembly East End did a naming ceremony for his baby,' recalls Pollard. 'We all sang "Circle of Life" from *The Lion King*, and then he put a dollop of jam on the baby's forehead. It was so cute. You laughed, but you also felt something.'

She adds that when she moved to London from New York in 2014, she didn't know anybody outside her husband's family. She was lonely, and her attempts to make new friends didn't stick. It was only when she found the London Sunday Assembly that she encountered that sense of belonging, meeting her people and even fulfilling her lifelong dream of 'becoming the lead singer in a rock band'.

'I've heard the same story time and again – people came to Sunday Assembly because they were new to London and needed friends and support,' she says. 'People who are religiously affiliated find their nearest religious institution when they move. But people who are not attached to a religious community often feel stranded in a new place.'

Over the years, a common pattern has emerged: many people attend regularly for two or three years, before finding a friendship group and moving on. That's not quite in keeping with the founders' original goals. They had hoped the 'church' would meet all the needs that are traditionally fulfilled by religious institutions, and that people would remain affiliated for life. But as time has gone by, Pollard has come to feel those goals are neither necessary nor realistic.

'If we can provide a space for people to meet face-to-face, sing together, have deep and meaningful conversations, and maybe even encourage them to support the greater community through volunteering, then we are providing an essential service,' she says.

One crisply autumnal morning, in November 2023, my husband, daughter and I arrived at Conway Hall to gauge the appeal of Sunday Assembly ourselves. An elegant, grade II listed building near Russell Square, the venue is as architecturally striking as any church. It's also the home of the Conway Hall Ethical Society, one of the oldest freethought organisations in the world, which began as a group of eighteenth-century dissidents rebelling against the doctrine of eternal hell. To someone who rejected Christianity for exactly that reason, it seemed the perfect backdrop.

We were greeted warmly, allaying my fear that we were somehow intruding on someone else's space. Although the sense of existing community was palpable, it didn't feel cliquey. And as new attendees we didn't feel scrutinised, despite the fact that our newly walking toddler could not be contained to a seat. I suspect that anyone who turned up alone and scared would quickly be taken under someone's wing.

Each Sunday Assembly has a special theme: 'Behind Closed Doors', a look at London's prisons; 'Seeds of Change', guerrilla gardening in focus; and the terrifying-sounding anniversary special, 'Send in the Clowns'. This week's theme was 'Aliens: What Are the Chances?', which was reassuring; I'd always opt for aliens over clowns.

The Spirituality Gap

The service featured a TED-style talk from biochemist Dr Peter Altman, who compared the mathematical probability of the origins of life (unfathomably unlikely) to the size of the universe (unfathomably large). Despite the mind-shredding nature of both these numbers – he showed us some slides with a lot of zeros on them – he calculated that the universe is much too small for life to have originated more than once. There was a quiet 'moment of reflection', during which time we were asked to ponder which was scarier: the idea that we're alone in the universe or the idea that we're not.

For me, that didn't take much reflection at all: option A is scarier, bring on the extra-terrestrials; and I didn't quite buy that the non-existence of aliens was mathematically so cut and dried. That said, it struck me that there was something awe-inspiring about whichever conclusion you landed on. If we're not alone in the universe, then conceivably we're part of a giant web of consciousness, populated in ways that exceed our wildest imaginings. But if we are alone, there is something astonishingly rare and precious about this planet, not to mention the glint in the darkness that is our lives. The feeling is life-affirming and, yes, 'spiritual', whichever way you slice it.

The songs, which included 'Rocket Man' by Elton John and 'Space Man' by Sam Ryder, were well chosen for the occasion. Just as in a traditional church service, some people were mouthing the words awkwardly, while others were belting them out with religious zeal. Of course, singing about spacemen isn't inherently weirder than singing about Jesus, and it is a real shame that our culture doesn't bring more opportunities for communal, mixed-ability, secular singalongs. Yet it was hard to shake the sense of the surreal: pop songs in a church?

Since our toddler was getting restless, we snuck out after the announcements, skipping the tea and biscuits. Had we stayed, we might have ended up joining one group of people who were heading out for lunch, or another who were heading to the pub. This kind of inclusivity is rare in secular spaces, especially in a city as suspicious and guarded as London. It's rather heart-breaking to think how many non-believers, new to an area and struggling to make connections, would be welcomed into the bosom of a community if only they believed in God. In that regard, I reckon Sunday Assembly performs a vital role.

'Overall, I think it's remarkable that this daft little idea from ten years ago has worked as well as it has,' says Lockwood. 'The most gratifying thing is when somebody says it's exactly what they've been looking for, or that it might even have saved their lives.'

Sunday Assembly's achievements in that span of time are significant, but one puzzling question for me is why gatherings of this nature haven't taken off in a bigger way. After all, there are a lot of 'nones' about. Many of us are seeking connections, and who wouldn't want to live better, help often, wonder more? The themes discussed *are* usually great ideas. The attempt to create new rituals is a valiant one; I would have loved something akin to a christening, minus the stuff about being born in sin, when my daughter was born. The Sunday Assemblers seem like thoroughly good eggs. So why isn't there a secular church on every street corner?

Part of the problem might be that these types of gatherings are not quite as inclusive as they appear. 'From the start, the assemblies were structured in much the same way as churches in the UK,' reflects Lockwood. 'That might have led us to attract the same kind of people who would go to a church anyway. In other words, it can be quite white and middle-class, although we have made a few steps in the right direction here.'

But there's another aspect too, outlined in Phil Zuckerman's book *Living the Secular Life*. Zuckerman makes the case that, for most secular people, being secular isn't at the forefront of their identity, and that only a tiny minority (he places the figure at 1 to 2 per cent) would ever get involved with groups like Sunday Assembly. That's because secularity is strongly linked to individualism. 'The very nature of being secular', he writes, 'involves an inherent reluctance toward joining or associating with structured, cohesive, like-minded groups.' Secular people 'prefer to take an à la carte approach to constructing their worldviews, their lives, their social networks, and their contributions to society'.[18]

It struck me that I'd been trying to play anthropologist without examining my own feelings in this department. If I was honest with myself, while I thought Sunday Assembly was a great idea, I thought it was a great idea *for other people*. Much as

I'd enjoyed my time there, I didn't want to go back every week. Sunday mornings were my opportunity to go for a long run and then watch a Netflix standup special while shoving a massive breakfast in my face.

Like Pippa Evans and Sanderson Jones, I'd been to church as a kid, but unlike Pippa Evans and Sanderson Jones, I didn't remotely miss the non-God bits. Secular by temperament even then, I'd found the church community claustrophobic, the singing corny, the organised fun unconscionable, the tea and biscuits bland. Church had cemented my sense of myself as Someone Who Doesn't Fit In.

You could say I'm unusual among secular people in that I'm obsessed with what I do and don't believe (Zuckerman told me that most 'nones' are simply indifferent to religion). But I'm every inch the individualist, and for many of us that's part of the draw – we don't want to be shackled to anything that looks, feels or quacks like an institution. Take out the shared belief system, and what's left, thinks Zuckerman, is something akin to non-alcoholic beer.

'It's really hard to create community out of thin air in such a deliberate way,' he tells me. 'Based on my study of this, I saw a lot of people who were looking for some kind of community. But when it came down to it, it felt a little forced, it felt a little fake, and it took effort to sustain.'

He explains that, in the United States at least, moving away from religion has historically also meant excising important aspects of social life. Churches often function as giant community hubs, and the Jesus part represents only a fraction of the overall offering. As a result, there have been multiple attempts to create non-religious congregations: not only Sunday Assembly but also a similar organisation launched in 2012, called the Oasis network, as well as explicitly atheist groups like Minnesota Atheists and Seattle Atheist Church. Going further back, there's the secular Religion of Humanity, founded by Auguste Comte in 1849, and the Ethical Culture society, a humanist 'religion' created in 1876 to cater to the faithless intelligentsia. There's also the Unitarian Universalists, a longstanding spiritual tradition promoting 'a faith of diverse beliefs'.

Atheist Churches: Pentecostalism for the Godless

In other words, the impetus behind Sunday Assembly isn't new but making it work over the long term can be tricky.

'You really have to have [a] dynamic leader,' says Zuckerman. 'One of the principles of Sunday Assembly was no structured leaders, no clergy. I like that ideologically, but I don't think structurally it works. Another issue is how you make a sustainable multigenerational community. If you don't have families, you're sunk, and how do you get that critical mass of families just to start?'

He adds that there's a location-dependent aspect too. If you grew up in the American Bible Belt, then your rejection of Christianity is going to feel like a defining aspect of who you are. You're going to gravitate towards others in the same position. The Oasis network, for instance, has chapters in Utah Valley and Salt Lake City, Mormon-dominated locations where non-believers may feel profoundly alone. Likewise, Sunday Assembly Nashville positions itself as something of a refuge from an overbearing religious culture. On the other hand, if you live somewhere that's highly secularised already, you're unlikely to spend your time seeking out other 'nones'. Zuckerman compares that to convening with others who no longer believe in Santa Claus.

'Religion is constantly explicitly stating who you are, what tribe you belong to, and what you believe,' he says. 'It's pounding that into you through church services, through rituals. When you're secular, you don't have those reminders of your identity, it's almost a default position.'

That said, he concedes that there will always be some secular people who do want to gather in a quasi-religious manner. He likes to talk about 'angry atheists and happy humanists'; in loose brushstrokes, the former have been traumatised by religion, while the latter are political progressives who want to make the world a better place. Both camps may stumble across an atheist church and feel like they've found 'their people'.

As for their common characteristics? 'I think there's a high intellectualism there,' says Zuckerman. 'A lot of them are voracious readers, debaters, discussers. The angry atheists want to join with other atheists almost as a sense of solidarity and refuge. The happy humanists just realise there's an affinity. They hear about humanism and they're like, "Oh, that's me, I'm home."'

Unlike Sunday Assembly, Seattle Atheist Church obviously *did* want to include the words 'atheist church' in its branding.

'With Sunday Assembly, you can get a hint but it's not obvious what goes on there – what are they assembling exactly?' says Jack Thompson, who sits on Seattle Atheist Church's board of directors. 'And while I love what they're doing, if you saw the Oasis network in an ad, what would you think it was? Maybe a spa or something? In contrast, when you hear "atheist church" you know generally what to expect. It's like a church but for atheists. Simple, easy, and the apparent oxymoron gives your brain something to wonder about.'

He concedes that some people are put off by the name; some find the word 'atheist' too aggressive while others don't want to go anywhere near a self-styled 'church'. That said, there's something about the stickiness of the term that works, especially given the rather more cerebral nature of this organisation.

'Our founders attended some of the meetings of the Sunday Assembly in Seattle, but they were turned off by how much supernatural was permitted, for lack of a better word,' says Thompson. 'This particular chapter was so open-minded that they were having people talk about the blessings of the Creator Spirit and things like that. So these folks decided to go ahead and form their own thing.'

Seattle Atheist Church was founded in March 2015, two years after Sunday Assembly. The group met every week in an old school building in the university district, before moving online during the pandemic. It has stayed online ever since, aside from a monthly open-air 'secular social'. While there are around 2,000 people on the meetup group, numbers have dwindled since going digital, with the services now attracting around twenty regulars.

As Thompson and his fellow director, Troy Kurt, explain, each service is about ninety minutes long. They start with some freeform discussion time, move through a 'moment of stoicism', and then host something akin to a TED Talk. Guest speakers have included the human rights activist Yasmine Mohammed, the author Sasha Sagan (daughter of Carl), and the very Phil Zuckerman featured in this chapter. They close with a moderated group discussion period, before moving onto the Discord server (a voice, video and text chat app) for informal chit-chat.

'We have talks on various topics, including secular ethics; self-awareness and the understanding of our emotions; communicating effectively with other humans; fascinating scientific discoveries and what they might suggest about ourselves, like the mapping of the connectome of the C. elegans brain, a roundworm; and self-improvement approaches like kaizen, stoicism, et cetera,' says Thompson.

This struck me as quite a 'thinky' list, in keeping with Zuckerman's characterisation of atheist churchgoers as 'voracious readers, debaters, discussers'. It was what you might expect from a techy metropolis like Seattle, one of the best-educated cities in the US[19] as well as one of the least religious.[20] Relatively few people here grew up evangelical, and – throwing no shade at all – I couldn't imagine Thompson or Kurt choosing to channel their spiritual impulses by dancing in the aisles to 'Rocket Man'.

Thompson, who has immersed himself in atheist thinking for many years, talked eloquently about the 'rationalist diaspora', and pointed me towards a wealth of blogs and online resources. I got the impression that what cohered the church members was first and foremost their intellectual appetite, coupled with an earnest desire for self-improvement. That might not be a huge draw for the average Joe, but it's clear that for the core membership, the sense of connectedness runs deep.

'Growing up as an atheist, I'd never really been in church,' says Kurt. 'I saw that when my religious friends got married, they had all their church people going, and when someone died their church was there for them. I didn't have that, and that sucked.'

Thompson mentioned another of their guest speakers, the evangelical preacher turned humanist chaplain Bart Campolo, who had talked about what it takes to build community in secular spaces. According to Campolo, you need to make sure there's as much heart there as there is head. Despite its prevailing intellectualism, this is a model Seattle Atheist Church strives to emulate.

'Lots of atheist groups get together and they bring their Richard Dawkins books and bash on religious people,' says Thompson.

'That's not something that can hold a community together. You know, as soon as conflicts come up, as they inevitably will, there's nothing there to hold people to the group. Campolo was making the case that it's all about love, right? There's got to be something deeper to connect us than just not being religious. So that's what we're trying to build.'

After looking into Campolo's back story, I decided to reach out to him myself. As detailed in a 2016 *New York Times* profile, he's the son of the famous preacher Tony Campolo, former spiritual advisor to Bill Clinton and something akin to evangelical royalty.[21] The younger Campolo became a successful preacher too, running youth groups and inner-city missions, but over the years the supernaturalist portion of his faith began to dwindle. Following a bike accident in 2011, he was able to admit to the ultimate taboo for an evangelical: he didn't believe in God.

That was the end of his Christian mission then, but he was a talented minister who didn't want to let those talents go to waste. He spent three years as the first humanist chaplain at the University of Southern California, before moving back to Cincinnati and working as a pastoral counsellor, coach, therapist, wedding and funeral celebrant, and host of the podcast *Humanize Me*. While he is busy by anyone's standards, he was happy to talk, remarking that 'humanising secular community building lies smack-dab at the centre of my heart'.[22]

In some respects, he says, his shift away from Christianity wasn't too great a departure. His mission had always been less about spreading the gospel, and more about creating welcoming spaces that enfolded those on the margins.

'My teenage youth group felt like a big club for nice kids,' he tells me. 'I was a nice kid, and I wanted to join, and I quickly realised the price of admission was to believe in Jesus. It wasn't going to heaven or escaping hell that brought me in, it was that I wanted to be part of that kind of loving, transformative community. When I finally came out on the other side, I still had the same values that drew me into Christianity.'

Unleashed into the secular world, his first thought was, 'Where's the church? Where's the congregation of people that want to pursue loving kindness in a secular way?' Atheist groups were not the answer. Those that Campolo attended were 'awful – every week they would get together and talk about how stupid it was to believe in God'. They tended to define themselves by what they didn't believe, not by what they were committed to; they didn't have charismatic leaders; they didn't want music; they had no interest in anything emotionally resonant.

'I'm thinking, "That's not how people make decisions. That's not how people come to new worldviews or get exposed to new ways of life,"' says Campolo. 'I was like, "There's a reason why you guys [atheists] have had the best narrative for 300 years, and yet you have no political power and make very little impact on society." You've got to speak to people's hearts.'

It's easy to see how this problem has arisen. Many atheists are quite rightly suspicious of cults and will baulk at anything that smacks of emotional manipulation. But if the eighteenth-century philosopher David Hume was right that 'reason is, and ought only to be the slave of the passions',[23] secular gatherings aren't going to prosper through force of argument alone. Campolo thinks these groups need three elements: a strong leadership, a clearly stated value system, and a sense of mission or outreach. They also need something that's often left out of these discussions: funding, and lots of it.

'If someone said to me, "Quit being a therapist and be the pastor of our congregation," I'd do that in a heartbeat,' says Campolo. 'But you've got to have a congregation where people are used to donating money or pay membership fees.'

This is something Matt Lockwood at Sunday Assembly knows all too well, remarking that many of the organisers get burnt out by the scale of their unpaid responsibilities. 'We also don't necessarily have the structures in place to support people who come to us with serious issues because we're all just volunteers. There's a reason why actual religious organisations have full-time employees!' he adds.

Although there are aspects of his former life that Campolo is glad to have left behind ('I don't miss having to say bullshit stuff to people when their kid died,' he says pointedly), there are other parts he misses dearly. He misses being part of a clearly defined movement that connects people wherever they are in the world.

He misses having the structures in place to help troubled youth, or to instil a moral education. Above all, he misses those 'grand moments of group transcendence' that sometimes arise when Christians get together.

'In a church, you could take fifty people who aren't even that great at singing, and they would still feel transported into a state of openness or even ecstasy,' he remarks. 'On a Christian retreat, you're all out there and the campfire's going and everyone's singing "Our God is an awesome God", and you feel this collective effervescence.* You feel the spirit. I would explain those experiences very differently now … and I don't think they are necessarily off-limits in secular spaces. But they're easier to do when you're pumping out the God stuff.'

While Campolo is ardently against 'crystals and New Age nonsense', declaring that 'there isn't a woo-woo bone in my body', he has become increasingly comfortable with the word 'spiritual' since leaving the fold. He doesn't mind its supernaturalist etymology, arguing that the 'spirit' part is nothing more than a linguistic fossil.

'If what we mean by "spiritual" is something unquantifiable, something we have all experienced but can't measure, then I think it's as good a word as any,' he says. 'What's more, the old use of the word "spirituality" has a very strong connotation of growth, and goodness, and purity, and righteousness. I'm not mad about those connotations.'

As we have seen, it's hard to get atheist churches up and running. Harder still to keep them going – to turn them into organic communities that buttress people's lives year after year. My gut feeling, however, is that the declining memberships may not tell the whole story.

Campolo persuaded me that there is a way to do it, and there's evidently some level of demand if you pitch it right. In countries like the UK and the US, Christianity is in continual, if not terminal,

---

* The term 'collective effervescence' comes from the French sociologist Émile Durkheim, who believed experiences of group ecstasy were the starting point for the world's religions.

decline, leaving behind a heterogeneous group of non-believers who may or may not be in the market for something church-like. I don't think we'll ever see nations united by their atheism, in the same way they were once united by religion. As Phil Zuckerman pointed out, the last stop on the train of secularisation is not so much atheism as indifference. But I do think that among the many millions of 'nones', each free to find their own spiritual tribe, there will be many thousands who feel at home in these kinds of spaces.

'A common refrain among my friends was, "Why do we need to go to an atheist church? Why can't I just go to the bar with my friends?"' Jack Thompson tells me. 'My thought was, "That's not quite the right question." We're learning about how to be better human beings. How to communicate more effectively together, how to understand ourselves better, how to improve ourselves, widening our social circle. So, nobody *needs* to go to an atheist church, but when all this good stuff is happening, wouldn't you like to?'

Chapter 8
Exercise: A Pilgrim's Progress

In April 2019, five months after my dad died, my family assembled in Edinburgh to get matching commemorative tattoos. I don't remember much about the trip – all my recollections of that time are a blur – but I do remember taking my newly inked self on a jog up Arthur's Seat. This is a long-dead volcano to the east of the city centre, believed by some to be the location of Camelot. On the way down, my running became so free, so effortless, and so downright ecstatic, it wouldn't have been an overstatement to call it a 'spiritual experience'.

I should point out that this is not my typical experience of running. I've been a runner for over a decade and, although my party line is that I love it, the dominant feeling is more often a desire for the run to be over. Scrolling through Strava, the running app I use, most of my outings are titled things like 'Tired slog' and 'Heavy plod' and 'Shaking off a shocking night's sleep'. Sure, I get a runner's high from time to time. I'd say that maybe a quarter of my regular jaunts have elements of what positive psychology calls a 'flow state'. But in running, as in life, the occasional bout of euphoria is offset by an overwhelming preponderance of grunt work.

On this particular run, the ascent had been just the right amount of challenging. At 250m above sea level, Arthur's Seat is hardly Mount Everest; any reasonably fit person could hike to the top without issue, and I had opted for one of the longer, gentler routes. But there were sections nonetheless that torched my quads and aggrieved my lungs, moments in which thinking was subsumed by raw sensation. If your mind is saying anything at all in that moment, it's something like 'Ouch!', 'Why did I sign up for this?', 'Nearly there!', 'Never again!' Once you stop and catch a breather, though, you forget the discomfort. It's a trick of memory that will doom you to repeat the experience – chasing not just the triumph of reaching the top, but also the painful parts, the screamingly 'present' parts, you encounter along the way.*

I reached the summit at around 8:30am, early enough to have the whole place to myself. The sky had a pearlescent quality, with scattered dark clouds and patches of buoyant blue. A halo of sunlight burst through the clouds. You could almost hear the angelic choir accompaniment. Beneath me were craggy rocks, undulating fields, and urban sprawl as far as the sea, a silver glimmer that grew hazier as it yielded to the sky.

After stopping for a while to savour the view (not to mention snap the requisite 700 photos), I began the descent. I turned on Jon Hopkins' *Singularity* album, which I was playing on repeat at the time. Most self-respecting trail runners would say that music sullies the experience, but this was the right album for the occasion. The *New Yorker* described it as 'an hour-long ode to spiritual transcendence',[1] while *Pitchfork* stated, rather grandly: 'Hopkins seems to model his music on the infinite cycles of destruction and rebirth that power the universe – but we, too, are part of the scheme.'[2]

I danced down the mountain, my stop-start footwork finding its match in the wobbly, off-kilter beats. After the exertions of the ascent, this part felt light and easy. I could have kept going indefinitely without getting fatigued. The movement, the music and the landscape were connected, and I was immersed in all of them, inseparable from the whole.

---

* The philosopher Mark Rowlands has written insightfully about this experience in his 2013 book, *Running with the Pack: Thoughts from the Road on Meaning and Mortality*.

Arriving back at the Airbnb, my tiredness reasserted itself, along with all the other thoughts and feelings that had temporarily abated. The grief of losing my dad was still very raw. This had been a reprieve, or maybe something of a salve; Dad had been a runner and cyclist himself, and he knew a fair bit about exercise-induced transcendence. I couldn't help but imagine I'd encountered a piece of him on the trail.

When I began reflecting on the spiritual aspects of running, my Arthur's Seat out-and-back seemed an obvious place to start. It had all the hallmarks of what the influential twentieth-century psychologist Abraham Maslow called a 'peak experience': the sense of functioning effortlessly, awareness of the present moment, positive feelings exceeding the more quotidian state of 'being in the zone'. Maslow claimed that peak experiences could be likened to 'a visit to a personally defined heaven from which the person then returns to earth'.[3] He saw them as a core aspect of spirituality and as part of the origin story of the 'high religions'. During a peak experience, there is supposedly a sense of something chiming deep within, an elevated perspective in which all is well with the world.

Maslow's writings are full of this kind of starry-eyed rhetoric. One of the founders of transpersonal psychology and the Human Potential Movement, he is perhaps best known for his hierarchy of needs: a pyramid in which more primal needs, like food and shelter, sit at the bottom, and 'self-actualisation' sits at the top. The self-actualised person, in Maslow's schema, is supposed to be 'fully illuminated or awakened or perspicuous', a person whose superior psychological development implies a superior spiritual development too. He believed that Western society was suffering a crisis of valuelessness, largely due to the decline of traditional religion, and that humanistic psychology could function as a kind of 'empirical spirituality' that could step into the breach. Peak experiences, in his view, 'give meaning to life itself'.[4]*

---

* This is one reason why much secular therapy-speak has an oddly spiritual aftertaste. The stuff about personal growth can trace its genesis to Maslow's writings.

When I felt myself to be at one with the music and the movement and the landscape, Maslow would have said I was tapping into my higher self. Other thinkers, of a more overtly religious bent, would have said I was connecting to God. Still others would have held that this quality of presence – being immersed in the present moment, without being distracted by thoughts of past or future – was spiritual in and of itself. I'm thinking especially about the German spiritual teacher Eckhart Tolle and his followers. In his explosively popular book *The Power of Now: A Guide to Spiritual Enlightenment* (1997), which one reviewer described as 'a sort of New Age reworking of Zen',[5] Tolle talks about 'the sense of freedom that comes from letting go of self-identification with one's personal history and life-situation, and a newfound inner peace that arises as one learns to relinquish mental/emotional resistance to the "suchness" of the present moment'.[6] He thinks that our incessant mental noise is what creates suffering and blocks our connection to 'Being' (ineffable reality). It's the present moment – a state that's all but inaccessible to the thinking mind – that holds the key to liberation.

In this view, any ritual that takes you out of the mind, and focuses your attention on the here and now, feels so nourishing precisely because it's a spiritual practice. Running may fit the bill for many of us, along with practices more explicitly geared towards that end, such as mindfulness meditation.

For Vanessa Zuisei Goddard, a writer and Buddhist teacher based in Mexico, running and Zen are a natural fit. As she details in her book *Still Running: The Art of Meditation in Motion* (2020), the Zen tradition treats running and other 'body practices' as a moving meditation, complementing the practitioner's seated meditation (or *zazen*). Because the body, in this tradition, is held to be inseparable from the mind, it becomes 'the means through which we realize our interconnectedness with all things'.[7] That's particularly the case when you apply techniques learned from seated meditation.

'I often use the phrase "moving into stillness" which I borrowed from the title of a book by yoga teacher Erich Schiffmann,' she tells me.[8] 'In "still running", you work to focus your mind so it isn't bouncing all over the place, and you pare down your movements

Exercise: A Pilgrim's Progress

until you're doing just what's needed to propel your body forward. In this type of movement, whether running or doing anything else, you can find a deep stillness.'

While the idea of 'still running' may sound like a contradiction in terms, it conveys something important about how it feels to truly absorb yourself in the activity. In Zuisei's book, she details various aspects of 'still running', closing out each chapter with a practical exercise. The end game is to completely immerse yourself in the activity, so much so that your very sense of self disappears.

In the interests of empirical research, I decided to try Zuisei's practice 'stop-start running', from the 'discipline' chapter of her book. As she explains: 'A distracted, undisciplined mind is a mind lacking clarity and leaking energy ... A concentrated mind, on the other hand, is stable and clear.'[9] She recommends a simple but deceptively difficult exercise: a ten-minute running meditation, in which the focus of your attention is the breath. Each time you realise you've become distracted, you need to acknowledge the intruding thought and let it go. You also – and here's the annoying bit – have to stop running.

Per Zuisei's instructions, I warmed up with a ten-minute jog, which took me to my local park, and found a spot of trail I knew well. I was keen to find a quiet corner, as I knew I'd look to all the world like I was playing a solitary game of musical statues.

I took a few deep breaths and got going. Compared to the breaths in a seated meditation, they had an urgent, throaty quality. They were a little ragged around the edges, even at a gentle jogging pace. I inhaled for a count of four steps and exhaled for a count of four steps. In-two-three-four, out-two-three-four, in-two-three-four – easy!

Hmmm, was that the right count though? I'd heard that to engage your parasympathetic nervous system, you really needed to increase the length of the exhale and decrease the inhale. Oh, and I should probably be breathing through my nose, shouldn't I? My mind jumped around, assessing the relative merits of mouth breathing versus nose breathing, 4-4 versus 3-5. I also wondered whether counting was even permissible, or whether the one-two-three-four was classed as a 'thought' that precluded me from being present in my body.

Then I realised that, in my attempts to get it right, I'd altogether lost the focus on my breathing. I stopped running, collected myself, and carried on.

Unsurprisingly, I had to pause many more times after that. My two repeat offenders were a compulsion to narrate the experience to myself, and a neurosis around whether I was doing it properly. I also got side-tracked by things going on around me (Tree! Dog! Squirrel!) and by worries about what people would think of my unorthodox running style. My timer went off after ten minutes and, as instructed, I let go of my regimented focus. I jogged home, allowing my mind to freestyle.

As in a seated meditation, this exercise had enabled me to identify some of my peskier habits of mind. I had a long way to go in terms of sharpening my concentration, but there had been pockets of focus, and I could absolutely see the payoffs. During those moments, I'd felt a sense of being anchored in the here and now. These moments seemed to yield an unusual spaciousness, unfurling a possibly endless stream of textures and sensations.

As Zuisei describes it, the purpose of this kind of practice is to develop skills, in this case, concentration and mindfulness, that you can use in everyday life. She herself spent almost twenty-five years living and studying at Zen Mountain Monastery in upstate New York, where as part of her spiritual practice she hosted running retreats. The point was not to train people to run better, but rather to help them become more embodied and self-aware.

'If you can indeed establish stillness during your runs, then you'll begin to see that you can do that with any kind of activity,' she says. 'You can do it on a hike, as you're working, when you're washing your dishes or doing your laundry. In my book, I gave the example of my friend Colt who ran so beautifully he was "not there" as he ran, he was pure movement – what in Zen we call "just running" itself. The same is true for us. We'll be able to disappear into the activity we're doing.'

In this regard, 'still running' sounds a lot like a normal runner's high or flow state. But it's a meditation practice too, and as such it may prompt one to enquire more deeply into the nature of reality.

'Hopefully this disappearance of the self will encourage you to ask, "What is the self if one moment it's there and another moment it's not? Where does it go?'" says Zuisei. 'My hope is that somebody who takes up "still running" as a practice will take that stillness, and the clarity and understanding that come from it, into all aspects of their lives.'

For someone like me, a secular person living in twenty-first-century Britain, the mind–body stuff is undoubtedly a big part of what it means to think of running as 'spiritual'. Physical exercise can bring you squarely into the present moment, helping you rein in the caprices of the mind. And if you're lucky, there may be the odd peak experience along the way.

But these aspects of running are only one small part of the equation. Throughout history, there have been many cultures for which running has played a more foundational role in their sense of spirituality, and that's still the case in many parts of the world today.

Take the mysterious 'marathon monks' of Mount Hiei in Japan, discussed in Zuisei's book, who are famed for running 1,000 marathons in 1,000 days.[10] The monks, also known as *gyoja* or spiritual athletes, run up to 52 miles a day through the mountains, while fulfilling a range of religious observances. After 1,000 days, they are considered a *Daigyoman Ajari*, 'Saintly Master of the Highest Practice'. This ritual has been unchanged since the 1300s, except for one alteration: the modern monks are no longer required to disembowel themselves if they fail to complete the course.

Viewed from the outside, the monks' motivations may seem opaque. The writer and endurance runner Adharanand Finn, who visited one of the marathon monks, was underwhelmed to hear that running for 1,000 days gives you lots of time to reflect on why we're alive. According to the monk: 'It is a type of meditation through movement. That is why you shouldn't go too fast. It is a time to meditate on life, on how you should live.'[11] As Finn noted in a *Guardian* article, this is a surprisingly quotidian way of framing such an extreme pursuit, but maybe we 'can take solace from their everydayness. If the monks are like us, then it figures that we are like the monks'.[12]

Another famous example is the Tarahumara, a remote community of Indigenous farmers living in Mexico, who are fabled for their exceptional running abilities. The Tarahumara, called the *Rarámuri* ('lightning-footed people') in their own language, were the subject of Christopher McDougall's 2009 bestseller *Born to Run: The Hidden Tribe, the Ultra-Runners, and the Greatest Race the World Has Never Seen*, and some of them can run hundreds of miles without resting. This ability has served them well while persistence hunting and when completing footraces, but it also carries a deep spiritual significance. According to a landmark 2020 study, the Tarahumara see running as 'spiritually meaningful, a form of prayer, a symbol of the journey of life'.[13]

This study, co-authored by Harvard anthropologist Daniel E. Lieberman, explores how Western awe at the Tarahumara's abilities can too easily bleed into tropes of the 'athletic savage'. As the researchers explain, Indigenous peoples are often 'stereotyped as impervious to pain and fatigue, as well as mysteriously in touch with nature'.[14] Lieberman's own research, which included participating in a Tarahumara footrace, has emphasised that the Tarahumara are just as susceptible to pain and injury as anyone else. If their abilities seem superhuman, it perhaps has more to do with their motivation than their physiology, a big part of which derives from their religious beliefs.

The night before a *rarajípare* footrace, participants assemble to dance *yúmari*, an ancient ceremonial ritual which petitions the god Onorúame for blessings. The race itself is considered an extension of this ritual, as well as a powerful form of prayer. During the run, supporters shout encouragements such as '*Iwériga, iwériga!*' or '*Iwérisa!*', which mean 'soul' or 'breath' and 'have stamina' respectively. As Lieberman and his collaborators explain: 'Both words thus point to the spiritual and physiological interconnections Tarahumara recognize between life, breath, soul, and strength.'

The Tarahumara aren't the only Indigenous people to treat running in such a reverential manner. For many Native American people, traversing the trails serves as a powerful connector with their lands. Dustin Martin, executive director of the Native youth development programme Wings of America, told *Outside* magazine: 'For me, running has become a pathway to communing with a higher power or higher calling, especially when it is in places my People have had ties to for time immemorial.' He belongs to the Navajo culture, which has a tradition of waking up early and running east towards the rising sun. The idea is to let the spirits and deities know that you are appreciative, working to be a stronger person, and ready to take advantage of the day. [15,16]

Then there are the San Bushmen of the Kalahari Desert in southern Africa, who can lay claim to being one of the oldest continuous cultures on Earth. Traditionally they are persistence hunters, for whom running is a matter of life and death. They also have animistic spiritualities that are inseparable from the lands they hunt in.

'There's a deep cosmology among the San Bushmen around running and the practice of hunting,' said Sanjay Rawal, director of the documentary *3100: Run and Become*, on a podcast. 'They say when they run and hunt, they're able to access the power of their ancestors, they're able to access the power of the Earth to overcome the feebleness and the weaknesses of the human body ... Using the human body to channel non-human or superhuman energies, that was man and woman's first religion. It's baked into us as mammals.'[17]

While many Western people enjoy the occasional jog in the park, 'using the human body to channel superhuman energies' remains a niche pursuit. To put it into perspective, around 48 million Americans participated in some form of running or jogging in 2023,[18] but only 87,000 of them completed an ultramarathon.[19]

For those not familiar with the term, ultrarunning is exactly what it sounds like: running, but more of it. Technically it refers to any distance greater than a marathon (26.2 miles or 42.2 kilometres), be that 50 kilometres down a canal towpath or a challenge even the Tarahumara might baulk at. At the more extreme end lies the Marathon des Sables, billed as 'the toughest footrace on Earth', in which competitors run 156 miles (251 kilometres) through the Sahara Desert in temperatures over 50°C.[20] Arguably even tougher is the Barkley Marathons, a course so ludicrous that only twenty people have completed the full five loops during the event's thirty-five-year history.[21] We might also cite the Self-Transcendence 3100 Mile Race (almost 5,000 kilometres), which was created by the Indian spiritualist Sri Chinmoy to help runners 'overcome the entire world's pre-conceived notions of possibility'.[22] Should you wish to rise to this challenge, you'll need to traverse a single half-mile city block in New York again and again over the course of several weeks, clocking an overall distance comparable to the breadth of North America (Forrest Gump, eat your heart out).

If you have any running experience yourself, you'll quickly see how astonishing these kinds of feats are and how far beyond the reach of most people. Personally, I've never been tempted to try: past a certain point, I get exhausted, injured or cranky. One time I came back from a long training run so glycogen-depleted that I found myself mesmerised by the sparkling colours emanating from a potato.

However, for those who manage to move past these pain points, it seems the experience can prove enriching on several levels. I first came across Miriam Díaz-Gilbert via her article 'The Spiritual Dimension of Ultrarunning', in which she explains: 'the long time commitment of ultrarunning affords ultrarunners the opportunity to think about what they are enduring, and to experience and talk about some kind of spiritual experience.'[23] A New Jersey-based writer, retired academic, and author of the memoir *Come What May, I Want to Run: A Memoir of the Saving Grace of Ultrarunning in Overwhelming Times* (2023), Miriam is also a devout Catholic and formidable endurance athlete, who has run thirty-four ultras since 2005. She seemed like the ideal person to speak to for this chapter.

While Díaz-Gilbert is physically talented in a way I'm not ('I stopped running marathons because I found that at the end of 26.2 miles, I still had some energy,' she tells me, mind-bogglingly), she isn't immune to the kinds of hardships that make the rest of us retreat to our sofas.

'The greater the time that you're running, the greater the time you voluntarily subject your mind to pain and suffering,' she says.[24] 'You run in heat, humidity, gale-force winds, rain, hail, muddy trails, freezing cold. There's sleep deprivation. You need to eat but sometimes the thought of food revolts you. There are blisters, there's body chafing, there's the possibility of injury. And then some of us hallucinate.'

Apparently, it's almost a rite of passage to encounter an animal on the trails, only to move closer and realise it's just a shadow. And never mind seeing colours in a potato: Díaz-Gilbert told me quite blithely about how, during a 100-mile ultra, she noticed a bunch of little people in her grilled chicken.

The point is that, despite these privations, ultrarunners keep going anyway. In many cases, that's why they bother in the first place. It's all but inevitable that you will slip into dark states of mind, but you may also find that you have the power to move beyond them, to find your limits as illusory as the shadow animals in the forest.

'This is something greater than myself,' says Díaz-Gilbert. 'I'm able to continue running because I get my strength from God, I get my strength from others. That's what it means for me to have ultrarunning be a spiritual experience.'

I wasn't surprised to hear that Díaz-Gilbert has had a few Maslow-esque peak experiences during her many hours on the trails. Early in her first 24-hour race, a magnificent rainbow appeared in the sky, spanning the lake she would be circling for hours on end. In another race, she ran by the ocean as the sun was setting and was still running as it rose. In yet another, with eight miles to go and exhaustion creeping in, two deer appeared at the edge of the trail, seemingly beckoning her to go on.

'There is this beautiful solitude and peace on the trails that nourishes the soul,' she says. 'In marathons, most people just want to get to the finish as fast as possible. But you're not going to enjoy the sights if you keep rushing it.'

Really, though, these experiences of beauty are only a small part of what most ultrarunners are seeking. Case in point: Díaz-Gilbert has completed track ultras, in which you jog round a 400-metre track for 24 hours. I'd be very surprised if you felt like you were at one with nature as you hauled your carcass around the 200th lap and surveyed the local high school for the 200th time. (Díaz-Gilbert countered this sentiment somewhat, remarking that sometimes the beauty of a fiery sunrise is a welcome sight for track runners as they reach the end of their ordeal.)

In the Self-Transcendence 3100 Mile Race, surely the absolute daddy when it comes to 'boring' races, runners are required to pound the same stretch of pavement for eighteen hours a day, for up to fifty-two days in succession. Here, you not only transcend your physical limits, but also your desire for variety and distraction. 'It's just your mind torturing you. With meditation it becomes possible,' said thirteen-time finisher Suprabha Beckjord, interviewed by the BBC.[25]

In fact, by removing the element of novelty, as well as stripping back your physical comforts, you may arrive closer to the heart of what extreme exercise is about for many people: a chance to find meaning within hardship.

'When I'm running, I think about the suffering of others, and I realise that my suffering during an ultra is nothing in comparison,' says Díaz-Gilbert. 'I meditate on Christ's suffering on the cross, I meditate on the suffering of the saints, I meditate on loved ones I have lost to cancer and the pain they have endured. And I run with purpose. I run for myself – for respite, for healing. I also run for others. For those who are sick, for those who need comfort. I pray for them when I'm running.'

Díaz-Gilbert wouldn't be the first Catholic ultrarunner to treat these events as a form of devotion or pilgrimage. She carries a rosary in her pouch, along with scripture passages and a copy of 'The Ultrarunner's Prayer' ('… Let it be an inner win. / A battle won over me. / May I say at the end / I have fought a good fight, / I have finished the race, / I have kept the faith').[26]

She added that other ultrarunners will take different approaches according to their own faith or background. Some, like Zuisei, turn to Buddhist philosophy, treating running as a meditation practice, while those with a purely secular background may be more likely to talk about personal development. For the Indigenous cultures we mentioned earlier, running often functions as a mode of prayer.

Almost invariably, though, they understand these sufferfests as in some way spiritual. What better word for an experience that strips away layer upon layer of your perceived limitations, paring your body and perhaps your soul down to the marrow?

In Díaz-Gilbert's 2018 research paper 'The Ascetic Life of the Ultrarunner', she argues that 'while suffering perceived as a source of happiness may sound like an oxymoron, to the ascetic and ultrarunner, suffering is natural'. What's more, rather than being self-destructive, this intense physical punishment is self-liberating – 'ultrarunning helps me triumph over my bodily weakness'.[27]

The Christian ascetic tradition, which began in Jesus's own time and continued through the medieval and early modern period, was not for the faint of heart. Ascetics denied themselves food, sleep or basic hygiene, and subjected themselves to a gory array of self-punishments. St Teresa of Ávila applied nettles to her infected sores. St Catherine of Siena starved herself and self-flagellated with an iron chain for an hour and a half, three times a day. Perhaps most disturbing was Simeon the Stylite, who lived atop a pillar, stood till his legs gave out, and developed a maggot-infested wound. When I heard what Simeon did with the maggots that fell out of the wound – put them back in, saying 'eat what the Lord has given you' – I could think of a few choice descriptors, but 'spiritual' wasn't one of them.[28]

Personally, it took me a while to see the parallels with ultrarunning. The ascetics struck me as strange, mentally unbalanced connoisseurs of suffering for suffering's sake. I did not have the same reaction to ultrarunners, despite knowing the extent of their self-imposed hardships. Perhaps that's because endurance exercise is coded within our society as intrinsically valuable, whereas physical torment divorced from physical prowess (for instance, reapplying the maggots to your wound) is not. What's more, ultrarunning fits neatly into our achievement-oriented mindset, in which glory lies just on the other side of a finish line. For the Christian ascetics, if there are any rewards to be had at all, they are situated in a putative afterlife. It's hard to relate to a practice that doesn't bring benefits or blessings, but simply offers oneself up as a mode of sacrifice.

Díaz-Gilbert has another take. In her paper, she comments on the kinship between the two, not just in terms of the adversity they voluntarily endure, but also in terms of their motivations. 'The life of an ultrarunner and an ascetic requires endurance, perseverance, and patience to approach the finish line and to find God. They share a spiritual challenge,'[29] she writes. Of course, the ultrarunner might be trying to run further than they ever have before, whereas for the ascetic it might not make sense to talk about goals at all. Still, the two are united through their sense of mission and focus.

There are crossovers, too, when it comes to how they deal with bodily weakness. For the pre-modern Christian ascetics, the body was seen as lesser than the soul, which meant the denial of the animalistic body was spiritually cleansing. While the typical twenty-first-century ultrarunner doesn't think this way, perhaps we can find the echoes of asceticism in their desire for self-transcendence or self-mastery. There's the weak self, the body, that feels the pain and wants to give up. And there's the strong self, the spirit, that's doing the mastering.

More contentiously, the delirium that often sets in along the way might bring its own spiritual benefits. In Aldous Huxley's long essay *Heaven & Hell* (1956), he talks about the 'antipodes of the mind' – non-ordinary states of consciousness that can be accessed through ascetic practices, as well as psychedelics.

'If men and women torment their bodies, it is not only because they hope in this way to atone for past sins and avoid future punishments; it is also because they long to visit the mind's antipodes and do some visionary sightseeing,' he writes. 'Empirically and from the reports of other ascetics, they know that fasting and a restricted environment will transport them where they long to go. Their self-inflicted punishment may be the door to paradise.'[30]

Although Huxley didn't mention ultrarunning, I wouldn't be surprised if endurance athletes embark on their own kind of 'visionary sightseeing'. This appears to be true of the Tarahumara runners, who, according to Lieberman and colleagues, often attain 'a heightened state of awareness and out-of-body feelings'[31] during long footraces. They may not be impervious to pain, but through knocking back the miles in a trance-like state, they might be able to override that discomfort.

I was coming to see that the spiritual dimension of exercise was a richer topic than I'd first envisaged. Exercise could be a gateway to transcendent experiences, personally meaningful experiences, and experiences so viscerally overwhelming that you slammed right into 'the antipodes of the mind'. It offered the chance for self-mastery and maybe some kind of redemptive narrative arc. It brought opportunities for self-knowledge and even (if you *really* got the hang of that whole 'still running' thing) enlightenment.

As discussed, physical exercise has one big thing in common with many religious rituals: it takes you out of your head. It gives you direct experience of the interface between mind and body. And while different people will think about that interface in different ways – a Catholic might contrast the frailties of the flesh with the transcendent nature of the spirit, while a Buddhist might see the mind–body as a site of interconnectedness – it is here that we may be most inclined to experience something beyond our workaday rational selves.

In Alex Hutchinson's book *Endure: Mind, Body and the Curiously Elastic Limits of Human Performance* (2018), he talks about the self-protective systems that set our limits in endurance sports. As athletes have intuited for years, and as scientists are now codifying, the outer edges of our capabilities are shaped as much by psychological factors as they are by physical ones.

'It turns out that, whether it's heat or cold, hunger or thirst, or muscles screaming with the supposed poison of "lactic acid", what matters in many cases is how the brain interprets these distress signals,' writes Hutchinson. 'Brain and body are fundamentally intertwined, and to understand what defines your limits under any particular set of circumstances, you have to consider them both together.'[32]

To me, this resonates deeply with Zuisei and Díaz-Gilbert's claims. Yes, mind and body are connected. And yes, by surpassing your apparent physical limits you can learn a lot about your capacity for self-mastery.

'You do need to cultivate quite a lot of mental strength to keep going in some of our workouts,' says Dr Suzanna Millar, a lecturer in the School of Divinity at the University of Edinburgh who moonlights as a Les Mills instructor, and who also happens to be my sister.[33] 'The struggles of a fitness class become almost like a safe microcosm of the struggles of your life. And it's tempting to think of that in terms of metaphor – that the skills you use in a fitness class are a metaphor for the skills you need in your life – but I think there's more to it than that. I think they're the same skills, and I feel like by struggling through fitness classes, I've learnt to bear with difficult situations in my life.'

Suzanna and I come from a fitness-focused family. Our two other sisters are marathon runners, our mum recently solo-hiked the West Highland Way, and our dad ran ten marathons in his forties before switching to multi-stage bike tours in his fifties. Endurance exercise is in our blood, and especially since Dad passed, I think we've all taken to it as a way of honouring his memory.

Suzanna's main 'thing' was always ballet, but that isn't something you can persist with indefinitely. You're subjecting your body to an incredibly intense strain. Injuries accrue, and few people can continue at a high level past their early twenties. With ballet on the back burner, Suzanna took up Les Mills workouts, choreographed group fitness classes including the likes of BodyPump (strength training with barbells), BodyBalance (a yoga–Pilates hybrid) and BodyCombat (a high-intensity workout inspired by martial arts). These workouts helped her through a turbulent period in her life: the double sucker-punch of losing our dad and the pandemic. After attending classes for a few years, she trained as an instructor and has subsequently taught about six classes a week in gyms around Edinburgh.

'After Dad died, the ritual of my Saturday morning Body-Pump class was one of the things that I really clung to,' she tells me. 'It was a safe space where I could go, and it had this journey that your instructor would take you through, without you having to come up with your own thing to do. So, for me it was a powerful way to get through grief. Some people would turn to religious rituals in that context, but the rituals of physical fitness, I think, can have a similar effect.'

In 2020, these inherently communal workouts went online. In common with many others around the world, Suzanna body pumped, balanced and combated from her living room. Many months later, she attended a two-day event called Les Mills Live in London, in which thousands of Les Mills acolytes assembled to do multiple workouts back-to-back.

'Les Mills was one of the things that got me through lockdown, so when [superstar instructor Glen Ostergaard] came on stage, I welled up,' she recalls. 'I think lots of people found it incredibly powerful and moving to have come together like that.'

I'd wanted to talk to Suzanna precisely because of the group nature of these workouts. If long-distance running has something in common with a pilgrimage or personal spiritual odyssey, then it follows that group fitness classes are somewhat like a church service.

This isn't an original observation: a 2017 *Atlantic* article titled 'The Church of CrossFit' made the case that 'gyms … are starting to fill spiritual and social needs for many non-religious people'.[34] It referenced a study called 'How We Gather' by Angie Thurston and Casper ter Kuile,[35] which found that for the overwhelmingly secular cohort of millennials, the likes of SoulCycle and CrossFit 'have become the locations of shared, transformative experience'. In other words, fitness empires seem to pull people together with an ease that atheist churches could only dream of.

However, Suzanna also goes to an actual church, meaning she is unusually well placed to draw some parallels.

'When everyone's moving together, it makes you feel part of something bigger than yourself, and that's amplified when you see the same people every week,' she says. 'Les Mills also feels like a community united around common goals and a common set of beliefs. At something like Les Mills Live, part of what was so powerful was just having that number of bodies in the room. But when you're coupling that with everybody subscribing to the same mentality and everybody physically doing the same thing, you're just buoyed on this big wave of "everybody together" and it creates this holistic experience.'

She adds that many of these classes have a ritualistic element that reminds her of the liturgies performed in churches. The class is always at the same time and in the same place. When you get there, you set out your weights and bar and mat in the same way. The workout itself will have the same structure no matter where in the world you do it. And the words and phrases she uses as an instructor are highly particular to that context.

'A priest friend of mine once said to me that he really likes liturgy and ritual, because they are something that happens around you and almost to you,' she reflects. 'Your role is to participate in that, rather than to go off and do your own thing. I think that's one of the things that I like about [the atmosphere of] fitness classes as well – it's something that's happening in the whole environment, and you just go with it, which I think has the effect of making the workout feel very safe and achievable.'

We talked for a while about the different facets of exercise as spirituality. If Les Mills is a church, then it's a broad church; those who are looking to mindfully explore their bodily sensations can try BodyBalance, whereas Les Mills Grit will encourage you to 'dwell in the pain cave' if self-mortification is more your jam. For Suzanna herself, though, there's another big factor at play, in that exercise forces her to honour her limitations. At the time of writing, she was struggling with an ongoing knee problem that was restricting her everyday activities. As far as I could tell, she had accepted the situation with a remarkable equanimity, but it's probably true to say that the more you love fitness, the more confronting an injury can be.

'For me, the recognition that I do have limitations is a spiritually important recognition,' she says. 'It creates a space for self-compassion and humility, which I suppose as part of a broader mindset reminds you that you are not the ultimate power in the universe. It might open you up to something beyond yourself.'

I'd concur that if there is any spiritual value to be had in exercise, dealing with injuries and off-seasons is bound to be part of it. My own relationship with running has had many such off-seasons and has taught me many different lessons at different times.

When I first started running, in my chaotic mid-twenties, I turned out to be surprisingly speedy and I chased those personal bests with all my might. Back then running taught me something about self-confidence. I didn't much believe in anything, least of all in myself, and I tended to sidestep my tricky emotions with a whole gamut of unhealthy coping strategies. Running allowed me to use those emotions as fuel, powering me to achieve something I could be proud of. From a spiritual perspective, you could say I was learning something about self-mastery.

Time passed, and I injured myself again and again. A caution settled in my muscles, and I could no longer override my body's warning signals quite so dauntlessly. Into my early thirties, running taught me something about listening to my body and letting go of my more deranged competitive impulses. The lesson here was all about loosening the ego.

By thirty-four, I'd settled into the groove of 'someone who used to be fast and was now just ticking over'. But then I met my husband, who was a runner himself, and a wiser one than I was. On our long runs together, I'd marvel at his ability to push past the pain barrier while still tuning into his body. It had something to do with finding ease, assuaging anxiety, teaching the body that a certain level of discomfort was safe to sustain. I started training for my first (and thus far only) marathon, and busted out a respectable 3:40. I don't believe I could have managed it had I still been in cahoots with the inner coach from hell. The lesson here is about balance, a lesson I'm still learning today.

I'm sure that for anyone more seasoned than me, there are many more twists along this road. It isn't always about chasing glory, and physical decline (or what the Buddhists would call impermanence) is an inevitable part of the package. But I hope that I'll be able to carry this relationship through many more seasons in life before I have to send my sweat-wicking T-shirts to the charity shop. I was inspired by talking to Díaz-Gilbert, who is in her sixties and still going strong.

'I'm a grandmother and I'm still running,' she says. 'For me, ultrarunning is as natural as breathing. It's about endurance, it's about perseverance, it's about patience, it's about discipline, it's about getting out of my comfort zone. It's my medicine, it's my meditation, it's my time to have a conversation with God. This is why I have longevity in running: it's because I enjoy the process. I'll run for as long as I can. And if I can't run, I'll walk.'

Chapter 9

Meditation: The Hurricane in Your Head

'Just take a moment or two to get comfortable,' says the man in my headphones. 'Beginning with some big deep breaths, breathe in through the nose and out through the mouth. And as you breathe out this time, close your eyes and allow the breath to return to its natural rhythm.'

I'm sitting cross-legged on the floor, listening to a guided meditation via the Headspace app. The app is replete with options and scrolling through its library for the first time, I experienced a kind of choice paralysis. Should I try 'Noticing Your Inner Critic' or 'Moving Toward What You Need'? Could I benefit from 'Strengthening Your Boundaries', 'Coping with Worries', or 'Navigating Change'? Or should I sample the seven-session collection, led by footballer Raheem Sterling, called 'Power of Mind with Raheem'?

In the end, I go for the no-frills option: a simple guided mindfulness meditation, narrated by Headspace co-founder and former Buddhist monk Andy Puddicombe. He asks you to notice the weight of your body, the different sounds around you, the sensations you may be feeling from head to toe. Then you move on to the breath. Which parts of your body move with the in-breath and out-breath? Is the breath long or short?

'Just counting the breaths as they pass, realising when the mind's wandered, each time returning to that sensation,' says

Puddicombe in soporific tones. 'And now letting go of that focus, just for a moment allowing the mind to be free.'

Ten minutes pass in this way and it isn't too painful, although I can't say I'm clear on what I'm supposed to get out of it. My breaths were medium-length, I guess? I think I counted a few dozen before I got distracted? I feel more antsy than I do enlightened, more bewildered than serene.

On one level, mindfulness meditation ought to be the simplest thing in the world. What could be more straightforward than taking a few minutes out of your day to observe your breath or bodily sensations? There's no complicated theory to learn, you don't have to subscribe to a particular worldview, and while different techniques abound, most could be distilled into a couple of sentences. The one I picked on Headspace is a classic example: find an object of focus, most commonly the breath, and bear witness to the thoughts that come and go, gently returning your attention to that object of focus as soon as you notice you've been sidetracked.

And yet if there's anything at all I know about meditation, it's that the practice can be fiendishly, offputtingly hard. I've made numerous attempts to incorporate it into my routine (mostly freestyle, without an app) and yet somehow it always ends up falling through the cracks. I'm too busy, I protest. If I have a minute to myself, I don't want to use it sitting aimlessly on the floor observing my breathing: I want to fill it with what Rudyard Kipling described as 'sixty seconds' worth of distance run'.[1]

This is an excuse, and I know it. A quote that regularly circulates on the internet (supposedly an old Zen proverb) says: 'You should sit in meditation for twenty minutes a day, unless you are too busy; then you should sit for an hour.' Zen proverb or not, it rings true to me. Those of us who think we're too busy, who can't pause our go-go-go mentality for five minutes, are precisely the people who could benefit from a spot of radical unbusyness. And if it's too hard to just sit and *be*, perhaps the meditation can help us unpack why.

Apps like Headspace and Calm have been an unequivocal success story, often credited as springboarding mindfulness into the mainstream. Headspace was founded in 2010 with a view to improving 'the health and happiness of the world'. It is now used in 190 countries, has over two million paying subscribers and, according to its own website, is 'proven to reduce stress by 14% in just 10 days'.[2] Rival app Calm, launched in 2012, has four million paying subscribers and a near-identical mission: 'to make the world happier and healthier'. In 2019, it became the 'world's first mental health unicorn'.[3] Disappointingly, a unicorn in this context refers to a startup valued at more than $1 billion.

Mindfulness meditation is well documented as being effective for stress, anxiety, depression,[4] sleep,[5] eating behaviours[6] and interpersonal difficulties.[7] Generally, what's being tested is something called mindfulness-based stress reduction (MBSR), an eight-week programme developed by American medical professor Jon Kabat-Zinn in the 1970s. Schooled in Zen Buddhism, Kabat-Zinn saw an opportunity to repackage Zen mindfulness practice for a wider audience. He stripped away any overtly religious elements, creating a product that would be palatable to the medical mainstream and amenable to scientific testing. As we will see, it is debatable whether those religious elements are really absent, or whether MBSR – like other practices we've covered in this book – is something of a Trojan horse.

As Kabat-Zinn explained in a 2011 journal article: 'From the beginning of MBSR, I bent over backward to structure it and find ways to speak about it that avoided as much as possible the risk of it being seen as Buddhist, "New Age," "Eastern Mysticism" or just plain "flakey." To my mind this was a constant and serious risk that would have undermined our attempts to present it as commonsensical, evidence-based, and ordinary, and ultimately a legitimate element of mainstream medical care.'[8]

Kabat-Zinn conceived of mindfulness as a 'public health intervention, a vehicle for both individual and societal transformation'. Starting out with one Stress Reduction Clinic in Massachusetts, now called the Center for Mindfulness, he quickly became the figurehead of a movement. True to his vision, mindfulness now has medical clout; the NHS recommends mindfulness-based cognitive therapy (MBCT) as a treatment for 'less severe depression'.[9] And since the practice is often perceived as fully secular, even the least crunchy, least New Agey, most left-brained among us might be persuaded to give it a try.

Jiva Masheder is a mindfulness and self-compassion teacher based in Brighton. 'People generally come to my MBSR courses because they're feeling stressed, anxious, overwhelmed,' she tells me over Zoom.[10] 'And when I ask people at the end, "What did you get from the course?", generally they say they have more of a sense of agency. They feel less stressed, more able to cope, they tend to sleep better, and relationships improve as well because people become less impulsive with what they say and do.'

For many of her students, the big takeaway from MBSR is the realisation that thoughts are not facts. Their inner critic might be hurling abuse their way, but once they've got some space from those thoughts, they realise they don't have to believe them.

'It's about getting a bit of freedom from the tyranny of what your mind says, to sort out what's a good, constructive, useful thought and what's the same old crap going round and round and round,' she says.

As positive as this sounded, I had questions. If the purpose of mindfulness meditation is to attune you to the present moment, then why are we judging the practice in relation to future mental health outcomes? And what if meditating *doesn't* make you feel better? What if you don't end up resembling the stock image of a blissed-out meditator on a mountaintop?

A thornier question still: does it even make sense to divorce mindfulness from its Buddhist underpinnings? When Buddhists promise liberation from suffering, is that the same as the 'healthier, happier you' that Headspace would have you strive for?

The story of meditation very likely begins deep in our ancestral past. According to one hypothesis, from psychologist Matt J. Rossano, it was 'campfire rituals of focused attention' – gazing at the campfire in a meditative way – that sparked our aptitude for symbolic thinking and separated us from our Neanderthal cousins.[11] In other words, we may have meditation to thank for our most recent evolutionary leap.

Whatever you make of this theory, meditation is clearly a cross-cultural phenomenon. Most religious traditions have their own techniques, and the word is used to bracket together a diverse array of practices, which belong together only in the most loose-knit way.

As well as mindfulness meditation, popular styles include transcendental meditation (a trademarked technique involving mantras), metta meditation (sending 'loving kindness' into the ether) and moving meditations like the 'still running' discussed in the previous chapter. The Buddhists don't have a monopoly on meditation – no one does. But when it comes to mindfulness specifically, it's no secret where Kabat-Zinn found his material.

'It's an often overlooked fact that mindfulness, the way that it's taught in all of these apps, is a practice that derives originally from Buddhism,' says C. Pierce Salguero, transdisciplinary scholar of health humanities at Abington College, Penn State University, when we talk.[12] 'But it has also undergone a pretty thorough transformation, to be turned from a more religious or spiritual practice into a secularised medical or mental health practice.'

As an expert in Buddhism and medicine (although, interestingly, not a Buddhist himself), Salguero has a lot to say about how mindfulness-for-health fits into its historical context. In his book *Buddhish: A Guide to the 20 Most Important Buddhist Ideas for the Curious and Skeptical* (2022), he explains how Buddhism itself has been reimagined in the West, laying the groundwork for the present mindfulness boom. Historically speaking, Buddhism has involved a rich tapestry of traditions, some of which are flagrantly religious or magical in hue. By contrast, the Buddhism many of us in the West recognise, in which the Buddha was something like an ancient psychologist, designing an empirical 'science of mind', emerged little more than a century ago.

'At the time, European discourse was talking about how backward the Asians were, and Buddhism was held up by colonial authorities as a prime example of superstition,' says Salguero, echoing what Shreena Gandhi told me about yoga. 'Buddhist authorities all over Asia engaged in a project of reimagining Buddhism in a more secular and scientific way, moving away from magical practices and rituals and emphasising the practice of meditation as a psychology and a philosophy.'

European and North American intellectuals, drawn to this rejigged form of Buddhism, started promoting meditative practices at home. Meditation became widespread, and with it, the perception of Buddhism as somehow more objective or empirical than other religions. When Kabat-Zinn set to work on making mindfulness 'commonsensical', the earlier colonial push to secularise Buddhism surely helped him along the way.

It isn't clear, though, that the endgame of a Buddhist mindfulness practice is quite the same as the endgame for MBSR. As Salguero explains in his book: 'Buddhist trainings that emphasize concentration often focus on generating what in the Pali language is called jhana, advanced states of absorption in which you become so concentrated on the object of meditation that the rest of the world melts away ... Trainings emphasizing insight, on the other hand, focus on perceiving your chosen object of meditation as a manifestation of suffering, impermanence, and non-self.'[13] In either case, the idea is to deconstruct our usual habits of mind and see 'reality as it is', as opposed to reducing anxiety or fostering calm.

'In general, the idea that Buddhist meditation is going to lead to inner peace is a misunderstanding,' says Salguero. 'What it does give you is the tools to be able to deal with a whole range of different kinds of experiences in a more detached and neutral way.'

At the bare minimum, he adds, you're going to experience sore knees and a sore back. People might also experience latent traumas and other kinds of negative emotions. 'If there's any inner peace to be had, it takes the form of your being able to sit there with equanimity while the emotional and physical pain pass through your body and mind.'

Salguero's description resonated with me, and even felt somewhat validating. Unlike the other routine self-care practices I am somehow *not* too busy for (exercise, taking a bath, brushing my teeth), meditation strikes me as an unknown quantity, and that's why I'm often reluctant to go there. For me at least, the benefits have never emerged in anything like a linear, predictable way.

Sure, sometimes it's relaxing, as the apps would have it. Sometimes I can see that it's helping train my concentration and focus, as any corporate mindfulness programme would have it. Other times, though, the experience is more complicated and confronting. I may find myself crying. I may find myself racked with existential confusion. I may find old issues resurfacing or new aggravations arising, or I may just sit there feeling frustrated and bored.

I've had powerful meditations too, in which new insights have bubbled up prolifically, or long-buried emotions have found release. On one occasion, I was trying to 'be present' with an overwhelming feeling of rage. Rather than getting lost in my thoughts about the rage, I tried to pay attention to the original feeling and how it hunkered in my body. I noticed my heartbeat, more emphatic than normal, and the coiled spring of my muscles primed for action. The feeling in its distilled form was not purely negative. It was powerful. It reminded me of fire – raw, amoral, magnificent, full of destructive potential. Afterwards, I felt something toxic had left my system for good.

Experiences of this nature have left me in a conflicted place. On one hand, I'm intrigued by meditation. I've tasted some of the possibilities on offer. I like a challenge, and there's a swashbuckling part of me that's fully on board with a quest through the gnarlier regions of the mind. On the other hand, if I've got ten minutes to spare for mental and spiritual maintenance, I'm going to default to something that reliably makes me feel safe or calm or connected. If you've ever tried meditating and felt less than beatific, it's easy to conclude that you're failing at it, or that the concept has been mis-sold.

'Maybe some strategic misinformation is being promoted about mindfulness, that it's just going to make you happy,' says Salguero. 'But if you practice mindfulness seriously, it's going to make you experience all your suffering in a way that is much rawer. You'll develop a lot more equanimity, maybe more bravery, because you're not fighting those forms of suffering as they come up. But it's certainly not going to make those kinds of things go away.'

In more recent years, the 'underbelly of the mindfulness movement', as Salguero described it to me, has attracted more attention. One powerful critique comes from Ronald Purser, an ordained Buddhist teacher and management professor at San Francisco State University. In his book *McMindfulness: How Mindfulness Became the New Capitalist Spirituality* (2019), he makes the case that mindfulness has been hijacked by consumerist culture. It has been reduced, he thinks, to an individual coping mechanism, engendering a passive acceptance of the systems that have caused our stress in the first place. This is particularly the case when corporations get involved, offering up mindfulness to their workers as opposed to improving their working conditions. For instance, Starbucks attracted ire in 2020 when it gifted its overstretched employees a Headspace subscription.[14]

As for the ways that mindfulness has taken off in Silicon Valley, there is clearly a stark contradiction in executives using a Buddhist-derived practice to get ahead in business. In Purser's view, practices like MBSR are being used to uphold the neoliberal status quo, masking the revolutionary potential of Buddhist teachings.

'Mindfulness has been oversold and commodified, reduced to a technique for just about any instrumental purpose,' he writes. 'It can give inner-city kids a calming time-out, or hedge fund tracers a mental edge, or reduce the stress of military drone pilots. Void of a moral compass or ethical commitments, unmoored from a vision of the social good, the commodification of mindfulness keeps it anchored in the ethos of the market.'[15]

Purser's tone is trenchant. After attending an MBSR programme, he does concede that 'MBSR is a saving grace for many people ... The course was accomplishing exactly what it was intended to do: teach people how to reduce their stress and anxiety, cope with pain, and live a more mindful life.'[16] But nevertheless, he contends, mindfulness stands to make us 'better adjusted cogs', docile in the face of exploitation.

His book is a bracing read and I found myself nodding along in places. That said, I sensed he didn't give the average Western meditator enough credit. Sure, meditating tech bros are a thing – microdosing, biohacking and breath-working their way towards corporate dominance. At the same time, there are many people whose inner explorations will lead them far off the beaten path of capitalism. To my mind, just sitting and being and doing 'nothing' is an inherently anti-capitalist practice, the antidote to our obsession with chasing future rewards. It is very likely to bleed into something spiritual too, even if that isn't always the terminology the practitioner would choose.

'Ron is articulating one response that Buddhists have had to the mindfulness movement, but the Asian Buddhist communities that I've been involved with have actually had a different response to Ron's,' Salguero says. 'The one I've heard most frequently is: the more people who practise mindfulness, the more wellbeing we'll have on the planet. The more people who practise mindfulness, the less suffering there will be across humanity. And moreover, the more people who practise mindfulness, the more people might be exposed to Buddhist ideas. For me, I think there's truth in both these responses.'

Jiva Masheder goes further, remarking that Purser has fundamentally misunderstood MBSR. As she sees it, his mistake is to conflate acceptance with resignation, which mindfulness teachers have never promoted. If there's any truth in his argument, she thinks it lies in his observation that mindfulness has been reduced to an individual coping mechanism. Traditionally, Buddhism would have been practised in a community setting (*the Sangha*) with a teacher, and MBSR courses are based on the same model. She thinks you're unlikely to get the full measure of mindfulness if you're doing it at home on your own.

A different kind of critique comes from Willoughby Britton, who made a splash in 2017 with a paper on the potential negative effects of meditation. Britton, who is a clinical psychologist and a professor of psychiatry and human behaviour at Brown University, was interested in experiences that could be 'described as challenging, difficult, distressing, functionally impairing, and/or requiring additional support'. Her team interviewed ninety-two Western Buddhist meditators who had reported these kinds of outcomes.

The resulting study, called 'The Varieties of Contemplative Experience', identified fifty-nine categories of negative experience, ranging from 'loss of the basic sense of self' to 'changes in motivation', 'the re-experiencing of traumatic memories' and even 'gastrointestinal distress'. A whopping 88 per cent of the meditators said their challenging experiences had spilled over into their everyday life. Shockingly, 17 per cent had felt suicidal and another 17 per cent had required inpatient hospitalisation.[17]

As the paper explains, many Buddhist traditions 'acknowledge periods of challenge or difficulty associated with the practice of meditation'. It adds that: 'Given that some of these effects might even run counter to the dominant paradigm of health and wellbeing, it is critical that the range of effects associated with Buddhist meditation be investigated in the modern Western context.'

For sure, these study participants aren't representative of the average person who downloads the Calm app. They were serious meditators, who had been selected for the study precisely because they'd had a tough time. Such experiences might be extraordinarily rare – the functionally impaired exception that proves the happy, healthy rule. But for researchers like Britton, they're too important to be ignored. Today, she offers trauma-informed mindfulness trainings called 'First Do No Harm', and provides support services to people who've run into meditation-related difficulties. As she remarked in a 2014 *Atlantic* article: 'As much as I want to investigate and promote contemplative practices and contribute to the well-being of humanity through that, I feel a deeper commitment to what's actually true.'[18]

Britton is not the only researcher to probe the dark side of meditation practice. As I have argued, there is a tension between mindfulness as a spiritual practice and mindfulness as a tool for personal thriving. According to Salguero, this very tension can sometimes cause people harm.

'You get a small minority of people who are interested in meditation for health and wellbeing purposes, who do some intensive practice or go on a retreat,' he says. 'They don't know about the Buddhist concept of non-self and they don't know that this is a practice designed to trigger those kinds of realisations. So, when they experience some of these effects, they don't have the context to understand what they're experiencing.'

It seems there are documented cases of people who have practised secular meditation and inadvertently 'cracked open the fiction of self'. We're talking about the kind of ego death experience we explored with the neuroscientist Dr James Cooke earlier in this book. For Cooke, this was a positive occurrence, but others are more panicked or perturbed by it. In some cases, they might call on a mental health professional, who is no more schooled in Buddhist frameworks than they are.

'They're diagnosed in many cases with serious psychiatric diagnoses like depersonalisation and derealisation,' Salguero remarks. 'If you read the symptoms, this sounds exactly like what Buddhists are going for with loss of self.'

Back to that Trojan horse: might someone who innocently downloads a meditation app independently reach some Buddhist realisations? After all, these apps have been stripped bare of any theoretical underpinnings. They don't purport to explain *why* you're calm, *why* you're relaxed (or as the case may be, why you've wound up re-evaluating your basic concept of personal identity). Any explanations you might find will likely be couched in physiological terms: you are calm because meditation calms your nervous system, not because you've happened across a truthful and spiritual insight.

Buddhist meditations, by contrast, are meant to guide you towards a particular way of seeing the world. It is intriguing to consider that the practical techniques adopted by MBSR might succeed in doing the same thing, even minus the supporting philosophy.

For that reason, Salguero thinks that meditators, however secular their inclinations, should be aware of the possible outcomes. In common with Britton, who came up with the idea, he thinks meditation ought to 'carry a warning label'.

'You can take the practice out of the temple, and you can secularise it, reinterpret it and put it into the hospital setting,' he says. 'But the practice was designed to produce these kinds of experiences. If you don't know anything about emptiness or non-self, then these experiences can be really disorienting.'

My husband, Nick Torry, is a seasoned meditator who first stumbled across mindfulness meditation in his late teens. His motivation was simple curiosity; he wasn't particularly trying to reduce stress, still less to probe the fictitious nature of the self. However, before too long, all those purported MBSR benefits made an appearance. 'I was noticeably less anxious and more easily able to control my emotions, I didn't stress out so easily,' he says.[19]

To begin with, his practice was purely secular. Although he knew it was linked to Buddhism, he didn't overthink it, and it wasn't till his early thirties that he decided to explore more deeply. He embarked on a Vipassana retreat – ten days of silent 'insight' meditation, in which practitioners sit for up to ten hours daily, observing the sensations that arise in their bodies.

'That was my first time associating meditation directly with the Buddhist background and the theory behind it,' he says. 'In the Vipassana retreat, there are lessons every day in why you're doing things a certain way, from a Buddhist perspective. It's something I still think about today, how things like craving and aversion are affecting the way I'm responding.'

In my twenties, before meeting Nick, I'd toyed with the idea of signing up for Vipassana myself. The 'go hard or go home' mentality appealed to me: I figured that anything with such a tantalisingly high difficulty level was worth investigating. I wanted to blast through my baggage with maximum efficiency. And I absolutely wanted those big splashy insights into the nature of reality.

There was only one problem: I couldn't meditate. The idea of sitting and being with my mind, even for five minutes, was frankly terrifying. The few times I tried, I fell asleep, which I now suspect was a self-protective mechanism. It was a bit like wanting to swim the Channel when you're scared to dip your toes in your local training pool.

Looking back, I'm glad I didn't subject myself to an experience I obviously wasn't equipped to handle. And from what Nick tells me, I was missing the point anyway: my hunger for climactic psychospiritual showdowns was unlikely to have been sated on the retreat. Sure, it was tough both mentally and physically, and once you got past those tricky bits, there was a certain serenity to be found. But it wasn't exactly brimming with big epiphanies. For him, those aspects of meditation tend to emerge more quietly over time.

'If you sit for long enough, you can't help but feel like there's some kind of oneness to everything and that the self is a more complex thing than we see day to day,' he says. 'There's also the power of the present moment, which if you allow yourself to sit in it, is just incredibly overwhelming and awe-inspiring. What is this thing that I am? What is this place that I am in? You start to experience those layers on layers of stuff that we don't usually allow ourselves to experience, in our very tunnel-visioned way.'

Though he isn't wedded to any one meditative technique, his goal is always the same: to loosen the grip of the narrative mind and experience a richer sense of the here and now. Whether it's body scanning, focusing on the breath, or following Eckhart Tolle's instruction to 'become very alert and wait for the next thought … like a cat watching a mousehole', the idea is to notice how expansive the present moment truly is. That awareness isn't necessarily relaxing – in fact, it can be ungrounding and destabilising – but it's exactly what meditation trains you to sit with.

'The benefit is learning to be stable within that and realising, "Hey, I'm still here. There's still this thing experiencing this mess of possible present moments,"' says Nick.

He thinks the spiritual aspects of meditation, such as they are, arise naturally from this process. If you realise, 'Hey, I'm still here,' it stands to reason that there's more than one 'you'. There's the 'you' that's having the thoughts, the compulsive narrator self, and there's the more mysterious 'you' in whom the whole drama is unfolding.

'What are these parts of myself which are conversing? Where do they come from?' says Nick. 'One of the simplest ways to explain it would be that within meditation you can commune with the mind, body and spirit. You can focus on what's going on in the body, you can focus on what's going on in the mind. But then, what's the thing that's doing that? I think it is helpful to at least be open to spiritual thinking, because at some point you're going to come across it.'

He finds this naturally engenders a stronger sense of personal agency. A lot of spiritual practices, he remarks, are meant to help the practitioner assert some control over their environment. Whether it's a dance to make the rains come, or a petitionary prayer for a sick relative, you're trying to connect to a higher power, entreating something to occur. With meditation, there's a parallel process at play. You're connecting to a higher part of yourself (whatever the self might be), and in the process you gain some mastery over your thoughts and emotions.

While describing himself as 'evangelical' about meditation, Nick is wary about the way the practice is often marketed. Sure, those stock image meditators might look peaceful, but that belies the reality: the more calmly and unflinchingly you sit there, the harder it is to distract yourself from the hurricane in your head.

'I think what most people experience when they first start meditating is just the noise of their minds,' says Nick. 'And the first thought someone has when that happens is "I'm not good at this" or "I can't do this", not recognising that they're going through exactly what the process is. It's as though they think there's this place in a holy box above them, which they're supposed to get into, and that if they're not doing that, they can't meditate. But that place either doesn't really exist or is just there in fleeting moments between the noise.'

After talking to Nick, I realised I was placing meditation precisely where it didn't belong: in an achievement-oriented framework. It wasn't just another task on an endless to-do list, an unpleasant enough framing in its own right; it was something I was bad at and was failing at. No wonder I don't reach the end of a long hard day and think, 'Ah, a meditation will be relaxing.'

I decided to try a new approach: an intentionally imperfect meditation with the explicit aim of being kind to myself. I waited till the baby was napping, put in my headphones, and played some music I found calming, creating a kind of cocoon of ambient sound. ('You need music to meditate? What an amateur,' scoffed my inner critic, whom I decided to ignore for once.) From there, I did all the things I would usually class as meditation no-nos. I focused loosely on my breathing but didn't berate myself too much once my thoughts wandered. In fact, I let them wander. I entered a state of dreamy expansiveness. I scratched an itch on my foot. I checked how much time I had remaining. I even checked a notification on my phone.

My inner critic piped up on each of these occasions, but I realised I was able to summon a kinder, wiser voice too. Scratching an itch? A very human response to itching. Checking a notification? A very human response to the ways that social media hijacks the reward pathways of our brains ('Although you should probably put your phone on airplane mode next time round,' said the wise voice, by way of caveat).

There's obviously a time and a place for something more structured, and I'm not sure what a meditation teacher would make of my approach. But what I needed in that moment was softness. I needed a reprieve from working, a reprieve from striving, a reprieve from trying to get it right. I needed to give myself what I lavished on my baby, the antsy little human I'd just rocked to sleep. My timer sounded after twenty minutes, and – in what was practically a first for me after meditating – I felt calm.

To better understand what was happening here, I spoke to Karin Peeters, a psychotherapist, coach and founder of two businesses: Vitalis Coaching & Therapy and Inner Pilgrim. She is a keen advocate of this self-compassionate approach. 'Mindfulness from the psychology perspective is about a moment-to-moment, non-judgemental presence onto whatever's happening,' she tells me.[20] 'One reason why people like therapy so much is because it has that element of unconditional love, holding space for anything that is arising in your life. Meditation teaches you to do that for yourself.'

Coming off the back of my most recent meditation, this way of explaining it blew my mind. I had long thought of meditation as a strategy for stepping outside my emotions, or for deepening my appreciation of the present moment, or even as a pathway towards a unitive mystical experience. But I had never once thought of it as an opportunity to be *nice* to myself. So much of the language you often hear around meditation – terms like emotional detachment, mental discipline, reining in the monkey mind – tends towards the hyper-masculinised and cold.

But as Peeters explains, the 'mind' in mindfulness doesn't refer to the cerebral so much as the feeling part of us. When a Buddhist talks about the mind, they point not to their head but to their heart.

'When we sit on the meditation cushion with mindfulness, we witness all of the turmoil unfolding in ourselves, ideally with a smile,' she says. 'It's like, "Oh my gosh, look at my thoughts going rampant, look at my feelings reacting, how fascinating. Look at my depression being so dark and wanting me to stay indoors all day and not engage with anyone. Look at my anxiety, creating absolute panic and telling me I'm not good enough. Look at me creating that inside of my own mind."'

It was the 'ideally with a smile' bit that got me. Sure, I'd borne witness to my inner turbulence, but only with a grimace. Peeters, by contrast, talked about self-compassion, about dealing with anticipatory fear ahead of meditating, about coming back to the body when overwhelmed. She added that sitting and focusing on the breath might not be right for everyone: you can recite a mantra, play music, even walk around gazing at the horizon if that's more peaceful for you. Once again, this blew my mind.

'It is most important to set your intention wisely,' she says. 'The intention is not to sit down on the meditation cushion for the allocated time. That is just a quantitative measurement. The intention is to be present to whatever happens inside me from a place of loving kindness. If the loving kindness shifts or the experiences that arise become too much to bear, then we just take a break.'

I was keen to talk to Peeters because of her dual focus as both a Western MBSR-informed therapist and a practising Buddhist. While she isn't a Buddhist teacher ('I am talking from my own understanding and any faults in it are entirely mine'), she did spend several years studying meditation in monasteries, and had a lot to say about how the religion intersects with MBSR.

For instance, she explained how Buddhist forms of meditation are intertwined with Buddhist conceptions of morality. Moving beyond the breath and the bodily sensations, the true object of our focus is meant to be our 'basic goodness'. From this perspective, that inner peace we may be looking for does not arise in a vacuum.

'One of my teachers, Lama Zopa, said someone asked him once what true relaxation means,' says Peeters. 'He said, "True relaxation means to live in virtue." For me that's so true – it's when we have nothing to hide, when we completely live according to our own ethics and integrity, that's when we feel at peace. So when we hear that meditation can be relaxing, it's meant in that way: turn your mind towards virtue, and relaxation will come.'

Although MBSR can be harnessed towards the greater good (Peeters points out that developing self-compassion typically makes us kinder all round), there is nothing to say that it has to be used that way. This, of course, was the basis of *McMindfulness* author Ronald Purser's critique: in the absence of any underpinning ethical framework, mindfulness can be appropriated to do just about anything you like. Its deployment in the boardroom may give your business the edge, but if you're using it to chill out in between a ruthless spate of corporate downsizing, that's not what a Buddhist would call relaxation.

'Mindfulness was created to guard our minds against what brings suffering and turn it towards what brings happiness, and what brings happiness is a life of virtue,' Peeters emphasises.

I got the sense from Peeters that while secularised mindfulness might have moved away from its Buddhist origins, that didn't have to be a problem. After all, Buddhism itself is intended as a framework for alleviating suffering. If your Headspace app does that for you, it would take a very salty Buddhist to begrudge you using it.

After our conversation, she put me in touch with 'an actual Buddhist monk', Geshe Tenzin Namdak, resident teacher at Jamyang Buddhist Centre in London. He didn't see anything wrong with Buddhist ideas being presented to a wider audience.

'MBSR is a secular aspect of Buddhism, but there are many more aspects of Buddhism that can be presented in a secular way and thus benefit more people who are not necessarily interested in spirituality or religion,' he said. 'Many of these secular aspects can go much deeper than MBSR. It just depends how deep people like to go, how much interest they have and how much positive transformation they like to expect.'[21]

On a similar note, Salguero remarked that there's nothing new about using Buddhist practices in the pursuit of better mental health. He told me that health – as opposed to loftier concepts like enlightenment – has been a focal point in Buddhist texts for millennia. What's more, its health benefits, both physical and mental, have always been one of its selling points during periods of cultural collision.

'I think modern mindfulness practitioners are doing what Buddhists throughout history have done whenever Buddhism arrives in a new culture,' he says. 'My textual research has primarily looked at the introduction of Buddhism to China in the medieval period, while other scholars have looked at its introduction to Tibet and Japan. Buddhism has spread into cultures all over the world in large part because of its health claims, so the fact this is happening now in the West is not surprising to me, as a historian.'

Now, it may be that something has got lost in translation, somewhere between the monk in his mountain monastery and me on my bedroom floor with a smartphone app. I'm sure I'm not the only person to have attempted mindfulness only to be derailed by the kinds of questions we've explored in this chapter, nor to be surprised by its difficulty level. When it comes to meditation, 'simple' emphatically does not mean 'easy'.

That said, the beauty of meditation is that it touches on something profoundly human. While I am loath to use the word 'universal' about anything so culturally loaded, this kind of reckoning with suffering is surely about as universal as it gets.

Both Peeters and Masheder alluded to the Buddhist parable of two arrows. The first arrow consists of all the pain we encounter as an unavoidable corollary of being alive. People die, you may get sick, your marriage may end, you may lose your job. It's a none-too-cheery prospect, and one we can't do much about; it's just the nature of the human experience.

'But then what we do in our minds is shoot ourselves with a second arrow, and that is suffering,' says Peeters. 'When we beat ourselves up, when we say, "I should be so much more peaceful, why can't I just deal with this like an adult?" That's the second arrow. Suffering is within our control, and mindfulness can help with that second arrow from both a psychological and a Buddhist perspective. Let's be kind, [life is] already hard enough – I don't need this extra layer on top.'

As reasons to meditate go, that strikes me as a pretty good one. With only the one arrow, rather than two, impaled in our psyches, perhaps we'll have the headspace to think beyond our daily grievances. We'll still be the walking wounded. But we'll be stronger and less paralysed by the huge collective challenges lying in wait.

Chapter 10

Nature Spirituality: The Door to the Temple

It's a balmy morning in early June, the first day of the year to make you say out loud, 'It's summer.' In honour of the new season, I have opted for a swimsuit and booked a slot at my local swimming lake.

I ease myself into the water, braced against the shock of entry. The bracing turns out to be unnecessary, as it just isn't cold today: a temperature I would initially describe as 'invigorating' quickly settles into a Goldilocks-worthy 'just right'. I pad through the mud until the water is at chest height and settle into an ungainly breaststroke, embarking on a gentle lap of the perimeter. I pass ducks going busily about their day, and dragonflies suspended in a coital slow dance. There are lush reeds ringing the water's edge and a patina of algae on its surface. The sky is as bright blue and the grass as bright green as it would be in a child's painting; the water glints and winks in the upbeat morning light.

Floating on my back, my thoughts become looser and dreamier in a way that reminds me of being a child on holiday. I used to spend hours in the campsite swimming pool, making up stories. I feel that no time has elapsed, or rather that time has looped back, as if I'm communing with some core version of myself that hasn't changed. Perhaps that's part of what it means to be 'in the now'.

When you go to the park, I muse, you're in nature, but when you immerse yourself in a lake you're really *in* nature. You're not zapping through it, as you do when running, or objectively admiring the scene. You're being held by nature, engulfed by it. I wonder whether we retain some cellular memory of our nine months spent floating in amniotic fluid. That said, I do have a mandatory orange inflatable tied to my middle, so if I'm feeling particularly safe and nurtured here, perhaps Mother Nature doesn't deserve all the credit.

Wild swimming, as we call it in the UK, has been having a boom moment. In recent years, more people than ever are taking to the nation's lidos, rivers, lakes and seas. I'd wager that many people find, as I did, that wild swimming has something magical about it, that the water can be a place where time stands still. Its physical and mental health benefits speak for themselves: boosting the immune system, reducing inflammation, promoting restful sleep. Then there are the more intangible aspects. In a 2022 poll from the Outdoor Swimming Society, admittedly a self-selecting cohort, 94 per cent of its members reported that the main reason they swam outside was 'joy', while 55 per cent said they also swam for spiritual reasons including 'connection with nature and deeper self'.[1]

Lucy Sam, a transpersonal life coach, is the author of a 2020 research paper entitled 'Nature as Healer: A Phenomenological Study of the Experiences of Wild Swimmers in Kenwood Ladies' Pond on Hampstead Heath'.[2] In order to write it, she interviewed five open-water swimmers to find out what made the experience so restorative. All the participants reported that they felt connected to nature in the pond, and that the place itself was significant, describing it as having 'an aura of healing' or the potential to open a door to the unexpected.

'They wouldn't all have labelled it spiritual, but a lot of them said things like "it took me outside of myself",' Sam tells me.[3] 'There was this sense of merging with nature, and a sense of awe and wonder, for instance when a heron landed next to them. They also found it meditative – it brings you into the moment. If you take any meditation practice, that's the whole thing, isn't it? Trying to still the mind so that you can merge with something greater. I think swimming maybe helps you sink into that.'

Our spiritual relationship with nature goes back to the dawn of humanity. Many ancient religious practices around the world involved some element of nature worship, or at least the attribution of spirits to the non-human realm. In fact, they might not have drawn a sharp delineation between the human and non-human at all.

In Christian-era Western Europe, a conceptual hierarchy began to emerge that placed a divide between humans and animals. The seventeenth-century French philosopher René Descartes deepened the schism. He contended that humans should become 'masters and possessors of nature', that animals are merely '*automata*' without minds, and that the universe is something akin to a giant machine. It's easy to see how this reasoning, once entrenched in the modern urbanised psyche, led us away from a relationship with the natural world and towards exploitation, viewing it as a 'resource' ripe for the plundering.

There have always been those who objected to this way of thinking, not least the English and German Romantic poets and the American Transcendentalists. Ralph Waldo Emerson, in his 1836 essay *Nature*, argued that nature is an expression of the divine, and that 'the happiest man is he who learns from nature the lesson of worship'.[4] If you've ever read Emerson or Henry David Thoreau and fantasised about going off-grid to live in a cabin, you wouldn't be the first. But it's only recently that the overarching 'world = machine' narrative, which has exerted dominance since the Industrial Revolution and the colonial era, has come under serious scrutiny from multiple angles.

In recent decades, an array of scientists, scholars and storytellers have been reconsidering the ways in which humans relate to nature. Some natural scientists argue in favour of Gaia theory, which holds that the Earth is a 'self-regulating complex system' – not so much a dead rock teeming with life, as an organism in its own right. In psychology, you have the fertile field of ecopsychology, which studies the emotional bond between humans and Earth; while 'deep ecology' stresses that nature's value has nothing to do with its utility to humans. In philosophy, theorists like Timothy Morton argue against the idea that we are 'embedded in nature' – instead asserting that there is in fact no binary between nature and civilisation at all.[5]

It is not so much that people are returning en masse to nature worship; it's more that some are challenging the idea that humans are separate from nature in the first place. Even the most hard-nosed traditionalist would struggle to argue the opposite these days: you only need consider the fact that bacteria outnumber human cells in our bodies for any strict division to feel trite.

Summing up the overall trend, the writer Charles Eisenstein has argued that our 'myth of separation', 'which holds us as discrete and separate selves in an objective universe of force and mass, atoms and void', is on the way out. It is giving way to a 'story of interbeing', which 'proclaims our deep interdependency … [with] the rest of nature … [and] unites us across so many areas of activism and healing. The more we act from it, the better able we are to create a world that reflects it. The more we act from Separation, the more we helplessly create more of that, too.'[6] He thinks we are now in the 'space between stories', in which the flaws in the old tale have become apparent before the new one has fully taken its place.

Eisenstein's 'Story of Interbeing' chimes with philosophies like Buddhism. In fact, the word 'interbeing' was coined by the Buddhist teacher Thich Nhat Hanh, who wrote: 'There is a cloud floating in this sheet of paper. Without a cloud, there will be no rain; without rain, the trees cannot grow: and without trees, we cannot make paper. The cloud is essential for the paper to exist. If the cloud is not here, the sheet of paper cannot be here either. So we can say that the cloud and the paper inter-are.'[7]

It also chimes with what many of us intuitively sense. I'm not sure if Descartes ever went wild swimming, but it's hard to think of nature as mechanistic and separate to yourself when you're bobbing around in a lake surrounded by ducks.

Lucy Sam, who talks about non-duality and the ecological self in her paper, says nature has afforded her several experiences of being connected to something greater. It happened the first time she swam in the Ladies' Pond, as well as on an occasion in Northern Cyprus, looking out onto the mountains and the sea.

'I had just come out of my yoga practice, and it was like everything stood still, but also moved,' she says. 'There was this merging, like I was connected with the universe. It was brief, just for a moment, but I was like, "Wow, there's not something outside of us. We're part of it, it's part of us." I think that's what ignited this feeling in me.'

Wild swimming isn't the only nature-oriented practice to have gathered steam in recent years. Another is the Japanese practice of *shinrin-yoku*, forest bathing, which involves immersing yourself in the sensory aspects of the forest. A sceptic might scoff that being in the woods doesn't need any special branding. But *shinrin-yoku* is more explicitly mindful than that. According to Dr Qing Li, founder of the Japanese Society of Forest Medicine: 'The key to unlocking the power of the forest is in the five senses. Let nature enter through your ears, eyes, nose, mouth, hands and feet.'[8]

As well as being meditative, forest bathing is often thought to be somewhat curative. That is to say, its physical and mental health benefits exceed those of a regular meditation. In studies, *shinrin-yoku* has been associated with lower cortisol levels, lower blood pressure, lower inflammation, greater parasympathetic nervous system activity and better immune system function (in part due to volatile compounds called phytoncides released from trees).[9]

Our presumptive sceptic might argue that none of this needs to be spelled out; we've always known that being in nature makes us feel better. You could even say it's what we're wired for, that our indoor, urban lifestyles are a historical aberration that simply doesn't suit our Stone Age circuitry. On the other hand, that quantifiable aspect is crucial when it comes to convincing funding bodies. The practice has been incorporated into the Japanese public health programme, while in the UK it is being recommended as a 'social prescription' within the NHS. You might go to your doctor complaining about burnout or anxiety, or even arthritis, and leave with a referral for forest bathing.[10]

It's easy to over-romanticise the curative powers of nature. The world of alternative medicine is awash with outlandish claims, while people dealing with chronic illnesses might take umbrage against the idea of nature as panacea. That said, it's true to say that nature can be healing in both a general and specific sense.

In the general sense, we know that 'biophilia' – which Edward O. Wilson defined as 'the urge to affiliate with other forms of life' – is a core human drive. According to a 2007 report, written by the appropriately named Dr William Bird, biophilia is one of the main theories linking health to the natural environment. Another is Attention Restoration Theory, which holds that the natural environment helps us improve our powers of focus and concentration; while another is Psycho-Physiological Stress Recovery Theory, which explores how biological markers of stress drop when we're in nature. The latter, along with biophilia, is 'assumed to be a result of some deep genetic code'.[11]

In the more specific sense, plenty of herbs and botanicals have medicinal uses. Willow bark for pain relief and snowdrops for brain health sound like the stuff of old wives' tales, but the 'old wives' had a point: those are the sources of aspirin and the dementia drug galantamine respectively.[12]

While describing nature as 'healing' isn't quite the same as calling it spiritual, there is a reason why alternative medicine and naturopathy (or indeed activities like forest bathing) are often bracketed with alternative spiritualities. They are all, to use a simple word, 'holistic'; each part is considered in relation to a greater whole. They reject mechanistic approaches to understanding ourselves and the natural world.

What's more, for a small but fast-growing proportion of the population, the healing aspects of nature are foundational to their spiritual practice. Take Wiccans and witches, who are renowned for their uses of herbal medicine and nature-related rituals. According to the website Celtic Connection, Wiccans 'strive to gain knowledge of and use the natural remedies placed on this earth by the divine for our benefit', and 'all of nature's creatures' must be treated 'as aspects of the divine'.[13] It is difficult to generalise about witches, and that's quite deliberate; the Wiccan religion lacks a formal structure, and not every witch would even describe themselves as Wiccan. But you'll find many a 'green witch' laying herbs on her altar, or 'lunar witch' basing her magick on the cycles of the moon.

Paganism, meanwhile, is a related and overlapping movement with similar tenets. Modern pagans might assemble at stone circles, celebrate the turning of the seasons, attend full moon ceremonies, or partake in ceremonial magic. Whatever their specific practices, the common denominator is that they venerate nature and see all living things as interconnected.

It should be noted that neopaganism and Wicca are modern movements with a distinctly Eurocentric slant. They shouldn't be confused with Indigenous animist practices, which are deeply embedded in the cultures that birthed them. Still, these contemporary 'religions' seem to be resonating more as time goes by. In the 2021 UK census, 74,000 people defined themselves as pagan (up from 57,000 in 2011) and 13,000 as Wiccan.[14] At least a million Americans belong to religions like paganism and Wicca, according to some estimates,[15] with the numbers practising non-mainstream faiths expected to triple by 2050.[16]

These kinds of philosophies and practices may be striking a stronger chord right now because, if we're part of nature and nature is part of us, we're not in a very good way. As poet and writer Rebecca Tamás put it in her book *Strangers: Essays on the Human and Nonhuman* (2020): 'However many jungles and wetlands we destroy, the nonhuman will not "go away", because it exists in our very own guts and on our very own skin. But the harder it is to find and access, the more ill, damaged, maimed and suppressed it is, the fewer opportunities we will have to grow new and spacious kinds of thinking.'[17]

If you're reading this, I'm sure I don't need to convince you about the grim reality of the climate and ecological crises. For anyone watching the news in the 2020s, extreme weather events and mass species die-offs just don't seem extreme anymore. In March 2023, the Intergovernmental Panel on Climate Change (IPCC) delivered its 'final warning' on the climate crisis, arguing that drastic action will be needed to keep global warming below 1.5°C. The UN secretary-general, António Guterres, described the report as: 'a clarion call to massively fast-track climate efforts by every country and every sector and on every timeframe. In short, our world needs climate action on all fronts: everything, everywhere, all at once.'[18]

During my visit to the swimming lake – during any such idyll – it would have been easy to make believe that the grim realities of climate change weren't happening. Our depleted soil, polluted air and unbalanced ecosystems may not be obvious to a casual observer on a beautiful summer's day. But even in privileged Britain, we can no longer bank on being able to close our eyes and pretend it all away.

My previous visit to the lake had been during the heatwave of summer 2022. In London, the mercury climbed past 40°C, confining us to homes that were ill-equipped to handle the heat. Nick and I sellotaped newspaper to our kitchen window, which didn't have a blind, and relied on a meagre desk fan to help us sleep. Six months pregnant and anxious for relief, I took a dip in the lake. The water itself was nice, if disconcertingly lukewarm, but the parkland around it had been sucked dry by weeks of drought. As in London's other 'green' spaces, there was no green to be found, just the lifeless yellow of grass that had turned to hay. Grassfires swept the country. During the Tory leadership debate, Liz Truss and Rishi Sunak were asked: 'What three things should people change in their lives to help tackle climate change faster?', and our next two prime ministers breezily issued recycling tips.[19] It was plain to see: there was no political appetite for climate action even as Britain was parched and scorched and burned. 2022 was the UK's hottest year on record,[20] while the ten hottest years globally have all occurred since 2010.[21]

On the one hand, the groundswell of people who care about the climate crisis is starting to reach critical mass. In a 2022 poll, three-quarters of Brits said they were 'very' or 'somewhat' worried.[22] Activists have thrown soup at paintings, glued themselves to streets, participated in school strikes for the climate, and assembled in their droves at peaceful protests like Extinction Rebellion's 'The Big One'. On the other hand, the complacency of our leadership, the compulsive greenwashing of our corporations, and the cartoonish villainy of our fossil fuel giants can make all that momentum feel futile, like we're running headlong into a wall.

Sure, nature may be a source of spirituality to many of us, bringing us beautiful moments of transcendence even as the climate crisis deepens. We may see ourselves as deeply connected to nature, embracing our 'interbeing' and rejecting the idea of nature as commodity. As the inestimable poet Mary Oliver put it, 'the door to the woods is the door to the temple.'[23] But for as long as the powers that be persist in wrecking the planet, where can this spirituality take us? Must we vacillate between denial and despair or is there room for hope too?

Some nature-focused groups are attempting to confront the emotional and spiritual burden of the climate crisis head-on. Alana Hyde Bloom is an activist and nature connection guide. When we spoke, she was preparing to lead a Wild Woman Camp Out in Dartmoor; it was an opportunity 'to shake free from the shackles of society, to step into the unknown and the restorative power of the natural world'. The camp-out sounded dreamy, and I wished I could drop everything and go. Participants could expect wild swimming, sleeping on the earth, 'embodiment practices' inspired by her background in dance and physical theatre, and drumming under the light of the full moon.

'The practices that we do throughout this weekend are about slowing down and allowing ourselves to build our relationship with the natural world,' says Hyde Bloom.[24] 'But it's also about stewarding our ecological awakening.'

Passionate and eloquent, Hyde Bloom feels that nature spirituality is all well and good, but climate change is the elephant in the room. You can't really talk about the subject, she thinks, without talking about ecological breakdown or land access or migration, or who has access to nature and who doesn't. This means that while she supports the boom in practices like wild swimming and foraging, describing them as 'great avenues of nature connection', she believes we need to adopt a respectful and politically engaged approach.

'All those things deeply nourish me, but if they're done in a vacuum without care and respect for the natural world, then they're just benefitting the individual and perpetuating the same systems,' she says.

As one of the original Extinction Rebellion rebels, who was there in the early days of the movement , she is every inch the activist. But she is keen to distance herself from some of the rhetoric of the frontline fight. As she explained, a lot of climate activism runs on the assumption that humans are a scourge on the planet. If humans weren't here, the story goes, the planet would be fine, plunged back into a state of Edenic innocence.

For Hyde Bloom, that's a long way off the mark. Following the depth psychologist and wilderness guide Bill Plotkin, she believes that humans have a critical role to play within ecosystems, as much as any other plant or animal. The problem is that we've cast ourselves out of Eden where we belong – separated from the natural world and upended from our ecological niche.

'There's this perspective that we don't belong here, when actually my experience is quite the opposite,' she says. 'This is our home. We have a responsibility. I've had very visceral experiences of feeling belonging with the natural world, and that I always belong there, that my belonging isn't debatable.'

'The "scourge on the planet" sentiment is one I recognise. It's almost doctrinal in some circles to say that our unchecked consumption, our plundering of the world's resources, marks us out as a cancer that needs excising. And while this might be a useful way to frame the neoliberal growth fantasy, it's an incredibly misanthropic way of talking about actual humans. If you see yourself and everyone else as something akin to a cancer cell, that's only going to reinforce the separation mindset. Plus, I'd guess it's hard to enjoy being in nature if you feel like your very presence is a problem.'

'My very personal sense of belonging has given me a space of joy and love and deep resourcing,' says Hyde Bloom. 'If we're not deeply resourced doing this work, we burn out. We mimic the same thing that's happening to the planet in ourselves.'

She emphasised that nature spirituality can manifest in different ways for different people. It can be grounded in subjective experience or born from scientific fact. It can look a lot like ancient animism, in which every life form has a soul or self or essence. Or it can simply involve a shift away from a human-centric worldview.

'In an ecocentric worldview, it's not just about being in service to humans,' she said. 'It's about being in service to the more than human, and I feel like, until we can stop situating ourselves at the centre of the world, none of our activism is going to be as poignant or effective as it could be. We're missing the core thing, which is that we're human animals situated within a much larger community of beings. So, if we poison the rivers and poison our air and poison our food, then we die along with everything else.'

This was as vivid a description of 'interbeing' as you'll find. And it left me with another question: what did she make of the quote-unquote 'bad guys'? It's one thing to let ordinary people off the hook, but it's quite another to include the fossil fuel executives and corrupt politicians in your story of belonging and interconnectedness. How does she deal with the impulse towards anger and blame?

'I don't think there is any short answer in terms of how to find equanimity here,' she says. 'But I imagine that many of those people have never experienced a sense of belonging with the natural world, or a sense of awe and wonder. Could it be a mirror? Like, the pollution and the destruction that these people are enacting on the Earth, they are also enacting on themselves?'

From Hyde Bloom, I got the sense that nature spirituality and climate activism could be two sides of the same coin. What's more, either one without the other was incomplete. If you immersed yourself in nature, but failed to engage with the bigger picture, any sense of connection you found in those moments would only take you so far. And if you spent all your time gluing yourself to government buildings, but never replenished with a long walk in the woods, you risked burning out and perpetuating your despair.

This perspective chimes with the US-based environmentalist Erik Assadourian, who believes that the green movement loses its way when it doesn't leave space for softness. Borrowing from his background in religious studies, he suggests that activists have taken all the angry, Doomsday-fixated parts of a religion, and omitted the parts that bring people joy or meaning.

'The theologian and environmentalist Martin Palmer said: "Environmentalists have stolen fear, guilt and sin from religion, but they have left behind celebration, hope and redemption,"' quotes Assadourian.[25] 'When I heard that, it captured my frustration. The most successful organising in history is religious organising, and I don't think environmentalism has that same self-determination right now. I have long daydreamed about using those same principles to create a deeper way of being connected with the Earth and each other.'

Assadourian is the founder of the Gaian Way, a new religious philosophy – and an official church, for tax purposes. The movement was founded publicly in 2019 and has subsequently blossomed into a thriving community of Gaians. Building on Gaia theory and deep ecology, Assadourian's working definition of a Gaian is: 'A person who believes that Earth (Gaia) is a living being and the root of *our being*, and of which we are a part. Gaia has an inherent right to life above all else, and it is Gaians' duty to restore and protect Gaia from harm.' This statement of duty is a big part of what differentiates Gaianism from, say, paganism; Gaians explicitly acknowledge the 'permacrisis' we're facing and address it as part of their spiritual practice.

Currently, most of their meetups are virtual – a book discussion here, a group meditation there – but Assadourian wants to support community development in the form of local Gaian Guilds, 'and not just because we might be about to experience the [permanent] loss of the internet – technology is fragile,' he points out. There are three so far, in Honolulu, New Orleans and Connecticut, and he hopes there will eventually be many more.

'You have Indigenous philosophies that are rooted in place, and then you have globalised missionary religions,' he says. 'With the Gaian Way, we want to move towards a synthesis – we're both rooted and global. We're competing in that marketplace of other global religions that don't necessarily aim to connect us to the Earth.'

A long-time environmentalist, Assadourian spent seventeen years researching sustainability at the Worldwatch Institute. But he had also studied comparative religion at Dartmouth College and knew a lot about what it takes for movements to prosper. Unlike professional environmentalism, religions are suffused with community spirit. They have rituals. They have parables. They have a cosmology, they have ceremony, they have celebration, they have ethics.

Assadourian hadn't originally intended to start a new religion, remarking that that would be 'a true form of hubris', but his 'community of Earth-centred individuals' seemed that way inclined. Just as a Sikh believes that it is their role to serve God, so a Gaian believes it is their role to serve Gaia. Just as a Muslim fasts during Ramadan, so a Gaian fasts during the new and full moon. And just as a Christian looks towards a heavenly afterlife, so a Gaian sees human life as the briefest flash of consciousness before we return to the Earth.

'The Gaian Way is working hard to create its own parables and stories, prayers and rituals that are based in supporting people's connection with the Earth,' says Assadourian. 'There's daily meditation, monthly moon fasting, and following the Wheel of the Year. There is a real core philosophy now, which in these first years has solidified, with a community of practitioners.'

Central to these practices are ways of dealing with our climate grief. Assadourian points out that, on one hand, the kind of grief I'm talking about is a privilege: he and I are probably not among the people who stand to be worst hit by the climate crisis. But we may experience fear about what's coming, sadness for those suffering already, frustration and rage towards the ship captains who have seen the iceberg yet stubbornly refuse to change course.

'What the Gaian Way offers is, one: a way to serve Gaia and lessen that grief by taking good action,' he explains. 'Two: ways to sit with that grief through meditation. Three: a philosophy for rebuilding after collapse. If we don't create these kinds of ecocentric cultures and philosophies, the default winners will be the current fascist tendencies that offer [the illusion of] security in the face of fear and lack. So, we're striving for a post-collapse renaissance that celebrates the Earth.'

If there is any hope to be found, Assadourian situates it far in the future, towards that post-collapse rebuilding on better terms. This is in keeping with what the eco-philosopher Joanna Macy calls 'the Great Turning', a movement away from an industrial growth society towards a genuinely life-sustaining civilisation.* In the meantime, Assadourian endorses an 'active fatalism', in which you know things are bad, but you're not defeated, and keep working to mitigate the crisis however you can.

---

* Not to be confused with 'the Great Reset' beloved of conspiracy theorists.

'There's lot of knowledge that we want to preserve, even in the worst times: midwifery, basic medicine, permaculture,' he says. 'My hope for the future of the movement is that we can take that knowledge and keep it alive in this transition stage. Our local guilds won't just meet weekly for forest meditation, but will say, "Hey, how can we support each other and the broader community through tough times?"'

While the Gaian Way is supposed to be an antidote to environmental tub-thumping, it doesn't exactly sugarcoat the situation. Throughout my conversation with Assadourian, I found myself grappling with an impulse to say: 'Hey, it can't be that bad.' After all, when you're chatting about things like total civilisational collapse, preserving midwifery, and a gameplan for when the internet breaks, your brain goes into self-protection mode. It was tempting to paint him as a prophet of doom, before regrouping with a nice anaesthetising scroll through Twitter.

I don't think Assadourian would be too surprised to hear this. He talked at length about our penchant for 'hyper-amusement' and distraction; our tendency to cocoon ourselves in bubbles that get more hermetic by the day. As satirised in the film *Don't Look Up* (2021), climate change is just one more item in a rolling cycle of celebrity gossip and manufactured outrage. It's easy not to engage with the permacrisis at all, at least until it crashes down on top of you.

'Even 200 years ago, there were the same critiques people are making now, that people are disconnected from nature and more focused on celebrities and trends,' Assadourian says. 'Back then, the light pollution blinded us from the stars, and cities inoculated us from understanding where our food came from. Now we don't even walk without having our heads down, looking at our smartphones. It's a step-by-step process of drawing us back into Plato's cave, where we only see the shadows as reality.'

My own take on this is that, if we are hiding in the cave, it's not because we're innately superficial or trivial. It's because we're scared. The more we distance ourselves from thoughts like 'This ham sandwich used to be a piglet' or 'Plastic recycling isn't the solution to our plastics problem', or even 'My sunscreen might be disrupting the ecosystem of the swimming lake', the easier it is not to crumble. There's real strength required to size up the situation as it is without succumbing to evasion or blind optimism. I can see how some people might want to wash their hands of the whole thing, to the point that they avoid connecting with nature at all.

My sense, though, is that in distancing ourselves from the fear, we're also distancing ourselves from the joy. And at this point in history, the light and the shadow come as a package deal.

Every month, the UK-based spiritual network GreenSpirit runs an online climate cafe in which people can talk through their feelings about the climate crisis. You're encouraged to bring an object that represents the feelings you want to express: it might be a bowl because you're feeling hollow, a stick because you're feeling vitriolic, some dry leaves because you feel despairing and everything's dried up. (At various points during the research and writing of this chapter, I felt my own choice of object would not have been so pretty.)

'You'd [put] some of these elements in the middle of the circle, and then you'd have a chance to go round the circle and express those emotions,' explains GreenSpirit secretary Hilary Norton.[26] 'But then the circle continues, and you try to look at things through different eyes. And you try to find something that you can do yourself to build hope.'

This ritual, inspired by Joanna Macy's group training exercise, 'The Work That Reconnects', is a time-honoured means of coping with climate grief. You start with giving gratitude – for the morning's spectacular sunrise, for the bluebells carpeting the woodland – and then you move onto stage two, 'honouring our pain for the world'. After that comes 'seeing with new eyes', that is, acknowledging your oneness with nature; this is followed by 'going forth', taking some form of action. As well as being used to structure climate workshops, this sequence may also 'unfold naturally over the span of a project, over the course of a day, several times in one day, or even over a whole phase of one's life'.[27]

Soberingly, this ritual was devised in the 1970s, which means people have been dealing with feelings of this kind since long before the crisis reached boiling point. Many of GreenSpirit's members are old hands in the environmental movement, and talking to Norton as well as Ian Mowll, the co-ordinator, I felt myself to be in the presence of wise elders who had been through the cycle of hope and despair many times before.

'We're not interested in spiritual bypassing, or cotton-woolling the situation,' says Mowll. 'Ever since I joined GreenSpirit in the year 2000, we've been very strong on climate change. We're often ahead of the game in certain societal trends, and that's because we're interested in digging and delving and questioning and relating to the world as it is.'

While GreenSpirit's roots lie in Christian mysticism, today it welcomes members from many different faith backgrounds and none, united by their appreciation of nature. As Norton remarked, 'nature is the first book of God', the original source of spirituality pre-dating any religious texts. 'When I say "God", I mean the source; some people believe in God and some people call it something different,' she clarifies.

Mowll describes some of its members as 'panentheist': they believe in the divinity of nature, but they also believe in 'the mystery of that which is beyond'. Still, he adds that imposing dogma is not the point.

'What I love about green spirituality is that religions tend to have a guru or teacher or text or organisation that says, "this is what it is",' he says. 'But when I go into nature, there's no one telling me what these things are. It's natural, it's organic, it's alive. I can get into nature and revive my soul and I can come back into human activity restored.'

GreenSpirit is perhaps more loosely structured than the Gaian Way, as well as more mystically inclined. But those differences are technicalities; Assadourian and Mowll had recently spoken on the same panel, and they separately told me how much they admired the other. It goes to show that whether you're a strict scientific naturalist, a panentheist, a Wiccan or a pagan or something else, nature spirituality can be a foundational part of your life. And perhaps it's key to staying sane if you want to look at the climate emergency face-on.

It's important to note as well that both groups are big on community and ritual. The atheist churches we've explored often run out of steam because they have nothing specific to mesh their communities together, nothing to hang their rituals on. Nature-based spiritualities don't have that problem. Adherents have something major in common, which makes community formation much simpler. And a ritual framework is ready-made in the form of the Celtic 'Wheel of the Year'.

'We will always honour the solstices and the equinoxes, and those times give us opportunities to think about our own journey through life,' says Norton. 'For instance, in autumn when the trees are shedding their leaves, that might be a time when we consider what we need to let go of. And winter might give us a time for being quieter, the whole of nature dies down but there's so much going on under the surface.'

On 1 May, a few weeks before my sojourn in the swimming lake, I hopped on a GreenSpirit Zoom call to celebrate the pagan festival of Beltane. Halfway between the spring equinox and the summer solstice, Beltane marks the season of hope, the very start of summer. It is one of eight festivals on the 'Wheel of the Year', and it celebrates all the things we in the northern hemisphere associate with this time of year: planting, fertility, sex, light, renewal, aliveness, love.

The GreenSpirit celebration involved folk songs, poems, a meditation and slides of bluebell woods in their full regalia. Members wore wreaths in their hair and shared descriptions of what they were growing in their gardens. What made the celebration feel so wholesome, I decided, was not only its inherent niceness but also the fact that it was truly grounded in a sense of place. My pre-Christian ancestors weren't doing reiki or snorting rapé, but they might well have frolicked in the bluebells in honour of Beltane.

I don't know if I left the meeting feeling hopeful as such, but I did feel less alone, and much more anchored in a very lovely present moment. Fears for the future had their place, but that evening I was watching the Beltane video call while chopping vegetables and putting my baby to bed. A mild spring breeze blew through my kitchen window as the sky turned dusky pink.

'What are we hoping for?' muses Norton. 'I don't think we're hoping for humanity to suddenly see the error of its ways, but at least we can hope that we build resilience, or that we have some sort of spiritual connection with the situation so that we're inspired to do something different. I'd also say that it feels like there's this wonderful loving energy in the universe, and if I slow down and quiet myself, I can tap into that energy. For me, that's where we have hope.'

Personally, I go back and forth on the hope question. But like every other Romantically inclined person since the Industrial Revolution, I do think something is broken in our society's relationship with nature. Healing that disconnect strikes me as innately spiritual, and if earth-spiritualities are having a moment now, it isn't a moment too soon.

Chapter 11

Shamanism: Beyond the Veil

I'm lying down in a forest, resting on a bed of pine needles and gazing up towards the treetops. I hear birdsong, the rustle of animals playing, a summer's breeze whispering through the leaves. After a while, I decide to get up and take a walk. I reach a clearing, where I happen across an ancient oak tree. It's gnarly and majestic and probably a thousand years old.

'The trunk has a door on it. You pull the handle and go inside,' says Jane. 'Do you want to go up towards the branches or down into the roots, or do you want to stay in the trunk?'

'Up to the branches,' I say without a second thought.

Without further ado, I'm perched on the top branch of the tree, kicking my legs like a child. It's playful, it's joyful, and I feel incredibly safe – but there's something bittersweet in the mix too. The scenario morphs into a specific memory: I'm sitting in the treehouse in my childhood garden, reading a book as dusk descends. My late father built this treehouse. It has a solidity, a protective quality, that I hadn't realised I was missing so keenly.

'Follow the images wherever they lead,' says Jane and, silly though it sounds, they lead me up and away, out of the treehouse and onto a hot air balloon. I'm floating higher and leaving it all behind, basking in the blue expanse of sky. Soon I'm up in the stratosphere, and then in deep space, drifting aimlessly among the stars.

For a short time, I'm bathing in pure white light, when I feel something (perhaps the realisation that the session is ending soon) tugging me back down to Earth.

'Let's go back down together,' says Jane, and we descend back through the tree trunk, returning to the forest floor.

Of course, I'm not actually in a forest, still less in a treehouse in 1998 or in the white-hot centre of a star. Physically speaking, I'm on a massage table in the Healing Space in Hackney, where shamanic healer Jane Egginton is guiding me through a 'journey'. Evidently, though, a big part of me is somewhere else. I think this is the first time I've been able to tap into my imagination so vividly since childhood, at least minus any chemical aids.

Before I came here, I had some preconceptions about shamanic healings. I assumed the treatment would be highly ceremonial – a smudge of sage here, a ritual chanting there – and probably quite culturally appropriative. 'Your power animal is an eagle,' the shaman would say, shaking his rattle, and I'd sit there awkwardly and wonder how two white-skinned British people had come to be cosplaying as Native Americans.

Perhaps, in another setting, this is what would have transpired. But there is nothing here for the critic in me to latch on to. A yoga teacher and travel writer who is trained in Celtic shamanism, Jane is a warm and grounded presence. Whatever the ontology of shamanism, and however fantastical my 'journey', I never felt like we were altogether away with the fairies.

I'd arrived at the Healing Space feeling unsure where to start. Although Egginton knew I was planning on writing about my experience, we agreed that this treatment would be just for me, that any conceptual overlay I wanted to place on it would come later. I had spent the train journey there trying to formulate what it was that needed healing. On one level, my life was going really well. Compared to many of the people who visit Egginton – heck, compared to myself on a different day, month, year – I had nothing to complain about. I was writing a book *and* I had a baby *and* I had an amazing partner who went halves on the housework and childcare. Sure, I was exhausted from months of disrupted sleep and, sure, I was working hard in a way I'd never worked before. Sure, I could have pointed towards an inventory of identity, lifestyle and friendship disruptions wrought by the whirlwind of new motherhood. But cry me a river, right? If I was frazzled, that was just the price you paid for 'having it all'.

On another level, though, I was worried about what might come up on that massage table. Since my daughter had been born, seven months previously, I'd had limited time for introspection, and I wasn't sure I was processing my experiences in the way I should. I mean, take giving birth. That hadn't been much fun. Was I supposed to do something specific to make sense of it, or to get it out of my system? Or was it cool that life had just… carried on? Then there were the various, less pleasant parts of my psyche that had bubbled up at times of extreme sleep deprivation. All I'd managed was to take note of what arose (oh, hi there, baggage from my teenage years!) and park it to deal with at another time.

So, when Egginton asked me what needed addressing, I went with the obvious. I was tired. So tired that to fully acknowledge the tiredness would have meant sinking into it, crumpling up into a heap I couldn't come out of.

Egginton asked me to set a mantra for the session, a single word I'd like to embody, and I went with 'relaxed'. 'It's not "I *want to be* relaxed", it's "I *am* relaxed",' she emphasised, pointing out the power of words to shape our reality. I shut my eyes and she set to work, guiding me into something like a hypnotic state through a combination of breathwork and visualisation. I don't remember this part of the treatment very well, but I think she encouraged me to stop striving and to fall back into something bigger than myself. At one point she called on the spirit realm to help out. By the time the stuff with the tree and the hot air balloon began, I was exactly as my mantra would have had it.

'There is a lot of bullshit in the spiritual world – I call it smoke and feathers,' Egginton tells me after our session.[1] 'It's about the show. But this is not a kind of fashion for me. I'm dedicated to it because I can see the difference it makes to people. It's almost like frontline work.'

In the previous chapter, I touched on animism, the ancient idea that everything in nature has a living spiritual essence. Shamanic practitioners are animistic, but they don't stop there. They believe that a shaman can directly interact with this spirit world through entering an altered state of consciousness or trance. In some cultures, the shaman arrives in that trance after ingesting plant medicines like ayahuasca, while in others they use practices like ritual drumming to the same effect. Egginton, for her part, uses a combination of voice, somatics and intention.

As the British shamanic practitioner Eddy Elsey, author of *Let Healing Happen: A Shamanic Guide to Living an Authentic and Happy Life* (2024), describes it: 'Shamanism at its core is a possession-based spiritual practice. If there's no trance, if there's no possession, if the shaman isn't becoming possessed by a spirit, then it's not shamanism. It's a very complex, intricate, and hardcore version of spiritual practice.'[2]

During a trance, the shaman may get taken over by ancestor spirits or local nature spirits, or their soul may travel out towards the astral realm. They return to ordinary consciousness with new insights, which, in Indigenous cultures, are geared towards their local community. Perhaps they've found a way to make the rains come, perhaps they've sussed out the tribe's fishing prospects, perhaps they've found a lost animal or located the cause of someone's illness.

Traditionally speaking, this kind of work would have been considered as practical as can be, in keeping with the kind of life-and-death concerns you'd have had as a hunter-gatherer. There is nothing here about self-improvement, psycho-spiritual healing, or attaining some nebulous sense of connection with the universe. And yet what could be more 'spiritual' than... well, talking to spirits? Of all the spiritual practices covered in this book, shamanism is probably the most ancient, and the most widely dispersed.*

According to the anthropologist Michael Harner, whose book *The Way of the Shaman* (1980) is regarded as a classic in the field: 'Archaeological and ethnological evidence suggests that shamanic methods are at least twenty or thirty thousand years old.'[3] He adds that 'these shamanic methods are strikingly similar the world over, even for peoples whose cultures are quite different in other

---

* Meditation and dance are two other strong contenders.

respects, and who have been separated by oceans and continents for tens of thousands of years'.[4]

For instance, there are the Tungusic shamans of Siberia, from whose language the word shaman (originally *samaan* or *s'aman-the*,[5] meaning something like 'excited man'[6]) derives. There are the Hmong shamans of East and Southeast Asia, and the Jhakri of Nepal, as well as disparate tribal groups across Finland, Mongolia, Tuva, Tibet, Central Asia and the Arctic Circle. Pockets of shamanism have been found in Australasia and Africa. Many Amazonian tribes have shamanic traditions, as do parts of Central America; Harner conducted his own fieldwork among the Jivaro people of the Ecuadorian Andes and the Conibo people of Peru.

Harner, who died in 2018, believed there was a common essence to all these traditions. 'Shamanism is not New Age. It is Stone Age,' he said.[7] Starting in the 1980s, he developed something called Core Shamanism, which maintains that this shamanic essence can be stripped of its cultural specifics and harnessed by contemporary spiritual seekers. Modern shamanism owes a lot to this thinking. The Nepalese shaman Bhola Nath Banstola has described the shamanic path as a 'common human heritage', reasoning that 'we all "drank from the same fountain" in different realities and lifetimes'.[8]

Unfortunately, there may be a bit of overreach in labelling certain cultures shamanistic. Native North Americans, for instance, have never used such a term to describe their own traditional healers, and it's unclear whether their medicine people are subscribing to the same 'ism' as, say, a Japanese Shinto practitioner or a Viking seer. As scholars like Alice Beck Kehoe have noted, the big risk is that we romanticise Indigenous practices, viewing them as offshoots of some ancient Ur-religion rather than meeting them on their own terms.[9] We bump up against a well-known racist trope, that of the 'noble savage'. And it gets worse still when Western practitioners, not content with the supposed core essence of shamanism, throw together elements from Indigenous cultures like a kid let loose on a dressing-up box.

I realised what a loaded subject this was when I tried to book a place on a sweat lodge ceremony. I'd been told that a sweat lodge was a powerful shamanic ritual, which was considered particularly healing for new mums. I contacted the organiser, telling him I wanted to take part within the context of writing about shamanism, but that I'd also be tackling the cultural appropriation angle and would want to maintain some critical distance from the topic. He took offence at both the terms 'shamanism' and 'cultural appropriation' and refused to let me participate. This was upsetting (I wanted to sweat!) and no doubt his concerns had some validity, but I decided it wasn't worth arguing my case to someone who wouldn't accommodate a questioning approach.

Despite that particular organiser's disavowal of the term, there are plenty of sweat lodges out there that actively market themselves as shamanic. You can book a shamanic healing, attend a shamanic drumming circle, sign up for a shamanic workshop or training, or even follow a guided shamanic journey on YouTube. A 2020 article in the *Evening Standard* asked, 'Are you having a spiritual meltdown? Best shamans in London',[10] and in 2019 *GQ* ran an article called 'The Strange Boom in Shamanic Healing'.[11] Meanwhile, gossip sites have had a field day with Shaman Durek, a supposed sixth-generation shaman beloved of Gwyneth Paltrow, who is engaged to Princess Märtha Louise of Norway and charges up to $1,000 for a private session.[12]

Aside from the standalone stuff, you'll often find shamanic elements inserted into other types of New Age practice. During a pregnancy yoga teacher training, I was perplexed to find that every day opened with a shamanic meditation. We used a compass to find each of the four directions, and pivoted to face north, east, west and south in turn, as the teacher called in the accompanying spirit guides. It felt like an odd way to start a day of pregnancy-safe core exercises and lectures about pelvic health.

I'm not sure this would have flown even a decade ago. Following the 2021 census, it was reported that shamanism was the UK's fastest growing religion; 8,000 people had written 'shamanism' in that 'other' box, up from 650 in 2011.[13] That's still a tiny proportion of the population, but it's unlikely to be reflective of the true number engaging in shamanic practices. As Egginton pointed out, shamanism isn't a religion, so why would you claim to follow it on the census? Anecdotally, from frequenting wellness spaces, it seems that shamanism has become trendy lately, perhaps even more so than paganism, Druidry and Wicca.

'I've also trained in Druidry, which is interesting, because if you think about Druids, they've got a very poor branding, haven't they?' says Egginton. 'It doesn't feel as though we fully embrace our own Indigenous traditions, and it's curious [as to] why that is.'

I had chosen to work with Egginton specifically because of her focus on Celtic shamanism. Those two dirty words – cultural appropriation – had been playing on my mind, and I hoped I might be able to bypass this concern by opting for a Celtic healing. I mean, without going the whole 23andMe route, I was pretty sure I counted as Celtic: my dad was Scottish with a dash of Irish, while my Mum is Northern English with a dash of Welsh. It seemed an appealing prospect to immerse myself in a pre-Christian form of spirituality that was anchored in these very lands.

Of course, it's never quite that simple. I downloaded the *Free Guide to Shamanism* from *Sacred Hoop*, a UK-based magazine for shamanic practitioners, and within the first few pages, editor Nicholas Breeze Wood had poured cold water over my fantasy. 'You might feel drawn to follow an animistic path from your own ancestors,' he writes, '…but be aware, if you come from a European culture the traditions are broken, and paths such as Wicca or the Druids, are modern inventions, and bear little in common with their ancient ancestors.'[14]

If that's the case, then it speaks precisely to the kind of vacuum that inspired me to write this book in the first place. If you're a white European person, the main spiritual tradition you're going to be able to trace through time is Christianity. You want something 'authentic'? Something historically grounded? Something that echoes the wisdom of your ancestors and has buttressed your community for generations? Well, then, don't waste your time with the New Age grab bag: go to church!

But as we've already explored, for many people this just isn't an appealing route. From where I'm sitting – and I'd wager that many other 'nones' would broadly concur – Christianity is a relic of everything society needs to relinquish. I have plenty of respect for those who do follow this path because I know the beating heart of the religion has little to do with its surrounding power structures. Nevertheless, as an institution it is interwoven with patriarchy, colonialism, disproportionate power and toxic systems of hierarchy and oppression. If I'm looking for my own Indigenous spirituality, I'd prefer one that hadn't travelled around the world stamping out other people's Indigenous spiritualities; and if I'm looking for ancestral wisdom, then I'll steer clear of whichever ancestors were involved in stealing other people's lands.

As we've already seen, practices like paganism and Wicca can offer an appealing alternative for many people, especially women. Sure, they may be modern constructs (probably for the best, considering that the original Celtic religions involved human sacrifice), but that isn't to say they're inauthentic or appropriative. Egginton notes that the witch trials weren't all that long ago, relatively speaking. By reclaiming these nature-based spiritualities, modern practitioners are siding with the kinds of people who've historically been silenced and worse.

'Not only could you be tortured, but your whole family could be killed, for showing any kind of magic, wisdom, connection to nature,' says Egginton. 'People were killed for just being into herbs. We've been so cut off from our power, frightened by it, that we look to other countries. But then when someone says "Celtic shamanism", it's like a remembering. The practices are really simple, they don't need to feel otherworldly or inaccessible.'

She doesn't feel qualified to drill too far into what Celtic shamanism means. In fact, she isn't keen on the word 'shaman' as it applies to her, remarking that 'if you're a shamanic practitioner in Peru, that's very different from me doing my year-long training'. But she does think her offering is particularly well suited to our modern state of disconnection. If the European animistic traditions have been broken, work like hers aims to heal that breakage.

As she put it: 'It's about connecting to nature, connecting to the cycles of the seasons, being in gratitude, being in humility, connecting with others, being in a state of love.'

While Celtic shamanism was the variant that spoke to her, she doesn't see anything inherently wrong with Westerners going elsewhere for their trainings. She spoke very highly of her colleague Ursula Ruddy, who is Irish but trained in South America.

'If you strip it down and take away the circus, what separates a shaman from a Catholic priest?' she says. 'They're just labels really, and different practices, but it all comes down to the same thing. What's important is how it's done. It needs to be done in love and respect, and with consideration to the people and traditions involved, rather than just spiritual window shopping.'

One man who could not be accused of spiritual window shopping is Chris Odle, who undertook a gruelling six-year apprenticeship in Amazonian shamanism before setting up an ayahuasca centre in the jungle with his wife. We met Chris already; as you may remember, he was the British astrologer who pushed back against the idea of horoscopes as an empirically verifiable science. His stance intrigued me, not least because his communication style was surprisingly down-to-earth, even when the content of our discussion was not. He mentioned that he had a lot to say on shamanism too, so I decided to hear him out.

'New Age versions of shamanism are a melting pot of different techniques and beliefs; it can go well, or it can be a bit of a dog's breakfast depending on what someone's doing with it,' says Odle.[15] 'A lot of people want to train, but the real shamanic stuff is not glamorous at all, and it's got nothing at all to do with personal will. So as this stuff becomes more accessible, there's a risk of it becoming more superficial as well.'

Nothing at all to do with personal will? That struck me as worth unpacking. In contrast with Egginton, who spoke about her work as a vocation, Odle maintains he was practically dragged down the shamanic path kicking and screaming. It all started in 2001 when, at the age of forty, he began experiencing recurrent insomnia coupled with disturbing dreams.

'Because it persisted, I started to research what it might be,' he says. 'It fit under the umbrella of a so-called shamanic calling or sickness, where spirits are calling you through an illness or psychic breakdown. Classically in a shamanic sickness, the only way you can resolve the symptoms is to train as a shaman: if you don't accept the calling you don't get healed. That sounds nonsensical in our paradigms, but in some Indigenous societies it is still a recognised thing.'

True enough, through a typical Western filter, the signs of a 'shamanic sickness' sound a lot like the symptoms of psychosis. If you told the doctor about your unsettling dreams and rapidly escalating visions, you might well end up medicated. You certainly wouldn't be encouraged to follow your spirit visions where they led, nor to grant them a reality on a par with your everyday life.

But Odle followed the call all the way to Peru, where he drank ayahuasca for the first time and subsequently began his apprenticeship. This involved lengthy *dietas* (periods of isolation, with dietary restrictions) and hundreds of ayahuasca ceremonies, in a brutal ongoing 'purification' that he credits with transforming his life.

'Particularly in the West, the barrier between our normal psyche and the ontological "other" is very clear, whereas in native societies it's very porous,' he told me. 'Their creation myths often involve people turning into animals, turning back into spirits, et cetera. So, the shamanic calling starts to break down those walls, and in the training, you continue that process by opening the barriers to other kinds of energies, whether you want to call them spirits or parts of yourself. At the same time, you are building your internal strength so that the energies you take on for other people don't affect you.'

In *The Way of the Shaman*, Michael Harner talks about the distinction between Ordinary States of Consciousness (OSC) and Shamanic States of Consciousness (SSC). A shaman, he says, can move between the two at will, and sees them as equally real in their own way. '"Fantasy" can be said to be a term applied by a person in the OSC to what is experienced in the SSC. Conversely, a person in the SSC may perceive the experiences of the OSC to be illusory in SSC terms. Both are right, as viewed from their own particular states of consciousness,' writes Harner.[16]

This couldn't be further from typical Westernised modes of understanding, which hold that subscribing to an SSC is almost the definition of madness. We grant that some people are blessed with a vivid imagination, but pathologise those who take their own imaginings too seriously, or who see or hear things that the rest of us cannot. And we would never suggest that the route back to sanity, for a budding mad person, lies in becoming madder still;

we don't have much discourse around learning to integrate the madness or navigate the 'energies' we've let in.

However, that's not to say the Western world is entirely lacking in sympathetic frameworks. In Chapter 3, we briefly met Stanislav and Christina Grof, pioneers of the notion of the 'spiritual emergency'. In their book of the same name, they write that many of the conditions we medicate are actually 'difficult stages in a natural developmental process', which, if correctly understood and supported, 'can result in spontaneous healing of various emotional and psychomatic disorders, favorable personality changes, solutions to important problems in life, and evolution toward what some call "higher consciousness"'.[17] That's shamanic sickness to a tee – and it also chimes with the Western religious motif of 'the dark night of the soul'.

On a similar note, the maverick Scottish psychiatrist R.D. Laing, who described insanity as 'a perfectly rational response to an insane world', aimed to revolutionise the treatment of psychosis in part by borrowing elements of shamanism. His approach, which was foundational to the 1960s anti-psychiatry movement, has left a mixed legacy, with the therapeutic community he established eventually dissolving into chaos.[18] Nevertheless, for plenty of thoughtful Westerners, something in Laing's philosophy rings true: the conceptual division between madness and sanity isn't all that clear-cut.

'I think discernment is the key, because some people are having a spiritual emergence, while other people are having a psychotic episode and do need a Western medical approach,' says Odle. 'During my shamanic sickness, I could see it both ways – I could see it as spirits, I could see it as something within my mind. So I was reasonably grounded, and I think that helped.'

Odle and his wife ran their Amazonian retreat centre, La Medicina, as a not-for-profit until 2022 before selling it on to a friend. They treated Westerners who made the pilgrimage, as well as working with locals for free. Though shamanic techniques were helpful for all their visitors, there were clear differences between the two groups. The locals would turn up with physical ailments, along with culturally specific illnesses such as *susto*, in which the person's spirit is believed to be in shock. There was even an illness caused by wearing clothes that had been hung outside and permeated by a particular kind of mist. The Westerners, by contrast, would arrive with a deep-seated psychospiritual malaise that probably requires no further explanation. Sometimes the problem would be more specific; Odle worked with a charity to help veterans with PTSD.

Throughout our conversation, Odle switched readily between shamanic and Western terminology, like a bilingual person translating on the fly. When thinking about shamanic viewpoints, it's tempting to see those viewpoints as *opposed* to modern Western discourse, as though it were possible to definitively settle the question 'Spirits or mental constructs? Which is right?' Talking to Odle, though, I sensed it didn't have to be that way. Such framing even began to seem somewhat irrelevant and daft, akin to asking about the respective veracity of Spanish and German.

To give the example of trauma, a shaman might describe this malady as soul loss, that a fragment of the person's soul broke away and flew off into a different astral region. Meanwhile, a modern psychologist might talk about splitting or compartmentalisation, in which the memory of the traumatic experience is parked somewhere inaccessible in the mind.

'I mean, what is the difference?' says Odle. 'I think far too many Westerners are dismissive of Indigenous ways of looking at the world, and [that indicates] a lack of respect, because the scientific paradigm is just one paradigm and the Indigenous one is just as valid. In fact, in terms of where the world is now, it's probably more useful to humanity.'

That said, he doesn't think the two 'languages' overlap exactly; both contain their fair share of untranslatable concepts.

'If you were to send a spirit to someone's house and they saw it, I'm not so sure it's so easy to explain that with current paradigms of Western science,' he says. 'Similarly, if someone had an ayahuasca experience and had profound realisations within that space, and then the next morning started saying, "Well, actually, it's just neurons firing," I don't know if that's the best way to go about it.'

At the retreat centre, he took pains to emphasise the mystical viewpoint, not necessarily because it was 'right' and naturalistic worldviews were 'wrong', but because it helped his guests break down the mental rigidity they so often brought with them.

'It was a deliberate choice to say, "You can't rationalise this, and maybe because you're rationalising all the time, that's why you're so unhappy. Maybe you need to learn to experience a different part of your psyche,"' he says.

Egginton had a similar perspective. I had so many questions; after all, shamanism was such a big, meaty topic, and I wanted to get my head around it. What had occurred during my treatment? To what extent was it shamanic? What are we to make of those non-ordinary states of consciousness that shamans can access: are they pure fantasy, or something more confounding than that?

Without trampling my curiosity, she repeatedly pulled me back to the same argument: that as a culture we over-intellectualise everything. It doesn't make us happy; it keeps us in separation mode; it's often at the root of our poor mental health.

'There's a lot of "thought" and "thinking" involved in what you just said,' she remarked in response to one of my questions (the audio playback confirmed this was true). 'The head always gets in the way. I want to take people out of that control of the mind because it doesn't help them, and it can actually make them ill.'

I knew what she meant, and it certainly chimed with the way my own session had panned out. I left the treatment feeling restored, as though my brain had been defragged. As I skipped towards the London Overground, colours sparkled, the music in my headphones acquired a cinematic quality and I wanted nothing more than to dance. I wasn't sure what had shifted exactly, but I was much more relaxed and much less tired, and a deep sense of peace buoyed me through the rest of a frantic week.

If Egginton was right, then I'd experienced all those benefits precisely because my thinking mind had been paused, my disbelief suspended. Or maybe not even suspended. The feeling was more one of something having been sloughed off, like removing a piece of too-tight clothing, allowing me to stretch out and unfurl. It was a sense of being held by something bigger than me, something loving and safe that wanted the best for me.

It didn't take long before I found myself second-guessing that sentiment. A fear response kicked in, telling me it wasn't safe to fall back on such a childlike belief. But there on the massage table, it had felt real, and the guided visualisations only compounded this feeling. I had moved from the earthy, grounded image of a tree, up into the outer reaches of the cosmos. I finished the journey inside a star, dispersing into the 'star stuff' we're all made of.

As the Grofs have put it: 'Whatever specific symbolic form the shamanic journey takes, the common denominator is always the destruction of the old sense of identity and an experience of ecstatic connection with nature, with the cosmic order, and with the creative energy of the universe.'[19]

My dad was in my journey too, of course, which was a little on the nose for a practice that classically involves meeting ancestral spirits. He and I had had a complicated relationship, and I didn't often sink into that gentler element of grief that presents as sadness. While in the 'treehouse' though, my protective barrier slipped, and I felt his love for me and mine for him very keenly. At the very least, I accessed the part of my mind in which the positive aspects of our relationship have been imprinted.

I told Egginton that the treatment had been helpful, but I hadn't been able to place exactly why. She said that was par for the course. 'When I had a healing with one of my teachers, he said, "Something's been cleared, but you don't need to know what it is,"' she adds. 'We hold on to so much with our heads, we even hold on to trauma. But if it's gone, it's gone. By contrast, my experience of having psychotherapy was that I found myself repeating the same story over and over again. The energy was going around in my head, but it wasn't being cleared from my body.'

Her comments bring to mind Bessel van der Kolk's seminal book *The Body Keeps the Score: Brain, Mind, and Body in the Healing of Trauma* (2014), which is often credited as bringing a somatic understanding of trauma into the mainstream. These days, few people working in mental health are exclusively wedded to talk therapies; most prefer to take an integrative approach that acknowledges the importance of the body. At the very least, they might encourage you to take some deep breaths to regulate your nervous system, or to ground yourself by placing your feet firmly on the floor.

'The body keeps the score, but also the body knows,' says Egginton. 'When you're feeling relaxed, you're in tune with your body and can go into your gut instinct. You know whether you want to eat pizza or pasta, or whether you want to go to Bermuda or Birmingham. You just know, you don't overthink it. And it's like when you fall in love. You don't get a spreadsheet out and go, "What if we get divorced or what if he has an affair or I don't like his nose?" It's just a feeling, a bodily knowing. This is something we've become disconnected from.'

She adds that a lot of her clients are women in their thirties and forties, who are at the top of their game professionally and are dutifully working hard in all aspects of their life.

'They're also working really hard at their spirituality and their mental health and their wellbeing; it's exhausting,' she says. 'We tend to go more into our heads and try harder. But what we don't do is get support. We're like mobile phones that never plug ourselves in – we're trying to do more and more things without plugging into source.'

Alongside her work at the Healing Space, Egginton volunteers with a mental health charity, treating people with serious diagnoses. Looking beyond these diagnoses, what she typically sees is big-hearted people who've been kicked around by society.

'Mental health for all of us is dependent on so many factors, including the social element,' she says. 'We like to put people in these diagnostic boxes, and then in psychiatric units. I don't think most shamanic communities would do that – a lot of traditions honour the mad person as the shaman, because they're literally out of their mind.'

When I started researching this chapter, I hadn't expected to spend so much of it deliberating the benefits of somatic trauma therapy, or the ontological status of the spirit world. My understanding of shamanism was perfunctory, and I imagined I would spend much more time dwelling on the cultural sensitivities around the subject, for instance, whether it was ever OK for Westerners to call themselves shamans.

As I learnt more, though, I began to feel there were other, stickier questions at play, which handwringing about access might distract from. Of course, the cultural sensitivity aspect is important, and nobody would deny there are bad ways of going about it. If you're dancing round in a headdress, commercially exploiting plant medicines, or commodifying someone else's sacred rituals, it's hardly an ethical grey area.

But Chris Odle was clear that Indigenous healers do want to pass on their knowledge, so long as they feel they're being honoured and respected. Sushma Sagar, the reiki healer we met in Chapter 6, had said the same thing. She'd trained in shamanism under Alberto Villoldo, an anthropologist turned shaman who'd apparently been given the go-ahead to spread the Inca people's teachings.

'The Indigenous people that he worked with said to him, "The planet is in trouble,"' she told me. '"And, quite frankly, we need as many people as possible to be using these practices in harmony with the Earth, and we want you to help us do that." They worked with him to create a version of shamanic medicine that could be done in the West.'

If that's the case, we are forced to reckon with how Western societies might integrate shamanic perspectives. Presumably, we don't want to dismiss them out of hand, or chauvinistically treat them as relics of a pre-scientific age. Equally, it can be challenging for us to know where to begin with concepts like non-ordinary consciousness – the 'firsthand knowledge of a hidden universe' that Michael Harner spoke of. In some ways, it's easier to say, 'that's a practice and worldview that belongs elsewhere, and one we don't have rights to'. Doing so allows us to broadcast our cultural sensitivity while disengaging from what's actually going on.

After talking to Odle, and particularly after my healing with Egginton, I'm convinced it doesn't serve us to be dismissive. Egginton remarked that her clients may or may not subscribe to a shamanic understanding of the world. But they've likely experienced something more important, something like a sense of safety, or love, or grounding.

'I don't think that people have to have a connection to spirit to benefit from this. I don't think you did, the music journalist at Glastonbury didn't, the barrister didn't, the GP didn't,' says Egginton. 'But it's not mental, it's how you feel. If you take an aspirin, you don't need to know how it works. You just know that it does.'

That, of course, is a common thread among many of the practices in this book. As we have noted elsewhere, there are many possible ways of explaining how something like reiki or tarot or manifestation 'works'. But getting stuck in explanatory mode can be counterproductive. You may remember the message I took from my ayahuasca ceremony, that over-intellectualising spirituality can tend to diminish, rather than deepen, our understanding of the subject. To really grasp what people mean by 'spiritual', we need to move beyond mental constructs and dive into the realm of the experiential.

I suspect that for many secular Westerners, the easiest way to do so might be through body-focused practices. This could involve physical exercise, sensory 'forest bathing', meditative body scanning or even, as we shall see, going to raves. What's great about these practices is that they don't require you to believe in anything as the price of entry. Whether or not you have what Egginton calls a 'connection to spirit', they can help you tune in to something beyond the chatter of the mind.

Chapter 12
Raves: God Is a DJ

Throughout this book, we've seen that many of the practices making waves in contemporary spirituality are a rich mix of old and new. For sure, some of the claims to antiquity are tenuous; it simply isn't accurate to state that the Law of Attraction is as old as the pyramids, or to draw an unbroken line between your vinyasa sequence and the Bronze Age Indus Valley Civilisation. In these cases, I think calling something 'ancient' isn't dissimilar to calling it 'exotic'; superficially, your practice has more clout if you can trace it to a more 'spiritual' time and place.

That said, practices like meditation, nature worship, use of entheogenic substances, and endurance exercise have formed part of humans' devotional toolkit for thousands of years. And while the surrounding teachings are highly context dependent, the actual techniques do have cross-cultural appeal. They are spiritual 'technologies', for want of a better word, that reliably seem to evoke a sense of the divine.

I want to finish with one of the world's oldest and most celebratory practices: dance, which has been core to human societies since Palaeolithic times. As Barbara Ehrenreich argues in her book *Dancing in the Streets: A History of Collective Joy* (2007), dance has bonded groups together, provided an essential release valve, and connected people with the spiritual realm. She cites the statistic, from anthropologist Erika Bourguignon, that 92 per cent of small-scale societies partook in ecstatic group rituals like dancing, with a view to entering religious trance states.[1]*

Ehrenreich writes: 'Compared to the danced religions of the past, today's "faiths" are often pallid affairs ... dependent on, and requiring, belief as opposed to direct knowledge. The prehistoric ritual dancer ... did not *believe* in her god or gods; she *knew* them, because, at the height of group ecstasy, they filled her with their presence.'[2]

Perhaps needless to say, that's not how we tend to think of it today. When we're throwing shapes on the dancefloor, we're generally not all that amenable to being filled with the presence of the gods. And yet the basic premise hasn't changed. For many people in the rave community, along with those partaking in 'conscious movement' practices like Ecstatic Dance, the combination of music and dance remains an important touchpoint with something greater.

Whether you're practising Biodanza, pumping your arms at an illegal warehouse rave, or tearing up Burning Man, you may have fleetingly touched on the numinous. You may also have found solace, connection, emotional healing and a visceral reminder that you're alive. The nineties rave classic 'God Is a DJ' by Faithless makes this point better than I ever could.

It's a Saturday evening, and I'm in a school hall decked out with psychedelic wall hangings. My good friend Emma has come along with me for the ride. We slip our shoes off, fill our bottles with lemon water, and each stick on a pair of headphones designed to amplify the sound. Hovering in the outer reaches of the room, clutching our bags to our middles, we're definitely not part of the inner circle. 'You can leave your bags over there, it's a safe place here,' someone tells us, and we waver for a minute before relenting and placing our valuables out of sight.

---

* The figure comes from a survey of the ethnographic literature conducted in the sixties.

We're here for an 'Ecstatic Dance and Cacao Ceremony', organised by Ecstatic Dance London. Neither of us have attended an event like this before, and we're game but a little nervous. My immediate reference point is that classic *Peep Show* episode about Rainbow Rhythms – 'Now we flow into red, the colour of primal urges' – which doesn't really paint Ecstatic Dance in the best light.

Ahead of the dance, the DJ tells the assembled group that we have a choice: we can hold on to our London-induced 'fuck-off energy', or we can channel other, more open-hearted places (I think he mentions Bali). He isn't targeting me and Emma specifically, but he might as well be. He's speaking to people who have their walls up. People who innately mistrust each other and wield their tote bags like shields.

Emma is going through a rough patch at work, and normally we'd have sliced up the situation every which way over a bottle of wine. Tonight though, we barely have a chance to talk, and we won't be drinking that bottle of wine. According to the instructions we received before the event: 'When we dance without the chitchat, something alchemical can happen on the dancefloor. A unified field of being emerges and we feel both wild and free, contained within ourselves and connected to something much, much greater than our individual selves.' The lack of wine doesn't get much of a write-up – the guidelines simply say 'Drug-Free, Smoke-Free, Alcohol-Free Environment' – but I know that sobriety is foundational to the 'conscious clubbing' movement. Many of us elder millennials grew up thinking we had to be drunk to dance in public. Events like this are built on the radical premise that in fact that's not the case.

So, Emma and I find ourselves sitting in a large ring of people, all holding hands (it's very kumbaya) and 'setting our intention' for the evening as we sip our little cups of cacao. The cacao, which I guess serves as a proxy for the alcohol and drugs, is much tastier than a Jägerbomb, and with deep roots in Central and South American Indigenous cultures, it's ceremonial in a way a sambuca shot is not. It's also mildly psychoactive, courtesy of a compound called theobromine, which gives you a caffeine-like rush without the jitters; phenylethylamine, which prompts the body to release endorphins; and anandamide, which derives its name from the Sanskrit word for 'bliss'.[3]

The Spirituality Gap

I don't need anything stronger. The music, when it begins, has a beguiling effect: two hours of deep house, rising from gentle beginnings through to an emotional peak and down again. It probably helps that I love deep house. It's a musical style I experience almost synaesthetically, as an intricate build-up of textures, waves and shapes. Beside the DJ booth is a video projector, playing looping visuals of mountains and deserts, forests and waterfalls and streams.

Although there's a strict 'no spectating' policy, I can't help but note that the other participants look in the main like yoga teachers; dozens and dozens of yoga teachers. It's not just that they're young or youngish, with lean bodies and a Lululemon aesthetic; it's that they all seem overwhelmingly at home in their own skin. And you can't really miss that they're dancing beautifully, inhabiting the music with ease.

For my own part, I had worried that I'd be too self-conscious to let go. I'm reassured to find that I do lose myself in the music, and I stop worrying about the gaucheness of my moves. It's as though I'm being carried along on a current, and to do anything other than dance would be to swim against the tide.

Emma is enjoying herself too. We're not in Bali yet; we stay tightly pressed against the periphery of the room, and our body language makes it clear that we don't want to be approached. But we're dancing non-stop, and we're losing track of time. And though I'm not spectating on Emma (promise!), I clock that she too is surfing on whatever wave has filled the room.

She and I slip away shortly before the end, feeling... if not ecstatic, then certainly better than we did beforehand. We haven't sorted through her work situation, or any of the other issues we're hauling around with us. But we're replenished, recharged, better positioned to face whatever life throws at us next. Our load has been lightened. It's strange getting the tube home at 10pm on a Saturday without the slightest hint of bleariness. I'd say in all sincerity that I did go on a 'journey' over the past two hours, and that I did touch base with something spiritual.

To learn more about Ecstatic Dance, I speak to Alena Pashnova, a certified dance movement therapist and the founder of Ecstatic

Dance Online. 'Dance is a universal concept,' she tells me.[4] 'No matter where, as a human tribe we've been dancing for centuries and centuries. For me, ecstatic dance is about knowing that, even if we're dancing individually, we're part of this dancing tribe.'

To take just a few examples, the Ancient Greeks had a strong cult of Dionysus, god of both ecstasy and terror. The 'maenads', as the female followers of Dionysus were called, engaged in frenzied dances, culminating in a state called *enthousiasmos*, 'having the god within oneself'.[5] Sufi Islam famously has its whirling dervishes, whose characteristic spinning movements are intended as a form of meditation; while Haitian Vodou practitioners dance until the spirit takes hold.[6]

As Barbara Ehrenreich explores in her book, something tragic was lost in the move towards hierarchical, large-scale civilisation. She talks about the suppression of communal festivities, which began in Europe in the sixteenth century. What cropped up around the same time was an epidemic of depression, which persists to this day. She also charts how polite society became suspicious of movement in general, succumbing to a 'routine immobilization'[7] in which entertainment was passively consumed, sports watched rather than played, and sex construed in terms of static positions. When you went to the theatre, you were supposed to remain silent and still, honouring the newfound divide between audience and performers. If you danced at all, it was only in a formal, stylised context.

Meanwhile, European colonialists were running into other societies that didn't share their hang-ups. Ehrenreich writes: 'When the phenomenon of collective ecstasy entered the colonialist European mind, it was stained with feelings of hostility, contempt, and fear ... The essence of the Western mind, and particularly the Western male, upper-class mind, was its ability to resist the contagious rhythm of the drums, to wall itself up in a fortress of ego and rationality against the seductive wildness of the world.'[8]

The Western world doesn't come out of this story well; it says a lot that you *almost* end up pitying the colonialists. So many normative features of our society, in this reading, are the signs of a people in denial of their essential humanity. But Ehrenreich also explores how the 'wildness of the world' can't be held back indefinitely.

Starting in the 1960s, the forces that had been repressed found a way to resurface, with an explosion of new musical genres that 'reopened the possibility of ecstasy' and positively compelled you to dance. A dam burst, and despite repeated attempts to contain the energies unleashed, there was no going back. It's no accident that ecstatic dance and raves – along with white teenagers' embrace of rock and roll – took off around this time.

'Dance stopped being something that was just about performance,' says Pashnova. 'People started recognising their ownership, that they could dance without being a professional dancer.'

Ecstatic Dance is usually said to have started life in the 1970s, in the Esalen Institute in Big Sur, California. It's here that the American dancer Gabrielle Roth devised her 5Rhythms technique, which is now practised in many countries around the world. As she explained it: 'I have found a language of patterns I can trust to deliver us into universal truths, truths older than time. In the rhythm of the body, we can trace our holiness, roots that go all the way back to zero. States of being where all identities dissolve into an eternal flow of energy.'[9] Since then, several different flavours of 'conscious dance' have arisen, Ecstatic Dance and Biodanza among them, which follow a similar credo.

A parallel and related development was the rise of the rave. First used in the late 1950s to describe the 'wild bohemian parties' of London's beatnik set, 'rave' soon became a free-floating term to describe any kind of party.[10] It didn't acquire its present meaning until the 1980s, when new electronic music genres sprung from the house music scene in Chicago and the techno scene in Detroit. The most notable of these was the squelchy sounding acid house, which was subsequently exported to Ibiza and then to London. A subculture emerged, centring around these new musical forms in conjunction with a 'heart-opening' new drug: the catchily named Methylenedioxymethamphetamine, better known as Ecstasy or MDMA.

First in clubs, then in abandoned warehouses, and then in open fields, thousands of young people convened for what became known as 'the Second Summer of Love'. As the authorities cracked down on these events, and commercial interests came to the fore, the utopian nature of the early raves was impossible to preserve. But pockets of the original rave spirit have always remained, spilling out into warehouse parties, club nights, festivals and underground gatherings.[11]

'Rave has legs, it's long lasting, and some of the original rave communities continue to do this together,' says Robin Sylvan, a religious studies scholar and ceremonial leader, when we talk over Zoom.[12] 'Then [there are] the young people coming up. The late teens and early twenties are a time of life when people are seeking initiatic experiences, so I think it's always going to appeal to young people that way, and that's what fuels its creativity and forward momentum.'

Sylvan is a seasoned raver, whose 2005 book *Trance Formation* pays homage to the 'tremendous spiritual and religious power' of raves. As he writes: 'For thousands of ravers worldwide, raves are one of their primary sources of spirituality and the closest thing they have to a religion. This is a theme that has emerged repeatedly in my research, and one that ravers have articulated again and again in my interviews with them.'[13]

At sixty-five, Sylvan is still involved in the community, and when we speak, he describes himself as an 'elder', who can hopefully impart some wisdom to the new kids on the scene. In his view, there are three key aspects that contribute to the spiritual dimension of raves. The first is the raw experience, which for many people presents as a moment of insight on the dancefloor.

'It's when you're dancing, and then all of a sudden, you're like, "Oh wow, I understand what this is all about,"' he tells me. 'That's life-changing for a lot of people, and from talking to people I found that it was almost universal. It correlates with the classic religious experiences that you can find in traditional religions.'

The music is as important here as the dance. Rave music is characterised by looping sonic arrangements and repetitive beats, felt deeply in the body, which excite the autonomic nervous system and shake us out of our normal, workaday modes of consciousness. Sylvan's scholarship has drawn parallels between raves and West African possession dances, in which complex, polyrhythmic drumming is used to initiate trance states.

'In my first book, *Traces of the Spirit*, I talk about the idea that popular music retains traces of the possession religion complex, because it still has this strong rhythmic component,' he says. 'There's still some element of it inducing trance states, even though you're not necessarily aware that that's what's going on. Electronic dance music is an offshoot of that.'

Then there are the ceremonial or ritual aspects. Ecstatic Dance has its cacao ceremonies and closing rites, and while 'normal' raves might seem more anarchic, they follow a specific template too.

'You're generally showing up fairly late at night, so you're in this liminal space outside the bounds of normal social structures,' says Sylvan. 'You're out on the dance floor for a while, and then usually those peak experiences will happen at two, three, four in the morning after you've been dancing for a long time. You're not having those experiences by accident – there's a whole structure that's been set up to move you in that direction.'

Religions, of course, are packed with rituals. It's not simply that you have your one-off encounter with the divine and then get on with your life: you'll keep going to church, or the temple, or the possession dance, and something about the set up helps you replicate that mystical experience repeatedly. Sylvan tells me he has come to understand ceremony as a kind of spiritual technology, and one that can work on the dancefloor as much as at the altar.

The third similarity is an overarching system of meaning. In the 1990s, ravers commonly used the acronym PLUR (peace, love, unity, respect) to describe their ethos, while many ravers today belong to a psychedelic, 'consciousness-expanding' counterculture. Meanwhile, the 5Rhythms community describe themselves as 'beat-driven, service-oriented, heart-based individuals who come together to embrace our tribal longings'.[14] It's not quite Buddhism's Noble Eightfold Path, but it comes close.

'Ravers share a lifestyle and a value system, which provides a roadmap for how to live your life,' says Sylvan. 'The community thing is important too. Most religions are not solo efforts, and some of the [regular] events I was going to in 1997 are still happening now.'

Sylvan makes a persuasive case for raves as sacred spaces, a case that seems all but watertight when you read the testimonials in his book. One interviewee says: 'I had the pretty distinct feeling that I had been living a black-and-white existence my whole entire life up until that day and it was suddenly like Technicolor kicked in.'[15] Another asserts: 'I'd never felt such unity. And I'd been in situations where it should have been there, like in a religious setting. But that just felt like there were so many issues that just kept that from happening.'[16] It doesn't feel too much of a stretch to link these sorts of testimonials with the conversion experience, which the nineteenth-century philosopher William James described as 'the process, gradual or sudden, by which a self hitherto divided, and consciously wrong, inferior and unhappy, becomes unified and consciously right, superior and happy, in consequence of its firmer hold upon religious realities'.[17]

Of course, given the association between raves and mindless hedonism, the notion of the rave as a site of spiritual awakening can be divisive. As Sylvan puts it bluntly: 'There is a common trope about raves just being a bunch of kids who are getting fucked up on drugs.' Raves have had a bad rap since the early days of the M25 scene – the nadir being the introduction of the UK's Criminal Justice and Public Order Act in 1994 – and the classic image of a raver gurning away in his bucket hat does not automatically read as 'spiritual'. These attitudes were crystallised during the pandemic, when special rules applied to 'places of worship'. Unless I missed it, raves were not on that list, and I am not aware that anyone attempted to justify their illegal knees-up on religious grounds.

But as Sylvan points out, one of the interesting things about current spiritual expression is the way in which it bubbles out of, and bleeds into, secular spaces. You'll note this has been a recurring theme of this book.

'I don't think people set out to create religious experiences through raves,' he says. 'There's a commercial aspect and it's almost like spirituality emerges out of this thing that no one was expecting it to. But when you step back, it makes a lot of sense. The bottom line for me is that music is one of the most powerful tools we have for inducing religious experience.'

When I hear tales of the original rave scene, I often feel sad that I was born too late to participate in it. Rave culture, as filtered through other people's testimonies, sounds like the purest distillation of 'good vibes' imaginable. Even if you never had a transportive experience on the dancefloor, you probably cemented friendships and had a great time waving your glowsticks around. It's telling that, in among all the questionable iconography that has cropped up on the scene over the years – the Mayan glyphs, Egyptian symbols and Hindu deities – the image most people associate with raves is a simple smiley face.

On the other hand, I went to a fair share of clubs in my youth and never once had a spiritual experience. I danced (round my handbag, awkwardly), and there were plenty of good beats that might have done something trance-inducing to my brain. But despite taking advantage of many a 2-4-1 drink deal, I'm not sure I ever really enjoyed myself properly, let alone brushed shoulders with the sublime. This alone is enough to put me on the alert: are the supposedly ecstatic elements of these events maybe a bit too good to be true?

Take the drug Ecstasy itself, which is indelibly associated with the rave scene. Ecstasy is an empathogen: it increases feelings of social connection and makes you feel loved-up. It's also a stimulant, giving you the energy to dance all night, and a mild psychedelic to boot. In a clinical setting, MDMA-assisted psychotherapy is being used, apparently with great success, to help people with post-traumatic stress disorder (PTSD).[18]

My own take is that drug-induced spiritual or mystical experiences are no less 'valid' than any other type of spiritual or mystical experience; people like Sylvan have argued convincingly that the Ecstasy tab functions much like a religious sacrament. But Ecstasy used recreationally is notorious for its comedowns, the Blue Mondays that follow a euphoric Friday night (intriguingly, these comedowns don't seem to be a feature of clinical usage).[19] What goes up must come down, and if we want to talk about dazzling peaks of bliss and transcendence and mystical unity, we must also consider what happens when the music stops.

Another contentious question is whether raves are safe places for all attending. They have always been billed as welcoming, inclusive spaces that make room for people of all ages, genders, sexualities, races and creeds. But I can imagine that, for some participants, a dancefloor pounding with sweaty, handsy, loved-up strangers might not feel especially sacred. These spaces may also feel intimidating for those who aren't accustomed to the scene.

The issues of safety and power are at the forefront of Alena Pashnova's mind. I asked her about the crossover between ecstatic dance events and typical raves, expecting her to talk about some of the happier parallels. Instead, she said she'd prefer to keep the two separate.

'A rave is a space where there are a lot of power dynamics,' she says. 'Without any acknowledgement of this issue or any solution, that could be triggering for a lot of people and could prevent them from having a healing dance practice.' Her Ecstatic Dance Online events were born in part from a desire to keep people truly safe – not only are you physically distanced from the other participants, but with the option of connecting online while turning off your camera, you can maintain a feeling of dancing together without even being observed.

'[My events] attract a slightly different crowd. We have a wide age range, and some people with disabilities, for instance,' she says.

She talked about the typical image associated with ecstatic dance events: young, able-bodied, mostly white people, who move beautifully. This can smack of elitism, alienating those who don't fall into that bracket. By contrast, Alena's online events are genuinely inclusive. When I dialled into one of her dances on a Saturday night, I noticed that about half the participants had their cameras off, and it was a relief to be able to do so myself. I could make whichever swooping, extravagant, ridiculous moves I liked, without worrying about the performative nature of dancing on camera, or the state of my living room.

'In many [in-person] ecstatic dances, there is a group of people who will stay in the centre for the whole dance just dominating the space,' says Alena. 'There are also people who stay at the edges, and there may be a lot of different processes involved in that. That is something that we avoid, through being in the same space without an actual physical structure and without a centre. Those power dynamics are not in your face.'

Arguably, in an online event, a big part of what makes the dance 'spiritual' is missing – the sense of being swept up on the wave of collective energies, or of finding ego dissolution in the crowd. Writing in 1912, the sociologist Émile Durkheim expounded his notion of 'collective effervescence', the joy, synchrony and harmony that emerges when people come together for group rituals. For Durkheim, collective effervescence was what distinguished the sacred from the profane in tribal societies, and eventually gave rise to religions.[20] My suspicion is that collective effervescence might be a hard thing to replicate in digital spaces, even if other aspects of group dances, like the sense of community, stay intact.

However, I don't think those soaring moments of mass rapture are quite what Alena is going for. Her events are billed less as an online dance party and more as a personal healing odyssey. To this end, she picks the DJs who offer the most eclectic sets and will help people access the full spectrum of their emotions.

'For me, an Ecstatic Dance that is only ecstatic, in the sense of feeling amazing, is not enough,' she says. 'I want people to sometimes bring sadness or anger, this shadow side that we sometimes don't have space to work with. I understand it's easier to hit that ecstatic state and to connect on that level. But I want to invite people to go deeper and process darker things through dance.'

This strikes me as an important point, and an antidote to what some might see as a strain of shallowness within rave culture. Remember that Dionysus, god of ecstasy, was the god of terror, too. If we choose to dive into the 'seductive wildness of the world', which our hyper-rationalist forebears were so anxious to keep at bay, that will likely involve a lot more than good vibes and smiley faces and happy times. It will mean engaging with the darkness too, and bringing our whole selves to the party.

'We all define our spirituality in so many different ways, but I believe that the core values are the same,' says Alena. 'It's difficult to be alive, but at the same time it's amazing to be alive. And we all have different stories, but at the same time, the same story. We're born, we go through life, we enjoy it and we suffer, and at the end we will die.'

Forget the conceptual spin or the wacky terminology that might accrue around this scene; for Alena, what makes a dance event spiritual is simply that it jolts you into your humanness.

You're not some robot working their way down a to-do list. You're here, embodied, feeling, moving, alive – a strange and miraculous human animal.

Sylvan too brings it back to the body, describing how the spiritual dimension of raves is first and foremost an embodied spirituality.

'It's a corrective to Western civilisation taking a left turn away from the body into the head, which is just not a very sustainable direction in the long run,' he says. 'If you look at where we are now with the climate crisis, that paradigm is killing us. So, people are craving some way to break free of that and get into their body.'

In addition to the Ecstatic Dance event, I had originally intended to make it to a classic rave – until I realised that throwing myself around in a field until dawn was incompatible with early parenthood. While I was experiencing plenty of altered states in the small hours, they didn't involve dancing and drugs. Then it occurred to me that maybe I could go to a rave after all: a baby rave. Over the last few years, there has been a growing trend for these daytime parties for parents and young children. As one attendee put it, 'it is not clubbing for kids, it's clubbing with your kids'.[21] Gimmicky, sure, but it sounded a lot more up my street than Baby Sensory classes.

And so, the three of us headed up to Alexandra Palace on a sunny Saturday afternoon in May. By sheer coincidence, this was the date of Ally Pally's 150th birthday party, and the palace and park had a festival feel. At not quite seven months old, my daughter had slept through most of the journey, and I can only imagine how it must have felt to have closed her eyes at the London Bridge interchange and awoken in the midst of an actual rave.

I have to admit the term 'rave' comes with some caveats in this context. Nobody here, presumably, had taken Ecstasy; nobody appeared to be in a trance state; and there were rather more inflatables, balloons and play tents than you'd find in your average abandoned warehouse. In keeping with the organisers' slogan, '2-4 Hour Party People', proceedings ran between 1:30pm and 4pm.[22] The West Hall was overrun with small children. And then there were the parents: tired-looking thirty- and forty-somethings, hoping to get a reprieve from the *Frozen* soundtrack and the ninety-minute YouTube megamix of 'Baby Shark'.

I'll say it again, though: this was an actual rave. There was rainbow lighting, dayglo outfits and a DJ set from Irish electronic breakbeat duo Bicep. Most of all, it turns out that children are the most natural ravers you're ever likely to encounter (and not just because they're dribbly). You simply don't get four-year-old wallflowers, inhibited five-year-olds, three-year-olds who've forgotten how to move. Unless something has gone badly wrong in their lives, young children don't second-guess themselves or worry about how they appear to others. They're untainted by the cynicism and notional sophistication that can get in the way of a damn good time.

It occurred to me, not for the first time, that so many spiritual practices are really just attempts to get back to basics. In the course of writing this book, I've heard it time and again: such-and-such practice puts you back in touch with your intuition. It takes you out of your head. Reconnects you with your community and the wider world. Taking it up a level, it connects you with some kind of knowing that was there all along, which you've forgotten amid the noise of the thinking mind.

That last point is a contentious one. What does it mean to 'know' something that vanishes under the glare of rational analysis? When my sceptic filter is on, that sounds like frustrating nonsense, but I've definitely had moments (on the dancefloor, out in nature, midway through a mushroom trip) when I've 'got it'. A part of me was hoping that, through writing this book, I'd be able to translate that 'knowledge' into something specific that my inner sceptic could get on board with. Of course, that was a wild goose chase – the ineffable can't be rationalised, by definition – but I've certainly had some fun along the way.

As the rave wound down, hundreds of parents and children spilled out into the sunshine. Nick and I grabbed a cold beer and parked ourselves on the grass in front of a reggae band. Our daughter was wide-eyed, befitting her first live music set and the start of her very first summer on Earth.

Gazing out onto the city sprawl before us, I experienced an abrupt jolt in perspective. Right now, someone in this panorama was having the best day of their life, and someone was having the worst. Someone had just met their life partner, and someone was in the throes of a break-up. Someone was having their Road to Damascus moment as someone else was losing their religion. Someone was being born as someone was dying.

You may know the term 'sonder', which appeared in John Koenig's *The Dictionary of Obscure Sorrows* and promptly went viral: it means 'the realisation that each random passerby is living a life as vivid and complex as your own'.[23] Well, this was like sonder on steroids.

'We thought of life by analogy with a journey, with a pilgrimage, which had a serious purpose at the end,' wrote Alan Watts, everyone's favourite 'philosophical entertainer'. '...But we missed the point the whole way along. It was a musical thing and you were supposed to sing, or to dance, while the music was being played.'[24]

Epilogue

When I first dipped my toes in the waters of contemporary spirituality, I can't say I found them very inviting. It was 2015. I was doing my yoga teacher training course, which involved spending my weekends under a railway arch in Hackney Wick, learning about energy channels and astral bodies. Most of the other students were serious yoga types. A young woman in the group sent round a censorious email, reminding us that we shouldn't be drinking alcohol as it made us 'vibrate at a low frequency'. One of the men claimed to have had a kundalini awakening while in corpse pose. I loved moving my body and found that yoga calmed me down, but otherwise it was as though I'd set foot on a different planet.

Those were the weekends. During the week, I wrote articles about pharmaceutical development and medical tech, architectural innovations and robotic process automation. If I filed anything that wasn't rigorously fact-checked, I'd risk my ongoing relationship with that editor. As for my social life, I liked to hang out in dark pubs with my journalist mates, putting the world to rights while sinking pints of low-frequency vibrations.

To say I felt divided would be an understatement. I loved yoga, but I couldn't work out how to reconcile what I was learning with my Western philosophical leanings. 'I shouldn't be here,'

I thought, week upon week. I even messaged the course tutor, who seemed like a smart guy, letting him know I was struggling.

When I spoke to him in person, though, I sensed that he just didn't understand where I was coming from. He suggested I might not be that theoretically minded, and perhaps I would be better suited to karma, bhakti or raja yoga (a path of service, devotion or discipline) than jnana yoga (the path of intellect). This was a bit of a worry, given that my idea of service was running into traffic to avoid chuggers; my idea of devotion was forswearing God forever; and my idea of discipline was using gin as a mixer.

In a way, it would have been easier to have jacked it all in, to have written some snarky articles about the asininity of the wellness world and doubled down on my identity as a jaded journalist. The problem was, I didn't think it was entirely asinine. There *was* something in all this that spoke to me, even though I couldn't articulate what that was. Trying to make sense of the subject, melding the two halves of my identity, became my personal fixation.

Eight years later, it's still a fixation, not to mention a fun intellectual exercise. But it's become much more than that too. Trying to integrate a sense of the spiritual, and work out what that might mean for me, has been part and parcel of my personal healing. (Past me would have hated the term 'healing', finding it vacant and soppy and mawkish and over-earnest, but she was headed in that direction regardless.)

As anyone who knew me in my youth will testify, I wasn't the world's most sorted person. I lived very much in my head. I was terrified of my feelings. Before I started yoga and running, I felt ostracised from my own body. Without going into all the ways that manifested, I had some serious 'work' to do. I refused to go to therapy because it sounded too woolly and nebulous. That reluctance to engage with one's softer side is often coded as being a male problem, but I guess it can affect a certain kind of woman too.

Then, I discovered a version of spirituality that was first and foremost about connection. I came to see myself as more than some disembodied Cartesian ego, and I started to respect my intuitions as well as my intellect. I started to move towards things that felt right even when, rationally speaking, I couldn't explain why or how. To this day, I feel out of place in many New Age spaces.

Epilogue

But I no longer feel as though I'm trying to bridge an uncrossable divide. In this book I have argued that there's a huge amount of crossover between spirituality and mental health – this conviction is born from personal experience.

For overthinkers like me, a lot of our spiritual practice necessarily involves suspending our need for control and certainty. Calming the thinking mind, and seeing what rises in its place, has been a common denominator in all the practices I've really chimed with.

However, I don't think my former self was misguided in her focus on critical thinking. Many New Age enclaves stand to alienate people, at best, precisely because they don't apply enough of it. In a field overrun with charlatans, it's important to keep your wits about you, and it's just as important to interrogate where these practices come from. Robin Sylvan wrote in 2005 about the 'hybrid, cut-and-paste nature of contemporary spirituality and religion'.[1] Too often, that means cutting and pasting elements that only make sense when embedded in their cultural context.

Many of us in the West are discovering some very old spiritual practices anew. When we partake in Earth-centred or shamanic spiritualities, take psychedelic substances, or use our bodies to enter altered states of consciousness, we're tapping into a core part of our human heritage. There are pressing reasons to do so. Remember that Rina Deshpande said of yoga: 'There's a generosity of heart there; it is intended to be shared and is helpful to many.' Kerry Moran said of ayahuasca: 'Many people believe that one of the reasons this plant is exploding all over the world is that it's bringing us in so that we wake up before it's too late.' Sushma Sagar said of shamanism: 'The Indigenous people that [Alberto Villoldo] worked with said to him, "The planet is in trouble … we need as many people as possible to be using these practices in harmony with the Earth."'

However, unlike the cultures that are already steeped in these practices, we often lack the tools for making sense of them. We may resort to borrowing those tools from elsewhere, which is fine if the belief systems in question are properly understood and integrated, but not so great if you're just spouting catchphrases or adding a mystical gloss for marketing purposes.

Epilogue

In other cases, we might choose to stick rigidly within our existing frameworks – the rationalist, physicalist paradigms that have dominated the West since the Enlightenment. There's nothing wrong with trying to understand spiritual concepts in scientific terms. But it can lead to an obsession with the quantifiable, and a refusal to acknowledge the value of a practice unless it's framed in terms of 'benefits'. Typically, the locus of these benefits is the individual capitalist actor, as opposed to wider society or the planet itself.

More broadly, I think entrenching a divide between the 'spiritual' and 'scientific' doesn't serve anyone. If spirituality is understood as the province of less scientific cultures, times and people, it's extremely othering. It fosters an image of these people as living in a sort of non-rational, uber-mystical Edenic innocence. But it's not great for secular Westerners either, who in this view have no authentic spirituality of their own and must forever be confined to a worldview that's blanched of any sense of the sacred.

The good news is that this dichotomy is breaking down, if it ever truly existed in the first place. Plenty of secular people are now starting to take this subject seriously, and are seeking spiritual sustenance outside the confines of organised religion. I am convinced that this shift in perspective holds some urgency, not merely on the level of personal healing, but on the level of societal and planetary healing too.

If mainstream Western society were a person, it might be a bit like me in my twenties – stuck in its 'head' (its dominant structures) while fearing and denying its 'body' (the societal 'other' and nature itself). It is also wildly self-destructive, whipping up exactly the kind of crises that will take it to breaking point and force it to start over with something new. If I sound grandiose here, I've gone off-course – this book was never intended as a treatise on humanity. But I have come to feel that bridging the spirituality gap, whichever way we can, will be key to how we evolve as a collective.

What will that look like? Well, it isn't about finding the one true path, and it isn't about prescribing a certain set of beliefs. I have long thought that arguing about spiritual beliefs is a bit like arguing about the duck/rabbit illusion – you see a rabbit, I see a duck, and it doesn't make sense to defend our positions too fiercely. Or to use a different animal-centred analogy, there's

Epilogue

the Indian parable of the blind men and the elephant. One man touches the elephant's trunk, and says, 'This elephant is like a snake'; another touches its ear and says, 'This elephant is like a fan.' The others touch its leg, side, tail and tusk, and describe the elephant as resembling a tree-trunk, a wall, a rope and a spear respectively. They come to blows, until a sighted man comes along and points out that none of them have the full picture. The filters you apply to your experience will be different from mine, as will the choice of wording that most resonates.

Personally, I don't know what a more 'evolved' secular spirituality might look like. But I'm pretty sure it won't be walled up within the self-focused, exclusionary world of wellness. I hope it will move towards something with a much stronger collective element, in which relationships with other humans and the nonhuman start to take centre stage. On a similar note, I hope we'll see a stronger bridge between spirituality and activism. Timothy Leary's counterculture-era slogan 'Turn on, tune in, drop out' might have worked for the 1960s, but it hardly seems appropriate for the 2020s and beyond, in which 'dropping out' feels like an abnegation of responsibility.

Above all, I think Western spirituality needs to acknowledge its own limitations. As we've seen in this book, there are many options available to us: maybe you swear by darkness retreats, or holotropic breathwork, or casting spells by the light of the full moon. But what we lack are well-trodden paths. In the absence of ancestral wisdom, time-honoured rituals, or even an agreed definition of the word 'spirituality', secular Westerners are almost having to start from scratch, meeting ourselves where we are with a necessary measure of humility.

And perhaps somewhere in that process lies our key to going deeper. The Buddhists talk about a 'beginner's mind': an attitude of open-mindedness and eagerness to learn that is often missing in experts. It's a state exemplified by The Fool in the tarot deck, who is forever starting afresh, taking a leap of faith into a great unknown. It isn't all rosy for The Fool – as we've seen, in the Rider–Waite deck he's about to step merrily off a cliff. But he's charging forward irrespective, full of possibility, with untold adventures lying in store.

Notes

Introduction

1 Kastrup, Bernardo, *Why Materialism Is Baloney: How True Skeptics Know There Is No Death and Fathom Answers to Life, the Universe, and Everything* (Iff Books, 2014), p. 203, Kindle edition.
2 Foster Wallace, David, 'This is Water', https://fs.blog/david-foster-wallace-this-is-water/.
3 Whiting, Kate, 'This is why polycrisis is a useful way of looking at the world right now', *World Economic Forum* (7 March 2023), https://www.weforum.org/agenda/2023/03/polycrisis-adam-tooze-historian-explains/.
4 Gibran, Kahlil, 'On Children', from *The Prophet* (Knopf, 1923).
5 Asadu, Chinedu, 'An Atheist in Northern Nigeria Was Arrested. Then the Attacks Against the Others Worsened', *Associated Press* (5 October 2023), https://projects.apnews.com/features/2023/the-nones/the-nones-nigeria.html.
6 Dias, Elizabeth and Graham, Ruth, 'The Growing Religious Fervor in the American Right: "This Is a Jesus Movement"', *New York Times* (6 April 2022), https://www.nytimes.com/2022/04/06/us/christian-right-wing-politics.html.
7 Pomeroy, Ross, 'A Surprising Explanation for the Global Decline of Religion', *Big Think* (29 August 2023), https://bigthink.com/the-present/a-surprising-explanation-for-the-global-decline-of-religion/.
8 'Religion, England and Wales: Census 2021', Office for National Statistics (29 November 2022), https://www.ons.gov.uk/peoplepopulationandcommunity/culturalidentity/religion/bulletins/religionenglandandwales/census2021.
9 'Religious "Nones" in America: Who They Are and What They Believe', Pew Research Center (24 January 2024), https://www.pewresearch.org/religion/2024/01/24/religious-nones-in-america-who-they-are-and-what-they-believe/.

10 See the Conspirituality podcast for examples, https://www.conspirituality.net/.
11 Feynman, Richard, 'The Pleasure of Finding Things Out' (1981), https://vimeo.com/340695809.
12 Yaden, David B., and Griffiths, Roland R., 'The Subjective Effects of Psychedelics Are Necessary for Their Enduring Therapeutic Effects', *ACS Pharmacology & Translational Science* 4(2) (2020), https://pubs.acs.org/doi/10.1021/acsptsci.0c00194.

Chapter 1
Ayahuasca: To Narnia and Back

1 Hay, Mark, 'The Colonization of the Ayahuasca Experience', *JSTOR Daily* (4 November 2020), https://daily.jstor.org/the-colonization-of-the-ayahuasca-experience/.
2 '1648–1768 – The First Written Reports of Ayahuasca Made by Jesuit Missionaries', *Ayahuasca Timeline*, https://ayahuasca-timeline.kahpi.net/ayahuasca-first-reports-jesuit-missionaries/.
3 '1851–1873 – English Botanist Richard Spruce Encounters Ayahuasca Use Among Indigenous Groups', *Ayahuasca Timeline*, https://ayahuasca-timeline.kahpi.net/richard-spruce-ayahuasca-amazon/.
4 Burroughs, William S., *Junky: The Definitive Text of 'Junk'* (Penguin Modern Classics, 2012), p. 127, Kindle edition.
5 Hicks, Bill, *Sane Man* (1989).
6 Watts, Alan, 'Psychedelics and Religious Experience', *California Law Review* 56(1) (1968), https://www.jstor.org/stable/3479497.
7 Millar, Abi, 'Trips and Traps: Psychedelics Seek Legitimacy in the World of Modern Medicine', *Volteface* (26 August 2020), https://volteface.me/feature/trips-and-traps/.
8 Taub, Benjamin, 'Do Our Brains Produce DMT, And If So, Why?', Beckley Foundation (5 July 2017), https://www.beckleyfoundation.org/2017/07/05/do-our-brains-produce-dmt-and-if-so-why/.
9 Pollan, Michael, *How to Change Your Mind: The New Science of Psychedelics* (Allen Lane, 2018), p. 328.
10 Interview with Dr James Cooke, conducted by author over Zoom, 2 December 2020.
11 Illing, Sean, 'The Extraordinary Therapeutic Potential of Psychedelic Drugs, Explained', *Vox* (8 March 2019), https://www.vox.com/science-and-health/2019/1/10/18007558/denver-psilocybin-psychedelic-mushrooms-ayahuasca-depression-mental-health.
12 Hartogsohn, Ido, 'The Meaning-Enhancing Properties of Psychedelics and Their Mediator Role in Psychedelic Therapy, Spirituality, and Creativity', *Frontiers in Neuroscience* 12 (2018), https://www.ncbi.nlm.nih.gov/pmc/articles/PMC5845636/.
13 Grob, C.S., Danforth, A.L., Chopra, G.S., Hagerty, M., McKay, C.R., Halberstadt, A.L. and Greer, G.R., 'Pilot Study of Psilocybin Treatment for

Anxiety in Patients with Advanced-Stage Cancer', *Archives of General Psychiatry* 68(1) (2011), https://pubmed.ncbi.nlm.nih.gov/20819978/
14 Nagel, Thomas, 'What Is It Like to Be a Bat?', *Philosophical Review* 83(4) (1974), https://www.sas.upenn.edu/~cavitch/pdf-library/Nagel_Bat.pdf.
15 Interview with Kerry Moran, conducted by author over Zoom, 8 February 2021.
16 Adams, Tim, 'Simon Amstell: "It's Difficult to Retain Depression If You're Jumping Around Every Morning"', *Guardian* (20 March 2022), https://www.theguardian.com/culture/2022/mar/20/simon-amstell-its-difficult-to-retain-depression-if-youre-jumping-around-every-morning.
17 Bradbrook, Gail, 'How Psychedelics Helped to Shape Extinction Rebellion', *Emerge* (25 March 2019), https://www.whatisemerging.com/opinions/psychedelics-and-social-change.
18 Beiner, Alexander, *The Bigger Picture: How Psychedelics Can Help Us Make Sense of the World* (Hay House UK, 2023), p. 73, Kindle edition.
19 Irvine, A., Luke, D., Harrild, F., Gandy, S. and Watts, R., 'Transpersonal Ecodelia: Surveying Psychedelically Induced Biophilia', *Psychoactives*, 2(2) (2023), https://www.mdpi.com/2813-1851/2/2/12.
20 Campbell, Joseph, *Myths to Live By*, (Stillpoint Digital Press, 2011), p. 269, Kindle edition.
21 Timmermann, C., Kettner, H., Letheby, C., Roseman, L., Rosas, F.E. and Carhart-Harris, R.L., 'Psychedelics Alter Metaphysical Beliefs', *Scientific Reports* 11 (2021), https://www.nature.com/articles/s41598-021-01209-2.
22 Davis, A.K., Clifton, J.M., Weaver, E.G., Hurwitz, E.S., Johnson, M.W. and Griffiths, R.R., 'Survey of Entity Encounter Experiences Occasioned by Inhaled *N,N*-Dimethyltryptamine: Phenomenology, Interpretation, and Enduring Effects', *Journal of Psychopharmacology* 34(9) (2020), https://journals.sagepub.com/doi/full/10.1177/0269881120916143.

Chapter 2
Yoga: Practice, Practice and All Is Coming

1 'Yoga Statistics', *Finder*, https://www.finder.com/uk/yoga-statistics.
2 Interview with Shreena Gandhi, conducted by author over Zoom, 20 December 2022.
3 Gandhi, Shreena and Wolff, Lillie, 'Yoga and the Roots of Cultural Appropriation', *Trauma Sensitive Yoga Nederland* (23 April 2021), https://www.traumasensitiveyoganederland.com/yoga-and-the-roots-of-cultural-appropriation/.
4 Foote, Andrew, 'Yoga Class Cancelled at University of Ottawa Over "Cultural Issues"', *CBC News* (22 November 2015), https://www.cbc.ca/news/canada/ottawa/university-ottawa-yoga-cultural-sensitivity-1.3330441.
5 Fenton, Siobhan, 'Russian Officials Ban Yoga Because it's Too Much Like a Religious Cult', *Independent* (30 June 2015), https://www.independent.co.uk/news/world/europe/russia-bans-yoga-as-part-of-crackdown-on-religious-cults-10355676.html.

Notes

6 Agency, 'Church Accused of Lacking Flexibility After it Bans Yoga Class for Being Too "Spiritual"', *Daily Telegraph* (9 February 2015), https://www.telegraph.co.uk/news/religion/11400824/Church-accused-of-lacking-flexibility-after-it-bans-yoga-class-for-being-too-spiritual.html.

7 Burgin, Timothy, 'History of Yoga', *Yoga Basics* (26 November 2007), https://www.yogabasics.com/learn/history-of-yoga.

8 Bryant, Kathleen, 'Yoga Sutra 1.2: Yogas Chitta Vritti Nirodha', *Yoga Basics* (17 October 2022), https://www.yogabasics.com/connect/yoga-sutra-1-2/.

9 Burgin, Timothy, 'The Hatha Yoga Pradipika', *Yoga Basics* (8 September 2020), https://www.yogabasics.com/learn/hatha-yoga-pradipika/.

10 Deslippe, Philip, 'Yoga Landed in the U.S. Way Earlier Than You'd Think – And Fitness Was Not the Point', *History* (20 June 2019), https://www.history.com/news/yoga-vivekananda-america.

11 Pagés Ruiz, Fernando, 'Krishnamacharya's Legacy: Modern Yoga's Inventor', *Yoga Journal* (2 September 2021), https://www.yogajournal.com/yoga-101/history-of-yoga/krishnamacharya-s-legacy/.

12 Smith, Laura, '41 Yoga Statistics: How Many People Practice Yoga?' *The Good Body* (26 September 2023), https://www.thegoodbody.com/yoga-statistics/.

13 Parikh, Jesal and Patel, Tejal, 'White Women Killed Yoga', *Yoga Is Dead* podcast (8 June 2019), https://www.yogaisdeadpodcast.com/episodes/2019/6/5/ep-1-white-women-killed-yoga.

14 Gilani, Nadia, 'Why I'm No Longer Talking to White People About Yoga', *Huffpost* (26 January 2020), https://www.huffingtonpost.co.uk/entry/yoga-whiteness_uk_5e2b2f07c5b67d8874b146fa.

15 Grouard, Salomé, 'How the West Ruined Yoga by Making it "the New Sexy" and India an "Exotic Playground"', *SCMP* (4 December 2022), https://www.scmp.com/week-asia/lifestyle-culture/article/3201818/how-west-ruined-yoga-making-it-new-sexy-and-india-exotic-playground.

16 Interview with Rina Deshpande, conducted by author over Zoom, 6 January 2023.

17 Deshpande, Rina, 'Want to Get Yoga's Life-Changing Benefits? The Key Is Not What You Expect', *Yoga Journal* (9 November 2022), https://www.yogajournal.com/yoga-101/philosophy/want-to-get-yogas-life-changing-benefits-the-key-is-not-what-you-expect/.

18 Tracy, Brian L. and Hart, Cady E.F., 'Bikram Yoga Training and Physical Fitness in Healthy Young Adults', *Journal of Strength and Conditioning Research* 27(3) (2013), https://doi.org/10.1519/JSC.0b013e31825c340f.

19 Tilbrook, Helen E. et al., 'Yoga for Chronic Low Back Pain', *Annals of Internal Medicine* 155(9) (2011), https://doi.org/10.7326/0003-4819-155-9-201111010-00003.

20 Gothe, Neha P., Khan, Imadh, Hayes, Jessica, Erlenbach, Emily and Damoiseaux, Jessica S., 'Yoga Effects on Brain Health: A Systematic Review of the Current literature', *Brain Plasticity* 5(1) (2019), https://doi.org/10.3233/BPL-190084.

21 Isath, Ameesh et al., 'The Effect of Yoga on Cardiovascular Disease Risk Factors: A Meta-Analysis', *Current Problems in Cardiolog* 48(5) (2023), https://doi.org/10.1016/j.cpcardiol.2023.101593.

22 Neumark-Sztainer, Dianne, Watts, Allison W. and Rydell, Sarah, 'Yoga and Body Image: How Do Young Adults Practicing Yoga Describe its Impact on their Body Image?', *Body Image* 27 (2019), https://doi.org/10.1016/j.bodyim.2018.09.001.
23 Woodyard, Catherine, 'Exploring the Therapeutic Effects of Yoga and its Ability to Increase Quality of Life', *International Journal of Yoga* 4(2) (2011), https://www.ncbi.nlm.nih.gov/pmc/articles/PMC3193654/.
24 Bridges, Ledetra and Sharma, Manoj, 'The Efficacy of Yoga as a Form of Treatment for Depression', *Journal of Evidence-Based Complementary & Alternative Medicine* 22(4) (2017), https://doi.org/10.1177/2156587217715927.
25 Interview with Laura Harvey-Collins, conducted by author over Zoom, 18 August 2020.
26 Gandhi and Wolff, 'Yoga and the Roots of Cultural Appropriation'.
27 Csala, Barbara, Springinsfeld, Constanze Maria and Köteles, Ferenc, 'The Relationship Between Yoga and Spirituality: A Systematic Review of Empirical Research', *Frontiers in Psychology* 12 (2021), https://doi.org/10.3389/fpsyg.2021.695939.

Chapter 3
Tarot: The Fool's Journey

1 Jung, C.G. (trans. Hull, R.F.C.), *Synchronicity: An Acausal Connecting Principle* (Princeton University Press, 1973), p. 120.
2 Van Erkelens, Herbert, 'The Unus Mundus (One World) as Meeting Ground of Science and Religion', in *Science and Religion: One World – Changing Perspectives on Reality* (Fennema, Jan and Paul, Iain, eds) (University of Twente & Kluwer Academic Publishers, 1990), p. 201.
3 Butzer, Bethany, 'Does Synchronicity Point us Towards the Fundamental Nature of Consciousness?: An Exploration of Psychology, Ontology, and Research Prospects', *Journal of Consciousness Studies* 28(3–4) (2021), https://www.ingentaconnect.com/contentone/imp/jcs/2021/00000028/f0020003/art00001.
4 Wigington, Patti, 'A Brief History of Tarot', *Learn Religions* (6 June 2018), https://www.learnreligions.com/a-brief-history-of-tarot-2562770.
5 Topolsky, Laura June, 'The Deck of Cards That Made Tarot a Global Phenomenon', *Atlas Obscura* (10 July 2015), https://www.atlasobscura.com/articles/the-deck-of-cards-that-made-tarot-a-global-phenomenon.
6 Greer, Mary K., 'Carl Jung and Tarot', *Mary K. Greer's Tarot Blog* (31 March 2008), https://marykgreer.com/2008/03/31/carl-jung-and-tarot/.
7 Ray, Sharmistha, 'Reviving a Forgotten Artist of the Occult', *Hyperallergic* (23 March 2019), https://hyperallergic.com/490918/pamela-colman-smith-pratt-institute-libraries/.
8 Bailey, Sarah Pulliam, 'Tarot Cards Are Having a Moment with Help from Pandemic', *Washington Post* (10 December 2021), https://www.washingtonpost.com/religion/2021/12/10/tarot-cards-pandemic-trend/.

9. Woodcock, Victoria, 'Why Tarot Is Trending Again', *Financial Times* (16 April 2021), https://www.ft.com/content/c4afbc05-a715-4b83-9323-44e4c4f95ca5.
10. 'Meet the Readers', *Psychic Sisters London*, https://psychicsisters.co.uk/collections/readings.
11. Dore, Jessica, *Tarot for Change: Using the Cards for Self-Care, Acceptance and Growth* (Hay House UK, 2021), p. 5.
12. Search term: 'tarot', Google Trends, https://trends.google.com/trends/explore?date=all&q=tarot&hl=en-US.
13. Search term: 'Nine of Cups', Google Trends, https://trends.google.com/trends/explore?date=all&q=nine%20of%20cups&hl=en-US.
14. Interview with Brigit Esselmont, conducted by author over Zoom, 16 January 2023.
15. Interview with Victoria Smith-Murphy, conducted by author over Zoom, 15 February 2023.
16. Jung, C.G. (trans. Winston, Richard and Winston Clara), *Memories, Dreams, Reflections* (William Collins, 2013), p. 294, Kindle edition.
17. Tomaine, Gina, 'Does Tarot Count as Therapy?', *Cosmopolitan* (4 November 2019), https://www.cosmopolitan.com/health-fitness/a29440976/tarot-therapy-mental-health-astrology/.
18. Jung, C.G. (trans. Hull, R.F.C.), *Synchronicity: An Acausal Connecting Principle* (Princeton University Press, 1973), p. 120.
19. Esselmont, Brigit, 'The Tower Tarot Card Meanings', Biddy Tarot, https://www.biddytarot.com/tarot-card-meanings/major-arcana/tower/.

Chapter 4
Astrology: Star Stuff

1. 'Campaigner, ENFP Personality', *16 Personalities*, https://www.16personalities.com/enfp-personality.
2. Emre, Merve, *What's Your Type?: The Strange History of Myers-Briggs and the Birth of Personality Testing* (William Collins, 2018), introduction.
3. Gecewicz, Claire, '"New Age" Beliefs Common Among Both Religious and Nonreligious Americans', Pew Research Center (1 October 2018), https://www.pewresearch.org/short-reads/2018/10/01/new-age-beliefs-common-among-both-religious-and-nonreligious-americans/.
4. Mclaughlin, Aimee, 'How Sanctuary Is Rethinking Astrology for the Digital Age', *Creative Review* (23 March 2020), https://www.creativereview.co.uk/sanctuary-astrology-app/.
5. Smallwood, Christine, 'Astrology in the Age of Uncertainty', *New Yorker* (21 October 2019), https://www.newyorker.com/magazine/2019/10/28/astrology-in-the-age-of-uncertainty.
6. Bruner, Raisa, 'High-Tech Astrology Apps Claim to Be More Personalized Than Ever. Gen Z-ers Are Turning Out to Be Believers', *Time* (23 July 2021), https://time.com/6083293/astrology-apps-personalized/.
7. Interview with Chloe Smart, conducted by author over Zoom, 16 December 2022.

8   Whitman, Walt, 'Song of Myself' (1855), https://resources.saylor.org/wwwresources/archived/site/wp-content/uploads/2012/11/Song-of-Myself.pdf.
9   Le Cunff, Anne-Laure, 'The Barnum Effect: Why we Love Astrology and Personality Tests', *Ness Labs*, https://nesslabs.com/barnum-effect.
10 Interview with Chris Brennan, conducted by author over Zoom, 13 January 2023.
11 Brennan, Chris, 'Explaining Astrology to a Skeptic', *The Astrology Podcast* (22 January 2023), https://www.youtube.com/watch?v=C2LsqdSZjKw.
12 Chapel, Nicholas E., '*The Kybalion's* New Clothes: An Early 20th Century Text's Dubious Association with Hermeticism', *Journal of the Western Mystery Tradition* 24(3) (2013), http://www.jwmt.org/v3n24/chapel.html.
13 Mehrtens, Sue, 'Jung and the Hermetic Law of Correspondence', *Jungian Center for the Spiritual Sciences*, https://jungiancenter.org/jung-and-the-hermetic-law-of-correspondence/.
14 Jung, C.G., *Jung on Astrology* (Routledge, 2017).
15 Van Erkelens, Herbert, 'The Unus Mundus (One World) as Meeting Ground of Science and Religion, in *Science and Religion: One World – Changing Perspectives on Reality* (Fennema, Jan and Paul, Iain, eds) (University of Twente & Kluwer Academic Publishers, 1990), p. 201.
16 Shakespeare, William, *Hamlet*, 1.5.165–6.
17 Sagan, Carl, *Cosmos: The Story of Cosmic Evolution, Science and Civilisation* (Abacus, 1983), p. 62.
18 'André Barbault's Prediction of the 2020 Pandemic', *Skyscript Astrology Forum* (29 March 2020), http://skyscript.co.uk/forums/viewtopic.php?p=114234&sid=75eb7b94789760c3d968353266e49a73.
19 Brennan, Chris, Surtees, Kelly and Coppock, Austin, 'Ep. 234 Transcript: 2020 Astrology Forecast: Overview of the Year Ahead', *The Astrology Podcast* (16 December 2019), https://theastrologypodcast.com/transcripts/ep-234-transcript-2020-astrology-forecast-overview-of-the-year-ahead/.
20 Dean, Geoffrey et al., *Understanding Astrology: A Critical Review of a Thousand Empirical Studies 1900-2020* (AinO Publications, 2022), p. 22.
21 Ibid., p. 15 quoting Dennis Elwell, 'Can Astrology Win Through?', *Astrological Journal* 33(1) (1991).
22 Ibid., p. 16.
23 Odle, Chris, https://apple-octopus-exss.squarespace.com/.
24 Interview with Chris Odle, conducted by author over Zoom, 16 February 2023.

Chapter 5
Manifestation: Magnetic Thoughts and Vision Boards

1   'It All Started Here', *Abraham-Hicks Publications*, https://www.abraham-hicks.com/.
2   Yarlagadda, Tara, 'Phineas Parkhurst Quimby: The Mind Can Heal the Body', *HowStuffWorks* (14 May 2019), https://people.howstuffworks.com/phineas-parkhurst-quimby-new-thought.htm.

Notes

3 Rusk, Connie, 'Noel Edmonds, 70, Believes "Cosmic Ordering" Brought him and Wife Liz Davies, 49, Together as they Talk about their Secrets to Long-Lasting Marriage', *MailOnline* (14 February 2019), https://www.dailymail.co.uk/tvshowbiz/article-6704991/Noel-Edmonds-70-believes-cosmic-ordering-brought-wife-Liz-Davies-49-together.html.
4 Byrne, Rhonda, *The Secret* (Simon & Schuster UK, 2006), introduction.
5 '#manifesting', TikTok, view count as of 26 July 2023, https://www.tiktok.com/tag/manifesting?lang=en.
6 Manson, Mark, 'The Staggering Bullshit of "The Secret"', https://markmanson.net/the-secret.
7 Byrne, Rhonda, *The Secret* (Simon & Schuster UK, 2006), p. 10, Kindle edition.
8 Ibid., p. 156.
9 Ibid., p. 14.
10 Ibid., p. 28.
11 Nafousi, Roxie, *Manifest: 7 Steps to Living Your Best Life* (Penguin, 2022).
12 Interview with Nick Trumble, conducted by author over Zoom, 4 April 2023.
13 James, William, *The Varieties of Religious Experience: A Study in Human Nature* (Longmans, Green and Company, 1902), 'Lecture IX: Conversion'.
14 Mulford, Prentice, *Your Forces and How to Use Them* (YOGeBooks, 2011), p. 48.
15 'About Abraham-Hicks', *Abraham-Hicks Publications*, https://www.abraham-hicks.com/about/.
16 Ahonen, Elias, 'The Moon "Created" his Lavish Reality… and Says You Can, Too', *Magazine by Cointelegraph* (23 May 2022), https://cointelegraph.com/magazine/carl-the-moon-runefelt-created-lavish-reality-thinks-you-can-too/.
17 Runefelt, Carl, TikTok (25 September 2022), https://www.tiktok.com/@carlrunefelt/video/7147406250806971650.
18 Interview with Evie Sparkes, conducted by author over Zoom, 21 February 2023.

Chapter 6
Reiki: A Spoonful of Wellness

1 Evans, Christopher H., 'Why You Should Know about the New Thought Movement', *The Conversation* (16 February 2017), https://theconversation.com/why-you-should-know-about-the-new-thought-movement-72256.
2 Dyer, W. Justin, Judd, Daniel K., Gale, Megan and Gibson Finlinson, Hunter, 'Perspective: What 18 Years of Research Tells us about the Mental Health of Latter-day Saints', *Deseret News* (20 June 2023), https://www.deseret.com/2023/6/20/23759342/latter-day-saint-mental-health-research.
3 Interview with Sushma Sagar, conducted by author over Zoom, 20 February 2023.
4 Sharp, Debbie et al., 'Complementary Medicine Use, Views, and Experiences: A National Survey in England', *BJGP Open* 2(4) (2018) https://doi.org/10.3399/bjgpopen18X101614.

Notes

5 'Rising Popularity of Complementary and Alternative Medicine Approaches', MentalHealth.net, https://www.mentalhelp.net/alternative-medicine/rising-popularity-of-complementary-approaches.

6 Nolsoe, Eir, 'Positive Vibrations, Chakras and Star Signs – What Spiritual Beliefs Do Britons Hold?', YouGov (11 January 2022), https://yougov.co.uk/topics/society/articles-reports/2022/01/11/positive-vibrations-chakras-and-star-signs-what-sp.

7 Kaufmann, Michael, 'The History of Usui Reiki and the Reiki Principles', Reiki-Meditation.co.uk, https://www.reiki-meditation.co.uk/the-history-of-usui-reiki/.

8 Ibid.

9 'Chakra', *Britannica*, https://www.britannica.com/topic/chakra.

10 Sagar, Sushma, *Find Your Flow: Essential Chakras* (Pop Press, 2020), p. 17, Kindle edition.

11 The Calmery, https://www.thecalmery.com/.

12 'Health: Reiki', ASA (12 October 2022), https://www.asa.org.uk/advice-online/health-reiki.html.

13 'Reiki Myths That Drive You Nuts', *International Association of Reiki Professionals* (2019), https://iarp.org/reiki-myths-that-drive-you-nuts/.

14 Davies, Joe, 'NHS Is Accused of "Endorsing Quackery" after Posting Job Ad for a Japanese Energy Healer who Will Treat Cancer Patients Alongside Chemo', *MailOnline* (15 August 2022), https://www.dailymail.co.uk/health/article-11112321/NHS-accused-endorsing-quackery-advertising-Japanese-energy-healer.html.

15 Gorski, David, 'No, Editors of *The Atlantic*, Reiki Does Not Work', *Science-Based Medicine* (9 March 2020), https://sciencebasedmedicine.org/no-editors-of-the-atlantic-reiki-does-not-work/.

16 Miles, Pamela, 'Reiki – Research', *Taking Charge of Your Wellbeing, University of Minnesota*, https://www.takingcharge.csh.umn.edu/explore-healing-practices/reiki/what-does-research-say-about-reiki.

17 Moriarty, Philip, 'Quantum Mysticism Is a Mistake', *iai News* (5 April 2023), https://iai.tv/articles/quantum-mysticism-is-a-mistake-philip-moriarty-auid-2437.

18 Tolboll, Morten, 'Who Is the Mystical Observer in Quantum Mechanics?', https://mortentolboll.weebly.com/observer-quantum-mechanics---the-matrix-dictionary.html.

19 Rosa, Linda et al., 'A Close Look at Therapeutic Touch', *JAMA* 279(13) (1998), https://jamanetwork.com/journals/jama/fullarticle/187390.

20 See for instance McManus, David E., 'Reiki Is Better than Placebo and Has Broad Potential as a Complementary Health Therapy', *Journal of Evidence-Based Complementary & Alternative Medicine* 22(4) (2017), https://doi.org/10.1177/2156587217728644.

21 'Reiki', National Center for Complementary and Integrative Health (December 2018), https://www.nccih.nih.gov/health/reiki.

22 Cell Press, 'Experts Denounce Clinical Trials of Unscientific, "Alternative" Medicines', *Science Daily* (20 August 2014), https://www.sciencedaily.com/

releases/2014/08/140820123248.htm#:~:text=Experts%20writing%20 in%20the%20Cell,such%20as%20homeopathy%20and%20reiki.

23 Catlin, Anita and Taylor-Ford, Rebecca L., 'Investigation of Standard Care Versus Sham Reiki Placebo Versus Actual Reiki Therapy to Enhance Comfort and Well-Being in a Chemotherapy Infusion Center', *Oncology Nursing Forum* 38(3) (2011), https://www.doi.org/10.1188/11.ONF.E212-E220.

24 'The Power of the Placebo Effect', *Harvard Health Publishing* (22 July 2024), https://www.health.harvard.edu/mental-health/the-power-of-the-placebo-effect.

25 Marchant, Jo, *Cure: A Journey into the Science of Mind Over Body* (Canongate, 2016), p. 291.

26 Interview with Michael Kaufmann, conducted by author over Zoom, 28 March 2023.

27 Marshall, Mallika, 'A Placebo Can Work Even When you Know it's a Placebo', *Harvard Health Publishing* (7 July 2016), https://www.health.harvard.edu/blog/placebo-can-work-even-know-placebo-201607079926.

Chapter 7
Atheist Churches: Pentecostalism for the Godless

1 Waite, Hannah, 'The Nones: Who Are They and What Do They Believe?', *Theos* (2022), https://www.theosthinktank.co.uk/cmsfiles/The-Nones---Who-are-they-and-what-do-they-believe.pdf.

2 'Are "Nones" Spiritual instead of Religious?', Pew Research Center (24 January 2024), https://www.pewresearch.org/religion/2024/01/24/are-nones-spiritual-instead-of-religious/.

3 Interview with Greta Christina, conducted by author over the phone, 29 June 2020.

4 Interview with Troy Kurt and Jack Thompson, conducted by author over Zoom, 24 April 2023.

5 Interview with Dr Phil Zuckerman, conducted by author over Zoom, 2 May 2023.

6 Evans, Pippa, 'There's a Space for us', TEDxShoreditch (1 December 2017), https://www.youtube.com/watch?v=gnCcwlnjIh4.

7 Brown, Andrew, 'The Sunday Assembly Is Not a Revolt against God. It's a Revolt against Dogma', *Guardian* (16 December 2013), https://www.theguardian.com/commentisfree/andrewbrown/2013/dec/16/sunday-assembly-revolt-god-dogma-atheist.

8 Evans, Pippa, 'Sunday Assembly Sets Foot in Australia', *ABC Listen* (27 June 2013), https://www.abc.net.au/radionational/programs/lifematters/sunday-assembly-melbourne/4785752.

9 Interview with Matt Lockwood, conducted by author over email, 19 December 2023.

10 Interview with Stephanie Pollard, conducted by author over Zoom, 20 July 2020.

11 Dawkins, Richard, Dennett, Daniel C., Harris, Sam, and Hitchens, Christopher, *The Four Horsemen* (Transworld, 2019), p. 38, Kindle edition.
12 Weiss, Bari, 'Meet the Renegades of the Intellectual Dark Web', *New York Times* (May 8 2018), https://www.nytimes.com/2018/05/08/opinion/intellectual-dark-web.html.
13 Hirsi Ali, Ayaan, 'Why I Am Now a Christian: Atheism Can't Equip us for Civilisational War', *Unherd* (11 November 2023), https://unherd.com/2023/11/why-i-am-now-a-christian/.
14 'Religion, England and Wales: Census 2021', Office for National Statistics (29 November 2022), https://www.ons.gov.uk/peoplepopulationandcommunity/culturalidentity/religion/bulletins/religionenglandandwales/census2021.
15 'How U.S. Religious Composition Has Changed in Recent Decades', Pew Research Center (13 September 2022), https://www.pewresearch.org/religion/2022/09/13/how-u-s-religious-composition-has-changed-in-recent-decades/.
16 De Botton, Alain, *Religion for Atheists: A Non-Believer's Guide to the Uses of Religion* (Penguin, 2012), p. 12, Kindle edition.
17 Booth, Robert, 'Alain de Botton Reveals Plans for "Temple to Atheism" in Heart of London', *Guardian* (26 January 2012), https://www.theguardian.com/books/2012/jan/26/alain-de-botton-temple-atheism.
18 Zuckerman, Phil, *Living the Secular Life: New Answers to Old Questions* (Penguin Press, 2014).
19 Balk, Gene, 'Seattle Is Most-Educated Big U.S. City – and 8 in 10 Newcomers Have a College Degree', *Seattle Times* (25 February 2019), https://www.seattletimes.com/seattle-news/data/seattle-is-most-educated-big-u-s-city-and-8-in-10-newcomers-have-a-college-degree.
20 'None of the Above: Survey Finds San Francisco 2nd Most Religiously Unaffiliated Metro Area', *CBS News* (16 March 2015), https://www.cbsnews.com/sanfrancisco/news/survey-unaffiliated-most-popular-religious-affiliation-san-francisco-bay-area-american-values-atlas-public-religion-research-institute/.
21 Oppenheimer, Mark, 'The Evangelical Scion Who Stopped Believing', *New York Times Magazine* (29 December 2016), https://www.nytimes.com/2016/12/29/magazine/the-evangelical-scion-who-stopped-believing.html.
22 Interview with Bart Campolo, conducted by author over Zoom, 16 May 2023.
23 Hume, David, *A Treatise of Human Nature* (1739–40), Book III, Part III, Section III, https://sites.pitt.edu/~mthompso/readings/hume.influencing.pdf.

Chapter 8
Exercise: A Pilgrim's Progress

1 Sanneh, Kelefa, 'An Electronic Soundtrack for Spiritual Awakening', *New Yorker* (23 April 2018), https://www.newyorker.com/magazine/2018/04/30/an-electronic-soundtrack-for-spiritual-awakening.

Notes

2 Howe, Brian, 'Singularity', *Pitchfork* (10 May 2018), https://pitchfork.com/reviews/albums/jon-hopkins-singularity/.
3 Maslow, Abraham H., *Religions, Values, and Peak-Experiences* (Rare Treasures, 1964), Chapter 16.
4 Evans, Jules, 'Abraham Maslow, Empirical Spirituality and the Crisis of Values', *Medium* (31 March 2021), https://julesevans.medium.com/abraham-maslow-empirical-spirituality-and-the-crisis-of-values-34148b775f1a.
5 Walker, Ether, 'Eckhart Tolle: This Man Could Change Your Life', *Independent* (21 July 2008).
6 Tolle, Eckhart, *The Power of Now: A Guide to Spiritual Enlightnment* (Namaste Publishing, 1997), preface.
7 Goddard, Vanessa Zuisei, *Still Running: The Art of Meditation in Motion* (Shambhala Publications, 2020), p. xii, Kindle edition.
8 Interview with Vanessa Zuisei Goddard, conducted by author over Zoom, 20 May 2023.
9 Goddard, *Still Running*, p. 46.
10 Ibid., p. 135.
11 Finn, Adharanand, 'What I Learned When I Met the Monk who Ran 1,000 Marathons', *Guardian* (31 March 2015), https://www.theguardian.com/lifeandstyle/2015/mar/31/japanese-monks-mount-hiei-1000-marathons-1000-days.
12 Ibid.
13 Lieberman, Daniel E. et al., 'Running in Tarahumara (Rarámuri) Culture: Persistence Hunting, Footracing, Dancing Work, and the Fallacy of the Athletic Savage', *Current Anthropology* 61(3) (2020), https://www.journals.uchicago.edu/doi/full/10.1086/708810
14 Ibid.
15 Hanson, Molly, 'What We Can Learn from Indigenous Runners', *Outside* (9 October 2023), https://www.outsideonline.com/running/news/people/what-we-can-learn-from-indigenous-runners/.
16 'Toward the Rising Sun', *Trail Runner* (26 April 2017), https://www.trailrunnermag.com/people/profiles-people/toward-the-rising-sun/.
17 'Running for Self-Transcendence, *Rich Roll* podcast (2 September 2018), https://www.youtube.com/watch?v=6JGCcF-GJyI.
18 'Number of Running and Jogging Participants in the United States in 2023', Statista (14 May 2024), https://www.statista.com/statistics/190303/running-participants-in-the-us-since-2006/.
19 'Ultrarunning Finishes', *UltraRunning*, https://ultrarunning.com/calendar/stats/ultrarunning-finishes.
20 Marathon Des Sables, https://marathondessables.co.uk/.
21 Brown, Angie, 'Jasmin Paris First Woman to Complete Gruelling Barkley Marathons Race', *BBC News* (24 March 2024), https://www.bbc.co.uk/news/uk-scotland-edinburgh-east-fife-68643341.
22 Goulding, Justin, 'Sri Chinmoy Self-Transcendence: The 3,100-Mile Race around a New York Block', *BBC Sport* (21 June 2019), https://www.bbc.co.uk/sport/48702452.

23 Díaz-Gilbert, Miriam, 'The Spiritual Dimension of Ultrarunning', *Huffpost* (12 July 2017), https://www.huffpost.com/entry/the-spiritual-dimension-of-ultrarunning_b_59662611e4b0911162fc3017.
24 Interview with Miriam Díaz-Gilbert, conducted by author over the phone, 24 April 2023.
25 Goulding, 'Sri Chinmoy Self-Transcendence'.
26 Lodge, Kristen, 'The Ultra Runner's Prayer', *An Outdoor Life* (3 September 2016), http://kristenlodge.blogspot.com/2016/09/the-ultra-runners-prayer.html.
27 Díaz-Gilbert, Miriam, 'The Ascetic Life of the Ultrarunner', *Spiritus: A Journal of Christian Spirituality* 18(2) (2018), https://www.miriamdiazgilbert.com/_files/ugd/51213a_b7330c6122e14e7f85607e64198f2586.pdf.
28 Harrington, Luke T., 'The Flagpole-Sitting, Maggot-Infested Saint of the Desert', *Christ and Pop Culture* (22 September 2017), https://christandpopculture.com/flagpole-sitting-maggot-infested-saint-desert/.
29 Díaz-Gilbert, 'The Ascetic Life of the Ultrarunner'.
30 Huxley, Aldous, *Heaven & Hell* (Vintage Classics, 2004), p. 44, Kindle edition.
31 Hutchinson, Alex, *Endure: Mind, Body and the Curiously Elastic Limits of Human Performance* (HarperCollins, 2018), p. 15, Kindle edition.
32 Interview with Dr Suzanna Millar, conducted by author over Zoom, 27 April 2023.
33 Beck, Julie, 'The Church of CrossFit', *Atlantic* (24 June 2017), https://www.theatlantic.com/health/archive/2017/06/the-church-of-crossfit/531501/.
34 Thurston, Angie and ter Kuile, Casper, 'How We Gather' (18 April 2015), https://caspertk.files.wordpress.com/2015/04/how-we-gather.pdf.

Chapter 9
Meditation: The Hurricane in Your Head

1 Kipling, Rudyard, 'If' (1910).
2 'About Headspace', Headspace, https://www.headspace.com/about-us.
3 'Calm Is the World's First Mental Health Unicorn', Calm (6 February 2019), https://www.calm.com/blog/calm-is-the-worlds-first-mental-health-unicorn.
4 Khoury, Bassam et al., 'Mindfulness-Based Therapy: A Comprehensive Meta-Analysis', *Clinical Psychology Review* 33(6) (2013), https://doi.org/10.1016/j.cpr.2013.05.005.
5 Chen, Tsai-Ling, Chang, Shu-Chen, Hsieh, Hsiu-Fen, Huang, Chin-Yi, Chuang, Jui-Hsiang and Wang, Hsiu-Hung, 'Effects of Mindfulness-Based Stress Reduction on Sleep Quality and Mental Health for Insomnia Patients: A Meta-Analysis', *Journal of Psychosomatic Research* 135 (2020), https://doi.org/10.1016/j.jpsychores.2020.110144.
6 Levoy, Emily, Lazaridou, Asimina, Brewer, Judson and Fulwiler, Carl, 'An Exploratory Study of Mindfulness Based Stress Reduction for Emotional Eating', *Appetite* 109 (2017), https://doi.org/10.1016/j.appet.2016.11.029.
7 Dekeyser, M., Raes, F., Leijssen, M., Leysen, S. and Dewulf, D., 'Mindfulness Skills and Interpersonal Behaviour', *Personality and Individual Differences* 44(5) (2008), https://doi.org/10.1016/j.paid.2007.11.018.

8 Kabat-Zinn, Jon, 'Some Reflections on the Origins of MBSR, Skillful Means, and the Trouble with Maps', *Contemporary Buddhism* 12(1) (2011), https://doi.org/10.1080/14639947.2011.564844.
9 'New NICE Guidelines on Depression Include Mindfulness as a Treatment for Less Severe Depression', The Mindfulness Initiative (30 June 2022), https://www.themindfulnessinitiative.org/news/new-nice-guidelines-on-depression-include-mindfulness-as-a-treatment-for-less-severe-depression2.
10 Interview with Jiva Masheder, conducted by author over Zoom, 26 June 2023.
11 Jaffe, Eric, 'Meditate on It', *Smithsonian* (1 February 2007), https://www.smithsonianmag.com/science-nature/meditate-on-it-147282062/.
12 Interview with C. Pierce Salguero, conducted by author over Zoom, 8 May 2023.
13 Salguero, C. Pierce, *Buddhish: A Guide to the 20 Most Important Buddhist Ideas for the Curious and Skeptical* (Beacon Press, 2022), p. 64, Kindle edition.
14 Kaori Gurley, Lauren, 'Starbucks Workers Want More Hours. Instead They Got a Meditation App', *Vice* (8 January 2020), https://www.vice.com/en/article/z3bxn3/starbucks-workers-want-more-hours-instead-they-got-a-meditation-app.
15 Purser, Ronald E., *McMindfulness: How Mindfulness Became the New Capitalist Spirituality* (Watkins Media, 2019), p. 17, Kindle edition.
16 Ibid., p. 104.
17 Lindahl, Jared R., Fisher, Nathan E., Cooper, David J., Rosen, Rochelle K. and Britton, Willoughby B., 'The Varieties of Contemplative Experience: A Mixed-Methods Study of Meditation-Related Challenges in Western Buddhists', *PLOS ONE* 12(5) (2017), https://doi.org/10.1371/journal.pone.0176239.
18 Rocha, Tomas, 'The Dark Knight of the Soul', *Atlantic* (25 June 2014), https://www.theatlantic.com/health/archive/2014/06/the-dark-knight-of-the-souls/372766/.
19 Interview with Nick Torry, conducted by author in person, 20 December 2023.
20 Interview with Karin Peeters, conducted by author over Zoom, 9 June 2023.
21 Interview with Geshe Tenzin Namdak, conducted by author over email, 25 June 2023.

Chapter 10
Nature Spirituality: The Door to the Temple

1 'OSS Survey Results', The Outdoor Swimming Society, https://www.outdoorswimmingsociety.com/oss-survey-results/.
2 Sam, Lucy, 'Nature as Healer: A Phenomenological Study of the Experiences of Wild Swimmers in Kenwood Ladies' Pond on Hampstead Heath', *Consciousness, Spirituality & Transpersonal Psychology* 1(2020), https://doi.org/10.53074/cstp.2020.110.
3 Interview with Lucy Sam, conducted by author over Zoom, 7 May 2023.

Notes

4 Emerson, Ralph Waldo, *Nature* (James Munroe and Company, 1836), https://archive.vcu.edu/english/engweb/transcendentalism/authors/emerson/essays/naturetext.html.
5 Blasdel, Alex, '"A Reckoning for our Species": The Philosopher Prophet of the Anthropocene', *Guardian* (15 June 2017), https://www.theguardian.com/world/2017/jun/15/timothy-morton-anthropocene-philosopher.
6 Eisenstein, Charles, *The More Beautiful World Our Hearts Know Is Possible* (North Atlantic Books, 2013), p. 16.
7 Nhat Hanh, Thich, 'Clouds in Each Paper', *Awakin.org*, https://www.awakin.org/v2/read/view.php?tid=222.
8 Li, Qing, 'Forest Bathing Is Great for Your Health. Here's How to Do It', *Time* (1 May 2018), https://time.com/5259602/japanese-forest-bathing/.
9 Li Qing et al., 'Phytoncides (Wood Essential Oils) Induce Human Natural Killer Cell Activity', *Immunopharmacology and Immunotoxicology* 28(2) (2006), https://doi.org/10.1080/08923970600809439.
10 'Forest Bathing for Mental Health and Mobility Issues as Social Prescribing in Scotland', *Forest Therapy Hub* (26 January 2022), https://foresttherapyhub.com/forest-bathing-for-mental-health-and-mobility-issues-as-social-prescribing-in-scotland/.
11 Bird, William, 'Natural Thinking: Investigating the Links Between the Natural Environment, Biodiversity and Human Health' (June 2007), https://www.centreforecotherapy.org.uk/wp-content/uploads/2021/07/Natural-Thinking-RSPB-report.pdf.
12 Pavid, Katie, 'Aspirin, Morphine and Chemotherapy: The Essential Medicines Powered by Plants', Natural History Museum (19 February 2021), https://www.nhm.ac.uk/discover/essential-medicines-powered-by-plants.html.
13 'What Is Wicca?', *Celtic Connection*, https://wicca.com/wicca/what-is-wicca.html.
14 Booth, Robert, Aguilar García, Carmen and Duncan, Pamela, 'Shamanism, Pagans and Wiccans: Trends from the England and Wales Census', *Guardian* (29 November 2022), https://www.theguardian.com/uk-news/2022/nov/29/ten-things-weve-learned-from-the-england-and-wales-census.
15 'Religious Landscape Study', Pew Research Center, https://www.pewresearch.org/religion/religious-landscape-study/.
16 'Other Religions', Pew Research Center (2 April 2015), https://www.pewresearch.org/religion/2015/04/02/other-religions/.
17 Tamás, Rebecca, *Strangers: Essays on the Human and Nonhuman* (Makina Books, 2020), 'On Panpsychism'.
18 Harvey, Fiona, 'Scientists Deliver "Final Warning" on Climate Crisis: Act Now or it's Too Late', *Guardian* (20 March 2023), https://www.theguardian.com/environment/2023/mar/20/ipcc-climate-crisis-report-delivers-final-warning-on-15c.
19 Horton, Helena, 'BBC Criticised over Climate Question in Tory Leadership Debate', *Guardian* (27 July 2022), https://www.theguardian.com/environment/2022/jul/27/bbc-criticised-over-climate-question-in-tory-leadership-debate.
20 'Record Breaking 2022 Indicative of Future UK Climate', Met Office (27 July 2023), https://www.metoffice.gov.uk/about-us/news-and-media/

media-centre/weather-and-climate-news/2023/record-breaking-2022-indicative-of-future-uk-climate.
21 Hockaday, James, 'When Were the 10 Warmest Years on Record?', *Yahoo! News* (18 July 2023), https://uk.news.yahoo.com/when-were-the-10-warmest-years-on-record-174557762.html.
22 Ball, Connie, Edser, Katie and Windsor-Shellard, Ben, 'Worries about Climate Change, Great Britain: September to October 2022', Office for National Statistics (28 October 2022), https://www.ons.gov.uk/peoplepopulationandcommunity/wellbeing/articles/worriesaboutclimatechangegreatbritain/septembertooctober2022.
23 Oliver, Mary, *Upstream: Selected Essays*, sourced at www.spiritualityandpractice.com/book-reviews/excerpts/view/28137/.
24 Interview with Alana Hyde Bloom, conducted by author over Zoom, 25 May 2023.
25 Interview with Erik Assadourian, conducted by author over Zoom, 4 May 2023.
26 Interview with Hilary Norton and Ian Mowll, conducted by author over Zoom, 4 May 2023.
27 'Spiral Journey: Programs in the Work that Reconnects', Work That Reconnects Network, https://workthatreconnects.org/spiral/.

Chapter 11
Shamanism: Beyond the Veil

1 Interview with Jane Egginton, conducted by author over the phone, 4 July 2023.
2 Elsey, Eddy, *The Chris Geisler Podcast* (26 June 2023), https://www.instagram.com/p/Ct8X6HIo4Xe/.
3 Harner, Michael, *The Way of the Shaman* (HarperOne, 2011), p. 40, Kindle edition.
4 Ibid., introduction.
5 Breeze Wood, Nicholas, 'So, What Exactly Is Shamanism Then?', *Sacred Hoop Special Issue* (2017), https://www.sacredhoop.org/Free-Guide-To-Shamanism/Sacred-Hoop-Free-Guide-To-Shamanism.pdf.
6 'Shaman and Native Mysticism', *Russian Life* (18 August 2000), https://russianlife.com/the-russia-file/shaman-native-mysticism/.
7 'Core Shamanism', *Foundation for Shamanic Studies*, https://www.shamanism.org/workshops/coreshamanism.html.
8 Nath Banstola, Bhola, 'Shamanism: A Common Human Heritage', *Sacred Hoop Special Issue* (2017), https://www.sacredhoop.org/Free-Guide-To-Shamanism/Sacred-Hoop-Free-Guide-To-Shamanism.pdf.
9 Beck Kehoe, Alice, *Shamans and Religion: An Anthropological Exploration in Critical Thinking* (Waveland Press, 2000), p. 2.
10 Ramsdale, Suzannah, 'Are You Having a Spiritual Meltdown? Best Shamans in London', *Standard* (15 October 2020), https://www.standard.co.uk/escapist/wellness/best-shamans-in-london-a4569396.html.

Notes

11 Hart, Anna, 'The Strange Boom in Shamanic Healing', *GQ* (6 August 2019), https://www.gq-magazine.co.uk/lifestyle/article/shamanic-healing.
12 Bennett, Jessica, 'The Shaman of Instagram', *New York Times* (3 July 2020), https://www.nytimes.com/2020/07/03/style/self-care/durek-verrett-instagram-shaman.html.
13 'Religion, England and Wales: Census 2021', Office for National Statistics (29 November 2022), https://www.ons.gov.uk/peop lepopulationand community/culturalidentity/religion/bulletins/religionenglandandwales/census2021.
14 Breeze Wood, Nicholas, 'So, What Exactly Is Shamanism Then?', *Sacred Hoop Special Issue* (2017), p. 13, https://www.sacredhoop.org/Free-Guide-To-Shamanism/Sacred-Hoop-Free-Guide-To-Shamanism.pdf
15 Interview with Chris Odle, conducted by author over Zoom, 1 June 2023.
16 Harner, *The Way of the Shaman*, introduction.
17 Grof, Christina and Grof, Stanislav, *Spiritual Emergency: When Personal Transformation Becomes a Crisis* (Tarcher, 1989), p. 8.
18 O'Hagan, Sean, 'Kingsley Hall: RD Laing's Experiment in Anti-Psychiatry', *Guardian* (2 September 2012), https://www.theguardian.com/books/2012/sep/02/rd-laing-mental-health-sanity.
19 Grof, Christina and Grof, Stanislav, *The Stormy Search for the Self: A Guide to Personal Growth through Transformational Crisis* (Tarcher, 1990), p. 119.

Chapter 12
Raves: God Is a DJ

1 Ehrenreich, Barbara, *Dancing in the Streets: A History of Collective Joy* (Granta Books, 2008), p. 5.
2 Ibid., p. 256.
3 'Does Chocolate Contain Drugs? – Molecules Found in Chocolate', *Science of Cooking*, https://www.scienceofcooking.com/chocolate/drugs-found-in-chocolate.htm.
4 Interview with Alena Pashnova, conducted by author over Zoom, 17 July 2023.
5 Ehrenreich, *Dancing in the Streets*, p. 35.
6 Guynup, Sharon, 'Haiti: Possessed by Voodoo', *National Geographic* (7 July 2004), https://www.nationalgeographic.com/culture/article/haiti-ancient-traditions-voodoo.
7 Ehrenreich, *Dancing in the Streets*, p. 213.
8 Ibid., p. 9.
9 '5Rhythms Cosmology', 5Rhythms, https://www.5rhythms.com/gabrielle-roths-5rhythms/5rhythms-cosmology/.
10 Evans, Helen, 'Out of Sight, Out of Mind: An Analysis of Rave Culture' (Wimbledon School of Art, 1992) http://hehe.org.free.fr/hehe/texte/rave/#hist.
11 Sylvan, Robin, *Trance Formation: The Spiritual and Religious Dimensions of Global Rave Culture* (Routledge, 2005), pp. 17–29, Kindle edition.
12 Interview with Robin Sylvan, conducted by author over Zoom, 3 July 2023.

13 Sylvan, *Trance Formation*, p. 8.
14 'Our Tribe,' 5Rhythms, https://www.5rhythms.com/who-we-are/5rhythms-onetribe/.
15 Sylvan, *Trance Formation*, p. 63.
16 Ibid., p. 64.
17 James, William, *The Varieties of Religious Experience: A Study in Human Nature* (Longmans, Green and Company, 1902), 'Lecture IX: Conversion'.
18 Mithoefer, Michael C. et al., 'MDMA-Assisted Psychotherapy for Treatment of PTSD: Study Design and Rationale for Phase 3 Trials Based on Pooled Analysis of Six Phase 2 Randomized Controlled Trials', *Psychopharmacology* 236(9) (2019), https://doi.org/10.1007/s00213-019-05249-5.
19 Sessa, B., Aday, J.S., O'Brien, S., Curran, H.V., Measham, F., Higbed, L. and Nutt, D., 'Debunking the Myth of "Blue Mondays": No Evidence of Affect Drop After Taking Clinical MDMA', *Journal of Psychopharmacology* 36(3) (2021), https://doi.org/10.1177/02698811211055809.
20 Durkheim, Émile, *The Elementary Forms of the Religious Life* (George Allen & Unwin Ltd, 1915), p. 226.
21 Cottrell, Hannah, 'The Brilliant London Rave where Parents Can Party with their Babies and the Little Ones Absolutely Love it', *MyLondon* (1 March 2023), https://www.mylondon.news/whats-on/brilliant-london-rave-parents-can-26328014.
22 'About', Big Fish Little Fish, https://bigfishlittlefishevents.com/about/.
23 Koenig, John, *The Dictionary of Obscure Sorrows* (Simon & Schuster, 2022).
24 Watts, Alan, from 'The Tao of Philosophy' lecture series (1972), https://alanwatts.org/transcripts/the-tao-of-philosophy/.

Epilogue

1 Sylvan, Robin, *Trance Formation: The Spiritual and Religious Dimensions of Global Rave Culture* (Routledge, 2005), p. 12, Kindle edition.

Bibliography

Beiner, Alexander, *The Bigger Picture: How Psychedelics Can Help Us Make Sense of the World* (Hay House UK, 2023)

Beres, Derek, Remski, Matthew and Walker, Julian, *Conspirituality: How New Age Conspiracy Theories Became a Health Threat* (PublicAffairs, 2023)

Brennan, Chris, *Hellenistic Astrology: The Study of Fate and Fortune* (Amor Fati Publications, 2017)

Burroughs, William S., *Junky: The Definitive Text of 'Junk'* (Penguin Modern Classics, 2012)

Byrne, Rhonda, *The Secret* (Simon & Schuster UK, 2006)

Campbell, Joseph, *Myths to Live By*, (Stillpoint Digital Press, 2011)

Crispin, Jessa, *The Creative Tarot: A Modern Guide to an Inspired Life* (Atria Books, 2016)

Dawkins, Richard, *Unweaving the Rainbow: Science, Delusion and the Appetite for Wonder* (Penguin, 2006)

Dawkins, Richard, Dennett, Daniel C., Harris, Sam and Hitchens, Christopher, *The Four Horsemen* (Transworld, 2019)

De Botton, Alain, *Religion for Atheists: A Non-Believer's Guide to the Uses of Religion* (Penguin, 2012)

Dean, Geoffrey et al., *Understanding Astrology: A Critical Review of a Thousand Empirical Studies 1900-2020* (AinO Publications, 2022)

Díaz-Gilbert, Miriam, *Come What May, I Want to Run: A Memoir of the Saving Grace of Ultrarunning in Overwhelming Times* (Resource Publications, 2023)

Bibliography

Dore, Jessica, *Tarot for Change: Using the Cards for Self-Care, Acceptance and Growth* (Hay House UK, 2021)

Ehrenreich, Barbara, *Dancing in the Streets: A History of Collective Joy* (Granta Books, 2008)

Eisenstein, Charles, *The More Beautiful World Our Hearts Know Is Possible* (North Atlantic Books, 2013)

Elsey, Eddy, *Let Healing Happen: A Shamanic Guide to Living an Authentic and Happy Life* (Rider, 2024)

Emre, Merve, *What's Your Type?: The Strange History of Myers-Briggs and the Birth of Personality Testing* (William Collins, 2018)

Finn, Adharanand, *The Way of the Runner: A Journey into the Fabled World of Japanese Running* (Faber & Faber, 2015)

Gilani, Nadia, *The Yoga Manifesto: How Yoga Helped Me and Why It Needs to Save Itself* (Pan Macmillan, 2022)

Goddard, Vanessa Zuisei, *Still Running: The Art of Meditation in Motion*, (Shambhala Publications, 2020)

Grof, Christina and Grof, Stanislav, *Spiritual Emergency: When Personal Transformation Becomes a Crisis* (Tarcher, 1989)

Grof, Christina and Grof, Stanislav, *The Stormy Search for the Self: A Guide to Personal Growth through Transformational Crisis* (Tarcher, 1990)

Harner, Michael, *The Way of the Shaman* (HarperOne, 2011)

Hutchinson, Alex, *Endure: Mind, Body and the Curiously Elastic Limits of Human Performance* (HarperCollins, 2018)

Huxley, Aldous, *Heaven & Hell* (Chatto & Windus, 1956)

James, William, *The Varieties of Religious Experience: A Study in Human Nature* (Longmans, Green and Company, 1902)

Jung, C.G. (trans. Winston, Richard and Winston, Clara), *Memories, Dreams, Reflections: An Autobiography* (William Collins, 2013)

Jung, C.G. (trans. Hull, R.F.C.), *Synchronicity: An Acausal Connecting Principle* (Princeton University Press, 1973)

Kabat-Zinn, Jon, *Wherever You Go, There You Are: Mindfulness Meditation for Everyday Life* (Piatkus, 2004)

Kastrup, Bernardo, *Why Materialism Is Baloney: How True Skeptics Know There Is No Death and Fathom Answers to Life, the Universe, and Everything* (Iff Books, 2014)

Koenig, John, *The Dictionary of Obscure Sorrows* (Simon & Schuster, 2022)

Lyte, Fire, *The Dabbler's Guide to Witchcraft: Seeking an Intentional Magical Path* (Simon & Schuster, 2021)

Bibliography

Macy, Joanna and Brown, Molly, *Coming Back to Life: The Updated Guide to the Work that Reconnects* (New Society Publishers, 2014)

Marchant, Jo, *Cure: A Journey into the Science of Mind Over Body* (Canongate, 2016)

Maslow, Abraham H., *Religions, Values, and Peak-Experiences* (Rare Treasures, 1964)

McDougall, Christopher, *Born to Run: The Hidden Tribe, The Ultra-Runners, and the Greatest Race the World Has Never Seen* (Profile Books, 2009)

Nafousi, Roxie, *Manifest: 7 Steps to Living Your Best Life* (Penguin, 2022)

Oliver, Mary, *Upstream: Selected Essays* (Penguin, 2016)

Pollan, Michael, *How to Change Your Mind: The New Science of Psychedelics* (Allen Lane, 2018)

Purser, Ronald E., *McMindfulness: How Mindfulness Became the New Capitalist Spirituality* (Watkins Media, 2019)

Rowlands, Mark, *Running with the Pack: Thoughts from the Road on Meaning and Mortality* (Granta Books, 2013)

Sagan, Carl, *Cosmos: The Story of Cosmic Evolution, Science and Civilisation* (Abacus, 1983)

Sagar, Sushma, *Find Your Flow: Essential Chakras* (Pop Press, 2020)

Salguero, C. Pierce, *Buddhish: A Guide to the 20 Most Important Buddhist Ideas for the Curious and Skeptical* (Beacon Press, 2022)

Satchidananda, Sri Swami, *The Yoga Sutras of Patanjali* (Integral Yoga Publications, 2012)

Sylvan, Robin, *Trance Formation: The Spiritual and Religious Dimensions of Global Rave Culture* (Routledge, 2005)

Tamás, Rebecca, *Strangers: Essays on the Human and Nonhuman* (Makina Books, 2020)

Tolle, Eckhart, *The Power of Now: A Guide to Spiritual Enlightenment* (Namaste Publishing, 1997)

Van der Kolk, Bessel, *The Body Keeps the Score: Brain, Mind, and Body in the Healing of Trauma* (Penguin, 2014)

Zuckerman, Phil, *Living the Secular Life: New Answers to Old Questions* (Penguin Press, 2014)

Acknowledgements

As any writer will testify, writing a book can be a lonely experience. It's tempting to frame the process as a solitary quest, facing down the empty page with as much heroism as you can muster. But writers are a self-dramatising bunch, and the truth is that you couldn't do it alone. So many people have helped me take this book from idea to reality, be that through practical support, helpful insights, or chiselling my writing itself into better shape.

The first person I have to thank is my agent, Anna Pallai, who saw the potential in my idea at an early stage, and never lost the faith. Without you none of this would have happened. A heartfelt thanks to the team at Duckworth, who have been unfailingly warm and enthusiastic, and have massively helped boost my confidence as a debut author. That's especially true of my two brilliant editors, Rowan Cope and Clare Bullock, whose input has improved this book immeasurably.

To all my interviewees – it is literally true to say 'I couldn't have done it without you'. Thank you for extending your time, energy and wisdom, and agreeing to be part of a project that accommodates diverging opinions. Each of you challenged me in a different way, and even (or perhaps especially) when we didn't see eye to eye, I truly appreciated your insights.

Acknowledgements

As for my friends – you have all been so encouraging, and an exhaustive list wouldn't be possible, but I'd like to give a shout-out to a few of you. Nat Healey, you are my ride-or-die, and have helped me through many a writing-related confidence crash. Lorna Hutchinson, you lived Chapter One with me – thanks for all the adventures and for reading my early drafts. Emma Godby, thanks for lifting me up on so many occasions. Laura Harvey-Collins, you've helped shape my thinking around yoga and spirituality. Honorary mention to my journalist mates, especially Ross Davies and Rod James, for sticking with me when I turned into a hippie.

A big thanks to my sisters, who exemplify my thesis that very smart people can come to very different conclusions about the big stuff. Bex Millar, you are the sharpest person I know, and the one most likely to call me out when my woo-woo tendencies run away with me. Steph Millar-Pollock, you have such a strong compass for what's important in life and what causes to fight for; thank you for inspiring me to make a stand. Suzie Millar, thank you for reading early drafts of the book, contributing to my exercise chapter, and for taking such a thoughtful stance on every issue.

Special thanks to my Mum, Kate Millar, who has been on the other end of the phone whenever I've needed it and has helped extensively with childcare. People ask me how I managed to write a book during maternity leave, and it's true that I made good use of nap times, but I'd probably have stalled at the first chapter were it not for you and Nick. A similar note of appreciation to my in-laws, Malcolm and Rebecca Torry, who have been incredibly helpful with childcare too and have been supportive about this project since the outset.

To my dad, Nicky Millar – I suspect you'd have disagreed with many of my conclusions, but I know you'd have identified with my questioning impulse. You were someone who always stood up for what you believed in and I'm grateful that you raised me to do the same.

Thanks to my husband Nick Torry, who has supported me on every level. You have lived all the highs and lows with me and have dealt with me at my most sleepless and grumpy. Thank you for giving me time every day to write, even while holding down work and your own projects. Thank you for believing in me more than I tend to believe in myself, and for refusing to indulge any defeatism. Thank you for getting where I'm coming from, and for understanding so deeply what I'm trying to do with this book. You've taught me a lot about spirituality minus the bullshit.

Jasmine – you were a newborn baby when I started this book, and you're a mischievous, chatty toddler as I reach the end of the process. By the time you come to read these words, you'll be a different person again, and I can't wait to get to know that person. I hope that whatever conclusions you come to about life's big questions, you always know you're on this planet for a purpose and that you are deeply loved.

To my readers: every time writing *did* start to feel lonely, I thought of all the people who have been wrestling with the same questions I have. This book is for you; thanks for coming so far with me on this quest.

Index

Abraham-Hicks (Esther Hicks) 92, 98–9
Abrahamic religions 5
Advertising Standards Agency (ASA) 115
AIDS epidemic 87
Allen, Tim 88
alternative medicine 111, 189–90
Altman, Dr Peter 136
Amstell, Simon 30
animal exploitation 25–6
animism 155, 191, 194, 205–6, 209, 210
Anka, Darryl 7
aparigraha (non-attachment) 47–8
Aquarius 77, 84
Archie (cat) 58, 59, 60
asana (physical posture) 42, 46
asceticism 98, 158–60
Asclepius 82
Ashtanga yoga 40–41, 43, 44, 51
Assadourian, Erik 195–8, 203
astrology 12, 65–6, 75–90, 107, 127, 211
    Barnum effect and 80
    birth chart 11, 12, 77–81, 83, 84, 86–8, 90

Co-Star app 77
divination, as form of 90
empirical aspects of 83–6
history of 82–6
Law of Correspondence and 82–3
Leo 79
memes 75, 77
mundane astrology 84
personality tests and 75–6
Pisces 76
randomised controlled trials and 86–8
Sagittarius 77
The Astrology Podcast 81–8
transits 87–8
atheism/atheist churches 2, 9–10, 12, 35, 97, 127–45, 163, 200–201
    Campolo and 141–4
    history of 138
    individualism and 137–8
    intellectualism and 139–40, 141
    New Atheism 2, 9–10, 132–3
    nones 7, 11, 12, 128, 133, 137, 138, 139, 145, 209
    Oasis network 138–40
    Seattle Atheist Church 129, 138, 139–40, 141

Index

Sunday Assembly 130–40, 143
  Temples for Atheists 134
Attention Restoration Theory 190
ayahuasca 10, 15–35, 37, 67, 208, 211, 212, 214, 219, 239
  animal exploitation and 25–6, 30
  ceremonies 15–16, 17, 20–22, 25–8
  DMT (N, N-Dimethyltryptamine) and 18, 20, 32–3, 34–5
  history of 16–17
  integration therapist 28–31
  psychedelics, attitudes towards and 17–20
  psychedelics, function of and 22–5, 31–5
  self-compassion and 27–8
  social change and 30
  spirituality gap and 34–5
  tourism 17, 31
  Western cultures, integration into 31

baby rave 233–4
Banstola, Bhola Nath 207
Barbault, André 87
Barnum effect 80, 88
Bashar 7
Beckjord, Suprabha 158
Beiner, Alexander 30
Beltane 201
Beth Israel Deaconess Medical Center 119
Bible Belt, American 9, 139
Biodanza 222, 226
biophilia 190
Bird, Dr William 190
birth chart 11, 12, 77–81, 83, 84, 86–8, 90
Blair, Tony 9
Bloom, Alana Hyde 193–5
BodyBalance 162, 164
Botton, Alain de: *A Non-Believer's Guide to the Uses of Religion* 133–4
Bourguignon, Erika 222

Bradbrook, Gail 30
brain 2, 18
  exercise and 161
  mind and 3
  placebo effect and 119
  psychedelics and 21–5, 26, 32, 34, 38
  social media and 180
  tarot and 60–61, 66
  yoga and 48, 49
breakups, relationship 20, 57, 58
Brennan, Chris 81–9, 84*n*
Britton, Willoughby 175–7
Buddhism 3–4, 9, 13, 29, 31, 42, 108, 150, 158, 161, 165, 188, 228, 241
  meditation and 167, 169–78, 181–4
  Zen Buddhism 3–4, 150, 152, 168, 169
Burroughs, William S. 16
Bush, George W. 9
Butzer, Bethany 61
Byrne, Rhonda: *The Secret* 92–5, 98, 116

Calm app 168–9, 176
Calmery, The 110–11, 114
Campbell, Joseph 33
Campolo, Bart 141–4
Campolo, Tony 141
capitalism 44, 47, 99, 105, 173–4, 240
Carhart-Harris, Robin 23
Catherine of Siena, St 159
Celtic Connection 190
Celtic shamanism 204, 208–11
Center for Mindfulness 169
chakras
  ayahuasca and 29–30
  reiki and 110, 111, 112, 113, 116, 120, 121, 122, 123
  yoga and 41, 42, 50, 51
Chalmers, David 3
Chapel, Nicholas E. 82
Chinmoy, Sri 155

Index

Christianity 6, 8, 9, 11, 32, 43, 76, 124, 128, 132, 133, 134, 135, 139, 197, 209
   ascetic tradition 158–60
   astrology and 76
   atheist churches and 142–4
   Christian Right 6
   defining 9
   Evangelical 6, 108, 141–2, 179–80
   mysticism 200
   reiki and 108, 124
Christina, Greta 73, 128, 133
Church of CrossFit 163
Church of Jesus Christ of Latter-day Saints 108
clairsentience 114
climate and ecological crises 30, 73, 78, 104, 105, 191–203
collective spiritual emergence 73
Colman-Smith, Pamela 61–3
colonialism 40, 45, 50, 210, 225
commodification 12, 43, 174
Comte, Auguste 138
conscious movement practices 222
consciousness 3, 10
   ayahuasca and 17, 19, 21, 22, 25–6, 29–30, 32, 34–5
   exercise and 160
   manifestation and 98–9, 101
   nature spirituality and 197
   raves and 222, 223, 224, 226, 227, 228, 229
   reiki and 112*n*, 117, 119, 124
   shamanism and 206, 212, 213, 215, 218
   tarot and 61, 62, 66, 69, 72
   yoga and 42, 51
consumerism 12, 52, 53, 174
Controlled Substances Act, US (1970) 18
Conway Hall Ethical Society 131, 135
Cooke, Dr James 22–5, 31, 33, 49, 176
Copernican Revolution 85

Covid-19 87
Crispin, Jessa: *The Creative Tarot* 69
cultural appropriation
   ayahuasca and 31
   shamanism and 208–10
   yoga and 39–50, 52–3

dance 154, 206*n*, 215, 221–35
Dawkins, Richard 131–3, 134, 141
   God Is Not Great 131, 132
   Unweaving the Rainbow 129
death 2, 3, 5, 17, 19, 24
   Death tarot card 57, 59, 66
   ego death/dissolution 21, 24, 32, 164, 176, 232
   fear of 25, 29
   grief and 10, 11, 20, 67, 149, 162, 197, 199, 216
deep ecology 188, 198
default mode network (DMN) 22, 23, 49, 107
Dennett, Daniel: *Breaking the Spell* 132–3
depersonalisation 177
derealisation 177
Descartes, René 187, 188
Deshpande, Rina 45–50, 52, 239
Deuteronomy 18:10–11 65
Devi, Indra 43
dharana (focused concentration) 46
dhyana (meditative absorption) 46
Díaz-Gilbert, Miriam 156–9, 161, 165
digital culture 7
Dionysus 225, 232
disconnection 30, 39, 40, 46, 52–3, 198, 202, 210, 217
divination 57, 65, 90
DMT (N, N-Dimethyltryptamine) 18, 20, 32–3, 34–5
Don't Look Up 198
Dore, Jessica: *Tarot for Change: Using the Cards for Self-Care, Acceptance and Growth* 63–4
Druidry 209
Durkheim, Émile 144*n*, 232

Index

Earth Mother 30, 37–8
ecstasy (emotion) 144, 222, 225–6, 232
Ecstasy (drug) 226, 230, 233
Ecstatic Dance 12, 222–6, 228, 231, 232, 233
Edmonds, Noel 92
Egginton, Jane 203–6, 208–9, 210, 211, 215–19
ego death/dissolution 21, 24, 32, 164, 176, 232
Ehrenreich, Barbara: *Dancing in the Streets: A History of Collective Joy* 221–2, 225–6
Eisenstein, Charles 188; 'Story of Interbeing' 188
Elsey, Eddy: *Let Healing Happen: A Shamanic Guide to Living an Authentic and Happy Life* 206
Elwell, Dennis 89
Emerson, Ralph Waldo; *Nature* 187
Emre, Merve: *What's Your Type? The Strange History of Myers–Briggs and the Birth of Personality Testing* 76
energy medicine 12, 108, 109, 110, 111, 114–15, 122
ENFP (Extroverted, Intuitive, Feeling and Perceiving) 75
entheogens 18
enthousiasmos ('having the god within oneself') 225
Erkelens, Herbert van 60
Ernst, Professor Edzard 115
Esalen Institute 226
Esselmont, Brigit 64–6
Ethical Culture society 138
Evangelical Christianity 6, 108, 141–2, 179–80
Evans, Pippa 130–31, 138
evolution 2, 8, 129, 133, 170, 174, 213
exercise 12, 147–65
    Church of CrossFit 163
    distress signals, brain and 161
    gyoja or spiritual athletes 153
    injuries and off-seasons 164–5
    Les Mills workouts 161, 162, 164
    limitations, honouring 164
    marathon monks 153
    Maslow and 149–50, 149*n*, 157
    moving meditation 150
    Navajo culture and 154–5
    peak experiences 149, 153, 157
    present moment and 149, 150, 153
    San Bushmen and 155
    self-actualisation and 149
    self-mastery and 160–61, 164–5
    self-punishments and 159–60
    shared, transformative experience 163
    still running 150–53, 157, 160, 165
    stop-start running 151–3
    Suzanna Millar and 161–3
    Tarahumara 153–5, 160
    track ultras 156–7
    ultrarunning 12, 155–7, 159, 160, 165
    visionary sightseeing and 160
Exodus 22:18 65
Extinction Rebellion 30, 192, 193

faith healings 108, 124
Feynman, Richard 7–8
Finn, Adharanand 153
5-HT2A 23
5Rhythms 226, 228
Free Guide to Shamanism 209
free will 9

Gacy, John Wayne 88–9
Gaia theory 12, 187–8, 196–8, 200
Gaian Way 196–8, 200
Gandhi, Dr Shreena 40, 43, 44, 49–50, 52–3, 171
Gemini 87, 89
Genesis creation story 8
Gibran, Kahlil 6
Gilani, Nadia
    The Yoga Manifesto: How Yoga Helped Me and Why It Needs to Save Itself 45
    'Why I'm No Longer Talking To White People About Yoga' 45

Index

God 3, 4, 29, 35, 37, 82, 90, 96, 104, 108, 124, 125, 150, 157, 159, 165, 197, 200
  atheism and 9–10, 11, 128, 130–31, 133, 137, 138, 142–4
  'God Is a DJ' (Faithless) 222
  importance of 6–7
Goddard, Vanessa Zuisei: *Still Running: The Art of Meditation in Motion* 150
gods 2, 4, 6, 7, 12, 16, 18n, 26, 33, 53, 128, 130, 131, 154, 222, 225, 232
Good Place, The 18
Gopnik, Dr Alison 22
Gorski, Dr David 115
GreenSpirit 199–201
grief 10, 20, 67, 149, 162, 197, 199, 216
Griffiths, Roland 10–11
Grof, Stanislav and Christina 73, 213, 216
Guterres, António 191
gyoja or spiritual athletes 153

Haitian Vodou practitioners 225
hallucination 3, 17, 32, 33, 156
hallucinogens 3, 20
Hanh, Thich Nhat 188
Harner, Michael: *The Way of the Shaman* 206–7, 212, 218
Harris, Sam 132–3
Harvey-Collins, Laura 51–2
hatha yoga 42–3
Hatha Yoga Pradipika 43
Headspace app 167, 168–9, 170, 174, 183, 184
healing
  ayahuasca and 15, 16, 17, 28, 30
  manifestation and 92–3, 97
  nature and 186, 188–90, 202
  reiki and 107–10, 112–15, 119, 122, 124
  shamanic 12, 204–11, 213, 216–18, 222, 231, 232
  yoga and 52
Healing Club 110

Healing Space 204, 217
heaven 8, 142, 149
hell 8, 17, 135
herbs and botanicals 190
Hermetic Order of the Golden Dawn 62
Hicks, Bill 17
Hill, Napoleon: *Think and Grow Rich* 98
Hinduism 6, 9, 16, 40, 42, 43, 230
hippie movement 18, 19, 20, 37, 43, 44, 127
Hirsi Ali, Ayaan 132, 133
Hitchens, Christopher 132, 134
Hittleman, Richard 43
Hmong shamans 207
Holy Spirit 8
Hopkins, Jon: *Singularity* 148
'How We Gather' (Angie Thurston and Casper ter Kuile) 163
Human Potential Movement 149
Humanize Me 142
Hume, David 143
Hutchinson, Alex: *Endure: Mind, Body and the Curiously Elastic Limits of Human Performance* 161
Huxley, Aldous: *Heaven & Hell* 160

India 6, 40, 42, 43, 47, 155, 241
Indigenous practices 31, 153–4, 158, 191, 196, 206, 207, 209, 210, 211, 214, 218, 223, 239
individualism 76, 105, 137–8
Indus Valley civilisation 42, 221
INFP 75
injuries and off-seasons 164–5
Instagram 5, 7, 27, 44, 54, 63, 78, 91, 93
Intellectual Dark Web 133
intellectualism 4, 9, 29, 53, 60, 70, 124, 139–40, 141, 215, 219, 238
intention setting 17, 100–101, 104, 182, 223
Intergovernmental Panel on Climate Change (IPCC) 191

Index

International Association of Reiki Professionals (IARP) 115, 119
Iran 6
Islamic revivalism 6
Islamophobia 133
Iyengar, B.K.S. 43

James, William 98, 229
Jamyang Buddhist Centre 183
Japanese Society of Forest Medicine 189
Jehovah's Witnesses 9
Jesus 8, 9, 42, 92, 108, 136, 138, 142, 159
Jhakri 207
Jivaro people 207
Jois, K. Pattabhi 43, 51
Jones, Sanderson 130, 131, 138
Jung, Carl
  astrology and 82–3
  depth psychology 29
  Synchronicity: An Acausal Connecting Principle 59–61, 71–2
  tarot and 59–61, 62–3, 70, 71–2, 83
Just Say No 18

Kabat-Zinn, Jon 169, 171, 172
Kabbalah 61, 72
Kalahari Desert 155
Kaptchuk, Ted 119
Kastrup, Bernardo 3; *Why Materialism Is Baloney: How True Skeptics Know There Is No Death and Fathom Answers to Life, the Universe, and Everything* 3
Kaufmann, Michael 120–24
Keats, John 129
Kehoe, Alice Beck 207
Kirlian photography 116
koan 3–4
Kolk, Bessel van der: *The Body Keeps the Score: Brain, Mind, and Body in the Healing of Trauma* 216
Krishnamacharya, Tirumalai 43
Kurt, Troy 140–41
Kybalion, The 82–3, 98

La Medicina 213–14
Laing, R.D. 213
Larissa (mythic tarot reader) 58–9, 67
Law of Attraction 12, 94–5, 97, 98–105, 108, 221
Law of Correspondence 82–3
Les Mills workouts 161–4
Li, Dr Qing 189
Lieberman, Daniel E. 154, 160
Light Centre, Moorgate 121
limitations, honouring 164
Lockwood, Matt 131–2, 134, 137, 143
LSD 11, 18, 19, 23, 30

Macy, Joanna 197
magic truffles 20
maintenance therapies 19
Manifest Daily 91–2
manifestation 91–105
  Abraham-Hicks and 92, 98–9
  control and 104
  future of 105
  history of 98
  Law of Attraction and 12, 94–5, 97, 98–105, 108, 221
  life partner and 102–3
  meritocracy and 105
  Nafousi and 91–3, 95–6, 105
  negative thoughts and 103–4
  positive thinking and 93–4, 98
  Runefelt and 99
  The Secret 92–6, 99, 100
  Trumble and 97–8, 99
  vision boards 94–5
Manson, Mark: The Staggering Bullshit of *The Secret* 93, 95, 97
mantra 47, 92, 102, 171, 182, 205
Marathon des Sables 155–6
marathon monks 153
Marchant, Jo: *A Journey into the Science of Mind Over Body* 119–20
Mars 84
Martin, Dustin 154–5
masculine energy 72–3

Index

Masheder, Jiva 170, 175, 184
Maslow, Abraham 149–50, 149*n*, 157
Matthew 6:20 5
McDougall, Christopher: *Born to Run: The Hidden Tribe, the Ultra-Runners, and the Greatest Race the World Has Never Seen* 154
meditation 12, 24, 38, 40, 42, 43, 46–7, 167–84
   apps 167–9, 176, 177, 183, 184
   Attention Restoration Theory 190
   Buddhism and 167, 169–78, 181–4
   Calm app 168–9, 176
   difficulty of 168, 175–6, 178, 184
   ego death and 176
   guided meditation 167
   Headspace app 167, 168–9, 170, 174, 183
   history 170–72
   intention setting and 182
   mindfulness and 12, 150, 167–77, 181–4, 189
   mindfulness-based cognitive therapy (MBCT) 169–70
   mindfulness-based stress reduction (MBSR) 169–70, 172, 173–5, 177, 182–3
   moving meditation 39, 150, 171
   negative effects of, potential/'The Varieties of Contemplative Experience' 175–6
   present moment and 170, 178, 179, 181
   self-compassion and 170, 180–82
   Torry and 177–80
   Vipassana retreat 178
MDMA 19, 228, 230
mental health 239
   ayahuasca and 19, 34
   meditation and 169, 170, 171, 176, 183
   nature and 186, 189
   reiki and 108
   shamanism and 215, 216, 217
   spirituality and 5, 12, 34, 239
   tarot and 70–71, 73
   yoga and 39–40, 47, 48, 49–50
meritocracy 105
Millar, Dr Suzanna 161–4
Mind 71
mindfulness 39, 152, 164, 167, 173–5
   meditation and 12, 150, 167–77, 181–4, 189
   mindfulness-based cognitive therapy (MBCT) 169–70
   mindfulness-based stress reduction (MBSR) 169–70, 172, 173–5, 177, 182–3
mindful stretching 41
Minnesota Atheists 138
Mohammed, Yasmine 140
Moran, Kerry 28–31, 239
Moriarty, Philip 116
Mormons 9, 108, 139
Morton, Timothy 188
Moses 32–3
Mount Hiei, Japan 153
Mount Kuruma, Japan 112
Mowll, Ian 200
Muhrer, Verle 88
Mulford, Prentice: 'The Law of Success' 98
Myers-Briggs test 75, 76
myth of separation 188

Nafousi, Roxie 91–3, 95–6, 105
Nagel, Thomas: 'What Is It Like to Be a Bat' 25
Namdak, Geshe Tenzin 183
National Center for Complementary and Integrative Health, US 117
Native Americans 154, 204, 207
Nature 34
nature spirituality 185–202
   biophilia and 190
   Buddhism and 188
   climate/ecological crises and 191–202
   Gaian Way and 196–8, 200
   GreenSpirit and 199–201
   healing and 186, 188–90, 202

herbs and botanicals and 190
history of 187–8
myth of separation and 188
'Nature as Healer: A Phenomenological Study of the Experiences of Wild Swimmers in Kenwood Ladies' Pond on Hampstead Heath' 186, 188–9
paganism and 191, 196, 200, 201
Psycho-Physiological Stress Recovery Theory 190
shinrin-yoku, forest bathing 189–90, 219
Wheel of the Year and 201
Wiccans and witches and 190
wild swimming and 185–7, 188–9, 192
Wild Woman Camp Out 193–4
naturopathy 190
Navajo culture 155
New Age 1, 2, 7, 10, 12, 16, 42, 66, 71, 82, 83, 98, 128, 144, 150, 238–9
meditation and 169–70
reiki and 116, 117, 117*n*
shamanism and 207, 208, 209, 211
New Atheism 2, 9, 132–3
New Thought movement 82, 92, 98, 108
New Yorker 76, 148
Newfrontiers 8
Newton, Isaac 129
NHS 115, 169, 189
Nigeria 6
nihilism 5
niyama (positive observances) 46
nones 7, 11, 12, 128, 133, 137, 138, 139, 145, 209
Norton, Hilary 199–202
Novella, Steven 118

Oasis network 138–40
observer effect 116–17
Odle, Chris 88, 90, 211–14, 218
Oliver, Mary 193
Outdoor Swimming Society 186

paganism 191, 196, 200, 201, 209, 210
Palmer, Martin 195
Parikh, Jesal 45
Pashnova, Alena 224–6, 231
Patanjali: *Yoga Sutras* 42, 46–7
Patel, Tejal 45
peak experiences 149, 153, 157
Peale, Norman Vincent: *The Power of Positive Thinking* 98
Peeters, Karin 181–4
personal growth 5, 149*n*
personality test 75–6
Pew Research Center 76, 128, 133
pharma industry 19–20, 237
Psychic Sisters, The 63
placebo effect 117–19, 124
Plotkin, Bill 194
PLUR (peace, love, unity, respect) 228
Pluto 87
Pollan, Michael: *How to Change Your Mind: The New Science of Psychedelics* 22
Pollard, Stephanie 132, 134, 135
polycrisis 5, 6
positive thinking 93–4, 98
possession-based spiritual practice 206
post-traumatic stress disorder (PTSD) 214, 230
pranayama (breathing techniques) 46
pratyahara (sense withdrawal) 46
present moment 149, 150, 153, 170, 178–9, 181, 201
psilocybin 18–20, 23, 25, 35
psychedelics 15–35, 49, 73, 121, 122, 160, 228, 230, 239. *See also individual psychedelic name*
psychiatry 18–19, 20, 175, 177, 213, 217
psychology
astrology and 79, 82–3, 86, 88
ayahuasca and 21, 27, 29, 31, 32, 34
depth psychology 29 *see also* Jung, Carl

Index

eco-psychology 187–8
exercise and 147, 149, 161
meditation and 170, 171, 175, 181, 184
nature spirituality and 187–8, 194
shamanism and 214
tarot and 59, 62–4, 70, 71–2, 73
Psycho-Physiological Stress Recovery Theory 190
psychotherapy 70–71, 122, 181, 216, 230
Ptolemy 84, 85
Puddicombe, Andy 167–8
Purser, Ronald: *McMindfulness: How Mindfulness Became the New Capitalist Spirituality* 173–5, 182–3

Quakers 9
quantum physics/mysticism 85, 94, 99, 116–17, 117*n*, 127
Quimby, Phineas 92

randomised controlled trial (RCT) 86–8, 118
raves 12, 221–35
  baby rave 233–4
  Biodanza 222, 226
  conscious movement practices 222
  Ecstasy 226, 230, 233
  Ecstatic Dance 12, 222–6, 228, 231, 232, 233
  'God Is a DJ' 222
  history of dance 221–2, 225–6
  raves 12, 219, 226–33
  sonder 235
Rawal, Sanjay 155
reiki 12, 107–25
  chakras and 110, 111, 112, 113, 116, 120, 121, 122, 123
  distance reiki 116, 127
  healing and 107–10, 112–15, 119, 122, 124
  history of 112
  Kirlian photography and 116
  marketing campaign complaint 115
  NHS and 115
  observer effect and 116–17
  placebo effect and 118–19
  popularity 111
  quantum mysticism and 116–17
  scientific evidence and 114–20
  self-care and 107–8
  sessions 108–11
  spiritual life force and 125
  therapeutic nature of 107–8
  training 120–24
  wellness culture and 108, 110, 111, 114
relational experiences 32
religion
  astrology and 90
  decline in importance of 6–7
  see also atheism
  exercise and 149–50, 153, 154, 155, 161, 162, 163
  health and wellbeing and 108
  Law of Attraction and 94
  meditation and 169–72, 182, 183, 187
  nature and 187, 190–91, 195–7, 200
  raves and 222, 227–30, 232, 235
  shamanism and 207–10, 213
  tarot and 65
Religion of Humanity 138
Rider-Waite deck 62–3, 67, 241
Rig Veda 42
Rocket yoga 40–41, 44
Romantic poets 129, 187
root chakra 29
Rosa, Emily 117
Rossano, Matt J. 170
Roth, Gabrielle 226
Royal College of Psychiatrists 19
Ruddy, Ursula 210
Runefelt, Carl (The Moon) 99

Sacred Hoop 208
Sagan, Carl 82, 129, 140; *Cosmos: The Story of Cosmic Evolution, Science and Civilisation* 83–4

Index

Sagan, Sasha 140
Sagar, Sushma 108–10, 218, 239
Salguero, C. Pierce 108; *Buddhish: A Guide to the 20 Most Important Buddhist Ideas for the Curious and Skeptical* 171–7, 183
Sam, Lucy; 'Nature as Healer: A Phenomenological Study of the Experiences of Wild Swimmers in Kenwood Ladies' Pond on Hampstead Heath' 186–9
samadhi (enlightenment or bliss) 1, 46, 49
samskaras 48–9, 107
San Bushmen 155
Saturn 87
scepticism 7, 79
Schiffmann, Erich 150–51
schizophrenia 33
science
　astrology and 75, 76, 81–90, 94
　atheism and 128, 129, 141
　exercise and 161
　Genesis creation story and 8–9
　manifestation and 94, 97, 99
　meditation and 169, 171, 176
　nature spirituality and 187, 194, 200
　psychedelics and 18, 19, 21, 22–4, 30, 31, 33–4
　reiki and 114–20, 124, 125
　religion and 8–9
　shamanism and 211, 214, 218
　spirituality and 11, 240
　tarot and 60, 66, 68
　yoga and 42, 43, 48–9, 52
Science-Based Medicine 115
Seattle Atheist Church 129, 138, 139–41
self-actualisation 149
self-care 64, 76, 77, 107–8, 172
self-compassion 27–8, 164, 170, 180–82
self-help 5, 54, 93
self-mastery 160–61, 164–5
self-punishments 159–60
self, sense of 23, 24, 39, 151, 175

Self-Transcendence 3100 Mile Race 155–7
Sessa, Dr Ben 19–20
Shaman Durek 208
shamanism 12, 114, 203–19
　animism and 205–6, 209, 210
　Celtic shamanism 204, 208–11
　Core Shamanism 207
　cultural appropriation and 208–10
　Free Guide to Shamanism 208
　history of 206–7
　journey 204, 208, 216
　La Medicina and 213–14
　mantra and 205
　Native North Americans and 207
　New Age practice and 208
　Odle and 211–14, 218
　popularity of 208
　possession-based spiritual practice 206
　psychosis and 213
　Shaman Durek and 208
　shamanic sickness 211–13
　Shamanic States of Consciousness (SSC) 212
　somatic trauma therapy and 217
　sweat lodge ceremony 207–8
　treatment 203–4, 215–17
　Western terminology and 214–15
　word 207
shinrin-yoku, forest bathing 189–90, 219
Simeon the Stylite 159
16personalities.com 75
Smart, Chloe 77–80
Smith-Murphy, Victoria 69–73
smudging 17, 204
Sola Busca deck 62
somatic therapy 29, 217
sonder 235
SoulCycle 163
Spark, The 75
Sparkes, Evie 99–102, 104–5
speaking in tongues 8
spirit, word 2, 72, 128, 144
spirit guides 1, 66, 108, 114, 121, 208

278

Index

spirituality
  activism and 241
  definition 2–4, 11, 50, 128–9, 241
  limitations of Western 241
  mental health and 5, 12, 34, 239
  secular spirituality *see* atheism
  spiritual emergency 213
  spiritual practice 114, 190
  the spirituality gap 4, 7, 11, 35, 240
  yoga and 53
  word 4, 10, 128, 144, 241
Spruce, Richard 16, 108
SQUID (superconducting quantum interference device) 116
SSRIs 19
still running 150–53, 157, 160, 165
stop-start running 151–3
Strassman, Rick 20
Stress Reduction Clinic 169
Sunak, Rishi 192
Sunday Assembly 130–40, 143
sweat lodge ceremony 207–8
swimming lake 12, 185–7, 192, 198–9, 201
Sylvan, Robin: *Trance Formation* 227–30, 233, 239
synchronicity 3, 11, 59–61, 69, 71–2

Takata, Hawayo 112
Tamás, Rebecca: *Strangers: Essays on the Human and Nonhuman* 191
Tarahumara 153–5, 160
tarot 12, 57–74
  Biddy Tarot 64–5, 67, 74
  Celtic Cross reading 58–9
  collective spiritual emergence and 73
  corporate world and 72–3
  Death card 57, 59, 66
  Devil card 62
  Eight of Wands card 58–9
  history of 61–3
  internet democratises 63
  Major Arcana 62
  masculine energy and 72–3
  mental health and 70–71, 73
  Minor Arcana 62
  organised religion and 65–6
  psychotherapy and 70–71
  resurgence of 73–4
  Rider-Waite deck 62–3, 67, 241
  shadow work 69–70
  Sola Busca deck 62
  synchronicity and 60–61, 71–2
  The Fool card 62, 241
  The Hanged Man card 57, 68
  The Hierophant card 70
  The Sun card 62
  The Tower card 73–4
  The World card 62
  tool for introspection 66–7
  Two of Cups card 68
TED Talk 130, 140
Temples for Atheists 134
Teresa of Ávila, St 159
The Astrology Podcast 81–8
Theos 128
therapy 5, 107–8
  astrology and 79, 80
  dance movement 224–5
  meditation and 181, 182
  psychedelics and 17, 19–20, 23, 24, 28–9
  reiki and 107–8, 115, 117, 119, 122
  shamanism and 213, 216, 217
  tarot and 59–60, 64, 70–72
This Is Your Brain on Drugs adverts 18
Thompson, Jack 129, 140–41, 145
Thoreau, Henry David 187
3100: Run and Become 155
Tibet 29, 38, 183, 207
TikTok 63, 64–5, 93, 99
Tolboll, Morten 117
Tolle, Eckhart: *The Power of Now: A Guide to Spiritual Enlightenment* 150, 179
Torry, Nick 177–80, 192, 234
track ultras 156–7
Transcendentalists, American 187
Trumble, Nick 97–8
Truss, Liz 192
Tungusic shamans of Siberia 207

Index

UC Berkeley 22
ultrarunning 12, 155–60, 165
Understanding Astrology: A Critical Review of a Thousand Empirical Studies 1900–2020 88–9
Unitarian Universalists 138
unitive experiences 32
University of Greenwich 30
University of Ottawa 41
University of Southern California 142
Uranus 87, 89
US Games Systems 63
Usui, Dr Mikao 112

veganism 26, 30, 67, 103
Vibhūti Pāda 48
vinyasa yoga 37, 40–41, 42, 54, 221
Vipassana retreat 178
vision boards 94–5
visionary sightseeing 160
visual cortex 23
Vivekananda, Swami 43

Waite, Arthur 61–2
Wallace, David Foster 4
Watts, Alan 235; 'Psychedelics and Religious Experience' 19
wellness culture 37, 50, 70–71, 108, 110, 111, 114, 208, 238, 241
WGSN 76
Wheel of the Year 197, 201
whirling dervishes 225
Whitman, Walt 78
Wiccans 190–91, 200
wild swimming 185–7, 188–9, 192, 193
Wild Woman Camp Out 193–4
Wilson, Edward O. 190
Winfrey, Oprah 129

Wings of America 154–5
witches 65, 77, 78, 110, 111, 114, 190–91, 210
Wollf, Lillie 40
Wood, Nicholas Breeze 209
World Economic Forum 5
World Values Survey 6
Worldwatch Institute 196

Yaden, David 10–11
Yale University 118
yama (moral disciplines) 46, 47
yoga 37–55
   aim of 49–51
   commodification of 43–4
   connector, as a 52
   cultural appropriation and 41, 44–50
   defining 39–42
   eight limbs of 42, 46–7, 51
   exercise classes and 38–9
   hatha yoga 42–3
   health benefits 48
   history of 42–3
   meeting yourself where you are 54–5
   noticing and 39
   scientific research and 42, 43, 48–9, 52
   word 42
Yoga for Health 43
Yoga Is Dead podcast 45

Zen Buddhism. *See* Buddhism
Zen Mountain Monastery 152
Zopa, Lama 182
Zuckerman, Dr Phil: *Living the Secular Life: New Answers to Old Questions* 129–30, 137–41, 145